高等职业教育新形态系列教材

# 双语太极拳初级教程

主　　编　张竹筠　范　伟
副 主 编　代流通　向成军　韩　彬
编　　委　冯建福　张倩菡　浑　涛
专家顾问　黄帝全　李朝旭　陈　娟
　　　　　李兆飞

北京理工大学出版社
**BEIJING INSTITUTE OF TECHNOLOGY PRESS**

**图书在版编目（ＣＩＰ）数据**

双语太极拳初级教程：英、汉 / 张竹筠，范伟主编
. --北京：北京理工大学出版社，2021.11
ISBN 978-7-5763-0493-0

Ⅰ．①双…　Ⅱ．①张…②范…　Ⅲ．①太极拳-教材

–英、汉　Ⅳ．①G852.11

中国版本图书馆 CIP 数据核字（2021）第 208413 号

---

出版发行 / 北京理工大学出版社有限责任公司
社　　址 / 北京市海淀区中关村南大街 5 号
邮　　编 / 100081
电　　话 /（010）68914775（总编室）
　　　　　（010）82562903（教材售后服务热线）
　　　　　（010）68944723（其他图书服务热线）
网　　址 / http://www.bitpress.com.cn
经　　销 / 全国各地新华书店
印　　刷 / 唐山富达印务有限公司
开　　本 / 787 毫米×1092 毫米　1/16
印　　张 / 17.25　　　　　　　　　　　　　　　责任编辑 / 江　立
字　　数 / 396 千字　　　　　　　　　　　　　　文案编辑 / 江　立
版　　次 / 2021 年 11 月第 1 版　2021 年 11 月第 1 次印刷　责任校对 / 周瑞红
定　　价 / 52.00 元　　　　　　　　　　　　　　责任印制 / 施胜娟

# 序 1

2020 年 12 月，联合国教科文组织保护非物质文化遗产政府间委员会第 15 届常会将"太极拳"项目列入联合国教科文组织人类非物质文化遗产代表作名录。太极拳作为承载多元历史文化的身体表达方式，因具健身、防身和修身多重功用也被列入国家文化、健康和体育发展战略。为了发挥学校"立德树人"和校园人文建设的任务，以及将"太极拳"这一世界遗产更好地传承与发展，编写团队选取了受众面较广的"简化太极拳"为主要教学内容，进而编写《双语太极拳初级教程》，作为高职院校中华优秀传统文化课程模块中通识性必修课程教材。

太极拳以其独特的运动形式、深厚的文化底蕴、显著的健身效果吸引着越来越多的人。它是一项让世界人民着迷的、具有丰富内涵的运动，尤其在当今社会高度文明、现代化的生活中，人们渴望自然、和谐、健康的生活方式，太极拳恰好是实现这些愿望的绝好运动。本双语教材旨在通过太极拳向世界传播中国价值和共建人类命运共同体的理念，推动太极拳运动的健康发展。

本教材有如下鲜明特色与创新：

1. 设计理念创新。

本教材遵循高职学生的认知规律，凸显"教书育人"的教材建设理念；一则以文育人：从"太极"起源，到太极拳的形成与发展，再到其蕴含的文化内涵，提炼出太极拳在教学过程中的实际教育作用价值；二则以体育人：总结现在太极拳最新、最权威的研究成果，凸显出太极拳作为身体运动对人体的实际意义和价值，树立大健康的教育理念，为学生终身体育锻炼打下基础。

2. 内容展现形式创新。

教材围绕一套经典的武术套路运动，立体化的展示单个技术动作的来历、作用、功法、用法、练法等内容，突出传统武术"打练结合"的特色，充分体现中华武术以攻防动作作为运动素材和健身手段的本质。借助当今信息网络技术实现智慧化教学和传播，教材配备了全套数字化教学资源，并且在 MOOC（慕课）平台和国内外特色国际课程推广平台配套发布，为学校开设 SPOC（小规模在线课程）和线上线下混合教学提供支撑。

3. 太极拳双语传习创新。

双语传习有利于无障碍交流，助推中外文化交流。作为双语教材首先将汉语的内容放到国际化语境中进行翻译整理，其次凸显教材的"活态"传承性，助推世界非物质文化遗产太极拳的发展。

电影电视及舞台剧制作人、编剧及导演，

中国功夫及武术演艺国际推手

傅华阳

2021 年 5 月 22 日

# Preface 1

As an indispensable part of China's current national cultural, health and sport development strategies, Tai-chi Chuan has been inscribed on the UNESCO Representative List of the Intangible Cultural Heritage of Humanity by the 15th Ordinary Session of the UNESCO Intergovernmental Committee for the Safeguarding of the Intangible Cultural Heritage in December, 2020. Deeply rooted in Chinese history and culture, Tai-chi Chuan has been traditionally practiced for multiple purposes including fitness enhancement, self-defense and mindful nurturing of well-being. Regarding it as an essential vehicle to cultivate students' moral values and strengthen humanity education, the authoring team of *Chinese-English Tai-chi Chuan Course for Beginners* select Simplified Tai-chi Chuan, one of the most popular Tai-chi Chuan forms, and write it into this textbook, serving as an inclusion of the fine traditional Chinese culture course module, a general but compulsory one for vocational colleges in China.

Tai-chi Chuan is a unique exercise that contains a vibrant culture and brings outstanding fitness results to practitioners who have been growing in number worldwide. It gains a wide appeal around the globe with its rich cultural and philosophical substance. Amidst of the fast pace of modern life, people are increasingly yearning for a more peaceful, natural and healthy life style. And Tai-chi Chuan is just the perfect answer to realize such desires. Through Tai-chi Chuan, this bilingual textbook aims to bolster mutual understanding and exchange, so as to advance the sustainable growth of Tai-chi Chuan, disseminate Chinese values and the concept of building a community with a shared future for mankind to the world.

The main features and innovative ideas of this textbook are as follows:

1. Innovative course design ideas.

By following the learning and cognition patterns of vocational college students, the textbook is centered around the idea of "teaching for cultivation". On one hand, it offers the overview of Tai-chi Chuan's culture to students. Spanning from its origin, its formation and

evolution to its cultural connotation, it emphasizes Tai-chi Chuan's vital role in educational application; on the other hand, this book embraces a comprehensive health education concept. It summarizes the most current and authoritative research findings of Tai-chi Chuan, highlighting its empirical values and implications as a fitness exercise, through which it helps students establish their "exercise for life" lifestyle.

2. Innovative form of content presentation.

The textbook revolves around a classic Tai-chi Chuan routine and vertically presents each posture by covering its origin, function, utility, application and exercise method. The traditional martial art characteristic of "combining practice with combat" is underscored to illuminate the nature of traditional Chinese martial art of utilizing combat and defense postures as basic movement elements and an exercise method. This course is also fully digitalized with up-to-date learning technologies for smart teaching and broad visibility. It has been released as a Massive Open Online Course (MOOC) and published on some major MOOC platforms at home and abroad. The digital version of the course provides schools a pathway to conducting a Small Private Online Course (SPOC) and the "online and offline" hybrid teaching.

3. Innovative bilingual teaching of Tai-chi Chuan.

The bilingual teaching of Tai-chi Chuan in Chinese and English facilitates learning and cultural exchanges between the east and the west. As a bilingual textbook, the original teaching content in Chinese is discerningly translated and compiled into English in the international context. Moreover, the bilingual version of this textbook itself exemplifies the dynamic progress of Tai-chi Chuan as an evolving legacy, through which it promotes its further development as a global intangible cultural heritage.

Fu Huayang

Director, screenwriter and producer of films, TV and theater

International promoter of Chinese Kung Fu and martial art performance

May.22，2021

# 序 2

我是一名临床肿瘤和血液病专科医生，现在美国佛罗里达州最大的肿瘤临床和研究院工作，同时我也是有近二十年练习陈式太极拳的太极爱好者。应挚友张兄竹筠教授之邀作序，我从一个医学工作者的角度来和读者分享我对太极拳的一些理解和感受。

世间万物，生生不息，其核心驱动力是平衡。平衡无处不在，小到分子和原子，大到整个宇宙。在医学领域，有肿瘤发展的致癌和抑癌机制、免疫系统的激活和抑制、血液系统的凝血和抗凝血等数不胜数的平衡，如果这种平衡被打破，问题就会出现，疾病就会发生。不断调节和保持机体本身和周围万物之平衡，是维持一个健康体质的基本要素之一，太极拳正是巧妙地利用阴阳之既相互对立，又相互统一、相互转化的特征，通过某种套路，把人的意、气、劲和形激活，并达到一种极致的平衡和协调，最终实现阴阳合一、内外合一、天人合一的境界，把人的潜能发挥到极致，达到"一动俱动，一至俱至"的能力，从医学角度达到预防和治病的目的。

古老的太极技艺能从梁武帝时期流传至今而不衰，用实践验证了它的实用性和哲理性。利用现代科技手段，它的科学性也不断被中外科学家所验证。正如书中所述，太极拳已经被科学证明其兼具健身、防身和养生功能。它不但可以调节中枢神经系统的平衡，还可以改善心血管功能，调节呼吸系统和消化系统功能，增加机体免疫功能。研究还表明，太极拳可以促进心理健康，用于治疗抑郁症、紧张性头疼、偏头疼、焦虑症和情绪低落等疾病；太极拳还可以治疗关节疾病，改善骨质疏松，减少骨折风险等等[1]。

肿瘤病人是一个特殊的群体，他们要承受的是机体和精神的双重伤害，大多数肿瘤病人患有抑郁病、焦虑症和情绪不稳定。通过手术、化疗、放疗，甚至最新的免疫治疗和靶向治疗，病人会有乏力、头晕、平衡失调、食欲不振、记忆力减退、注意力下降以及肌肉萎缩、

---

[1] Ryan Abbott, JD MTOM and Helen Lavretsky. *Psychiatr Clin North Am*. 2013 March, 36(1): 109-119.

无力等毒副作用。现代临床研究证明，练习太极拳能有效改善病人的柔韧性和平衡度，增加肌力、改善食欲、记忆力并能提高注意力，太极拳能明显地有助于治疗后康复和改善病人的生存质量[①]。太极拳已被很多美国知名医院列为辅助医学或综合医学的一个重要组成部分。到目前为止，全世界已经有超过 301 个已经完成和正在进行的太极拳临床应用实验[②]。

太极拳防病治病的作用显而易见，把太极拳作为全民大健康教育的一部分，对改善国民整体素质、防病治病具有长远的意义。但是，太极拳套路的复杂性和语言语义上障碍，限制了它在中外的广泛推广应用。我们在美国的太极队，致力于推广太极、弘扬中华民族文化。我们也对把太极引入癌症病人的康复很有兴趣。在国外推广太极拳最大的障碍，是没有一套简单易学的、标准的英文版太极拳教科书。这本双语太极拳教材，以流传广泛的 24 式简化太极拳为蓝本，把太极的套路动作和传统太极的内涵精髓，通过中英文双语，利用立体教学方式，填补了太极拳教学的空白。张竹筠教授首次提出的太极"八纬度模型"，能够帮助初学者揭开太极拳神秘的面纱，更好地理解太极的精髓。本书引经据典，首次参考了自 1947 年以来重要的中英文文献，增加了本书的科学性和可靠性。我相信，《双语太极拳教程》一定会再次掀起全民学习太极的热潮，促进全民健康，促进太极的国际交流和推广；一定会使更多人喜欢太极，并终生受益于太极拳练习。

美国佛罗里达州肿瘤和血液病临床研究所

张文卿　医学博士

2021 年 5 月 22 日

---

① Lee Smith, Dan Gordon, Adrian Scruton and Lin Yang. *Future Science*. OA 2016 2 (4).

② www.clinicaltrials.gov.

# Preface 2

I am an oncologist and hematologist currently working in the largest private Hematology Oncology Group in the State of Florida, US. As a Tai-chi enthusiast, I have been practicing Chen-style Tai-chi Chuan for almost 20 years. Thanks to the kind invitation from professor ZHANG Zhujun, I would like to share my understanding and experience of practicing Tai-chi Chuan in the view of a Tai-chi enthusiast and a medical professional.

Everything in our universe continues endlessly and is centrally driven by balance. Balance is ubiquitous and can be seen in all scales, from the tiniest of atomic interactions to the magnetic poles keeping our vast earth at orbit and the balance of whole universe. In our own bodies, the forces of balance maintain our homeostasis, such as oncogenes and tumor suppression genes; immunoactivation and immunosuppression; coagulation and anticoagulation and so forth. Should balance be disrupted, problems arise and diseases occur. Constantly adjusting to maintain the balance within our bodies and our surroundings is the fundamental key to healthfulness. Tai-chi Chuan embodies the philosophy of Yin and Yang, in which opposites are united  and are allowed to be transformable. Using a well-designed form, Tai-chi Chuan integrates and activates the people's intent (Yi), vital force (Qi), intrinsic energy (Jin) and physique(Xing) to achieve a delicate and refined balance. Ultimately, the harmony between Yin and Yang, the internal and the external, practitioner and universe will reach the level of all-in-one. As described in the book by professor Zhang, at this level, the practitioner can optimize the body's full potential and achieve the capability of "harness all movements that are connected to each other as a single movement; conduct one movement in the right place, and all other connected movements timely follow to enhance it." By manipulating fluidity and balance with purposeful movements, the hope is to restore balance within, therefore restore the body homeostasis and prevent and treat certain diseases.

The ancient art of Tai-chi Chuan has been passed on from the time of Emperor Wu of Liang Dynasty to present. Its practical values and philosophical significance have been well-proven by both practice and scientific validation. Tai-chi Chuan has been shown to benefit fitness, self-defense and wellness. Not only does it adjust the balance of the central nervous system, but it also enhances the cardiovascular, respiratory, digestive and immune system function. Clinical research has demonstrated that Tai-chi Chuan can promote mental health, as well as treat anxiety/depression, tension headaches, migraines and mood disorders. Furthermore, it can also be used in the management of certain joint disorders; it can alleviate osteoporosis, reduce the risk of fractures and so on[4].

Cancer patients are a distinct patient group that have a higher prevalence of comorbid depression, anxiety, and emotional distress. They suffer from not only physical illness but also mental stress. Beyond facing the reality of the diagnosis, our treatment modalities themselves including surgery, chemotherapy, radiotherapy, immunotherapy and target therapy can cause side effects like fatigue, dizziness, imbalance, loss of appetite, memory loss, difficulty focusing, muscle atrophy and weakness. Modern clinical researchers have demonstrated that Tai-chi Chuan can remarkably improve flexibility and balance, while also enhancing muscle strength, appetite, memory and concentration. It can significantly improve post-treatment recovery and patient's quality of life[5]. Hence, it has been listed as an important component of alternative medicine or integrative medicine by many leading U.S. hospitals. By far, there are more than 301 completed and on-going Tai-chi Chuan related clinical trials worldwide[6].

Obviously, Tai-chi Chuan helps to prevent and treat certain diseases. The inclusion of Tai-chi Chuan in public health education system plays a profound role in strengthening the public health, disease prevention and treatment. However, the complexity of Tai-chi Chuan form and language barrier pose a significant difficulty in popularizing Tai-chi Chuan nationally and internationally. In the United States, our Tai-chi Chuan team is dedicated to promoting Tai-chi Chuan and its traditional Chinese culture serving as its foundation. We're also interested in introducing its principles to the rehabilitation program for cancer patients. The biggest challenge of mass

---

4 Ryan Abbott, JD MTOM and Helen Lavretsky. *Psychiatr Clin North Am.* 2013 March, 36(1): 109-119.

5 Lee Smith, Dan Gordon, Adrian Scruton and Lin Yang. *Future Science.* OA 2016 2 (4).

6 www.clinicaltrials.gov.

distribution is the absence of a simple and standard English version of Tai-chi Chuan textbook. The advent of this bilingual Tai-chi Chuan textbook rightfully fills the gap in Tai-chi Chuan education. It adopts the popular simplified 24-style Tai-chi Chuan as the basic form, encapsulates the quintessential traditional Tai-chi Chuan movements passed down over generations, and presents them both in Chinese and English in a multidimensional education module. Professor ZHANG Zhujun, for the first time, proposes the "Eight-dimension Model" of Tai-chi Chuan to help beginners better understand the essence of Tai-chi Chuan and decipher its philosophical complexity. The textbook has referenced most of the major literatures on Tai-chi Chuan in Chinese and English since 1947. I sincerely believe that the publishing of <<Chinese-English Tai-chi Chuan Course>> will widen the impact and popularity of Tai-chi Chuan, deepen the international exchange and promotion of Tai-chi Chuan, and spark more interest in the public to learn Tai-chi Chuan in order to reap the many physical and psychological benefits it can offer.

ZHANG Wenqing, MD

Oncologist and Hematologist

Florida Cancer Specialists and Research Institute

May.22，2021

# 目　录

第一章　太极拳概述 …………………………………………………… 1

第一节　太极拳简史 …………………………………………………… 1
第二节　太极拳的八维度特征与功能 ………………………………… 5
第三节　太极拳与其他学科 …………………………………………… 9

Chapter 1　Overview of Tai–chi Chuan …………………………… 17

Section 1　Brief History of Tai-chi Chuan ………………………… 17
Section 2　8-Dimension Features and Functions of Tai-chi Chuan …24
Section 3　Tai-chi Chuan and Other Disciplines …………………… 30

第二章　太极拳技术原理 ……………………………………………… 43

第一节　太极拳基本技法 ……………………………………………… 43
第二节　太极拳技术要求 ……………………………………………… 45
第三节　太极拳呼吸方法 ……………………………………………… 50

Chapter 2　Technical Principles of Tai–chi Chuan ……………… 52

Section 1　Basic Techniques of Tai-chi Chuan …………………… 52
Section 2　Technical Requirements for Tai-chi Chuan ……………55
Section 3　Breathing Method of Tai-chi Chuan …………………… 63

第三章　现代科学健身中的太极拳 …………………………………… 66

第一节　太极拳对中枢神经系统的作用 ……………………………… 66
第二节　太极拳对心血管系统的作用 ………………………………… 67
第三节　太极拳对呼吸系统的作用 …………………………………… 69
第四节　太极拳对消化系统的作用 …………………………………… 70
第五节　太极拳对免疫功能的作用 …………………………………… 71
第六节　太极拳对心理健康的作用 …………………………………… 73

**Chapter 3　Tai-chi Chuan in Modern Fitness Science** ················· **78**

Section 1　The Effect of Tai-chi Chuan on Central Nervous System ·········· 78

Section 2　The Effect of Tai-chi Chuan on Cardiovascular System·········· 80

Section 3　The Effect of Tai-chi Chuan on Respiratory System ·········· 82

Section 4　The Effect of Tai-chi Chuan on Digestive System ·········· 83

Section 5　The Effect of Tai-chi Chuan on Immune System ·········· 85

Section 6　The Effect of Tai-chi Chuan on Mental Health ·········· 88

**第四章　太极拳的基本形态和功法**················· **95**

第一节　基本形态 ·················· 95

第二节　常见功法 ·················· 105

**Chapter 4　Basic Forms and Practicing Methods of Tai-chi Chuan** ········· **112**

Section 1　Basic Forms ·················· 112

Section 2　Common Practicing Methods ·········· 123

**第五章　教学与训练**················· **132**

**Chapter 5　Teaching and Training** ·················· **138**

**第六章　简化太极拳**················· **146**

第一节　简化太极拳简介 ·················· 146

第二节　简化太极拳动作图解 ·········· 147

第三节　简化太极拳技击原理与用法 ·········· 181

**Chapter 6　Simplified Tai-chi Chuan** ·················· **193**

Section 1　Brief Introduction to Simplified Tai-chi Chuan·········· 193

Section 2　Diagrams of Simplified Tai-chi Chuan Movements·········· 194

Section 3　Simplified Tai-chi Chuan Attacking Principles and Application ·········· 241

**附录　简化太极拳路线图**················· **255**

**Appendix　Road Map of Simplified Tai-chi Chuan** ·········· **256**

**致谢**················· **257**

**Acknowledgements** ·················· **258**

# 第一章　太极拳概述

## 第一节　太极拳简史

### 一、太极拳的概念

#### （一）太极

在理解太极一词前，先要正确理解什么是"太"和"极"。"太"可解释为很、极或极大、至高；"极"可解释为顶点、最高位、中正的准则、达到最高限度。"太"和"极"组合成复合词"太极"，即含有至高、至极、绝对、唯一，以及中正之意。太极一词源出《周易·系辞》："易有太极，是生两仪。两仪生四象，四象生八卦。"太极派生为万物的本源，气的运动分阴阳，由阴阳二生四时，因而出现天、地、风、雷、水、火、山、泽八种自然现象，推衍为万事万物。《辞源》中解释了"太极"本义是指原始混沌之气。太极之理即阴阳相互对立、相互统一、相互转化之理。在我国宋朝时期已经形成了完整的太极学说，其代表人物是周敦颐、朱熹。周敦颐著有《太极图说》，朱熹以为太极即是理，总天地万物之理就是太极。太极拳以此解析运动原理。

#### （二）太极拳名称的由来

"拳"即拳法、拳术，为徒手搏击的一种武术。从汉画像石的资料来看，先秦时期已经产生了拳术。冠以"太极"之名的拳术，并接受太极理论指导和解析的拳术，称之为太极拳。太极拳是中华武术的著名拳种之一。早期，因其动作如长江之水，滔滔不绝、绵绵不断，故称之为"长拳"，也称"绵拳"；又因其内含八种基本技法（掤、捋、挤、按、采、挒、肘、靠）和五种步法（进步、退步、左顾、右盼、中定），所以又称"十三势"。清朝乾隆年间，山西王宗岳第一个全面系统地用太极哲理解释拳意，著有《太极拳论》，这是"太极拳"这一名称最早的文字记载，从此普遍采用"太极拳"这一名称。[①]

---

① 于翠兰. 简化太极拳［M］. 南京：江苏科学技术出版社，2006.2（1）.

1

## 二、太极拳的形成与发展

### （一）太极拳起源

关于太极拳的起源，专家学者历来都是众说纷纭，莫衷一是。参考各类文献综合分析，我们认为太极拳可分为古代太极拳和近代太极拳。据吴图南先生在《吴图南太极拳精髓》一书中记载，梁武帝时期，徽州府休宁人程灵洗精通太极拳，其师韩拱月创立十五势。唐朝时期徽州府歙县许宣平、安庆人李道子皆以太极拳为修养身心之具。许宣平创有三十七势太极拳，李道子所创太极拳，名先天拳，亦名长拳。元明时期张三丰（1247—约1412）深通道法，创立十三势，拳技绝伦[①]。清康乾年间，山西人王宗岳，曾在洛阳、开封设馆教书，悉心研究拳术理论及拳械技艺，著有《太极拳谱》，后人称之为《太极拳经》，其内容包括"十三势论""太极拳论""太极拳解""十三势歌""打手歌""十三势行功心解""十三势名目"等。古代太极拳记载于文献，偏碎片化，未能有完整、连续的传承谱系，传说或推断的成分较大。

据中国武术史学家唐豪等人考证，太极拳最早传习于河南省温县陈家沟陈姓家族中，创编人是陈王庭。陈王庭文武兼备，谙熟黄老之学，他在练武实践中结合古代导引吐纳术和古典哲学"易经"的阴阳学说及中医"经络学说"理论，综合吸收了明代各家拳法，博采众家之长，特别是戚继光的三十二式长拳，创编了太极拳、器械及对练套路。在其三百多年的流传中，派生出多种流派。[②]我们认为唐豪先生考订的太极拳可以称之为近代太极拳，有明确的连续的传承谱系。

明末清初时期是太极拳发展的成形时期。明洪武七年，从山西洪洞迁至河南温县陈家沟（时名"常阳村"）的陈氏一族，精习拳术。明崇祯至清康熙年间，第九世的陈王廷（1600—1680）于晚年在民间和军队中流行拳法的基础上，取众家之长编创出太极拳早期拳架。陈王廷所编拳架注重动作与呼吸协调。陈王廷遗词中有"《黄庭》一卷随身伴"，可见，早期太极拳结合的导引吐纳术，主要取自道家的《黄庭经》。清朝中叶，太极拳走完了它的幼稚期，进入了成熟期。这一时期的代表人物有陈氏十四世的陈长兴（1771—1853）、永年人杨露禅（1799—1872）以及兼得杨露禅和陈清平（亦被写为"青萍"）之传的永年人武禹襄（1812—1880）。

进入20世纪上半叶后，太极拳在北京的发展日益兴盛。拳派繁衍，传说频生，太极拳考据学也随之兴起。在太极拳拳技方面，由杨露禅编传的"绵拳架"，经其子杨健侯（1839—1917）和其孙杨澄甫（1883—1936）修润定型为后世广为流传的杨式太极拳套路。民国初年永年李亦畬之徒郝为真（1849—1920），至北京传授武禹襄创编的武式太极拳。河北完县人孙禄堂（1861—1932）得郝为真传后，以武式太极拳为基础，融合形意拳和八卦掌技法，创编成孙式太极拳。河北大兴人吴鉴泉（1870—1942），于1921年受聘入北京体育研究社执教后，将师承其父全佑（1834—1902）的杨式拳架，进行删难就简、突出轻柔的整理，

---

① 吴图南. 吴图南太极拳精髓［M］. 北京：人民体育出版社，1991.1. 第265页.

② 中国武术拳械录编纂组. 中国武术拳械录［M］. 人民体育出版社，1993，（132）.

创编成吴式太极拳。故此，太极拳出现了分支迅速、流派繁衍的景象①。近百年来，拳师们，以经典的太极理论和太极拳论为指引，创立了李氏太极拳、和氏太极拳和王其和太极拳。

## （二）太极拳的传统流派

### 1. 陈氏太极拳

陈氏太极拳是太极拳发展史上一个非常重要且流传最广泛的流派。传承代际谱系表明，陈氏太极拳是杨氏太极拳、孙氏太极拳、吴氏太极拳、武氏太极拳等流行太极拳的母拳。陈氏太极拳有陈氏老架和陈氏新架之分，传承脉络清晰。

陈氏老架太极拳为明末陈王廷所创。据后人著录的《陈氏拳械谱》中记载，陈王廷所创之拳共五路，现仅存一路"十三势"，二路"炮捶"，其余都已失传。所谓"十三势"，就是最早的太极拳，计一百零八式，俗称"陈式老架"。这套拳的特点是：架式宽大低沉，运行螺旋缠绕，强调由松入柔、运柔成刚、刚复归柔，其间插有快速发劲、跳跃和震脚等动作。陈氏第八代传承人陈鑫为太极拳理论集大成者，著有《陈氏太极拳图说》《太极拳引蒙入路》《三三六拳谱》《陈氏家乘》等经典著作。

陈氏新架太极拳为清代河南陈家沟拳师陈长兴所创。他忠于陈氏老架太极拳的套路内容和架式宽大低沉的特点，删除了老架中一些刚烈、跳跃动作，使之柔和平稳，以适应年老体弱者锻炼，所以当时人们称之为"略"。后来，他的族侄陈清平在此基础上，又创造了一套小巧紧凑的拳式，架式由简入繁地逐步加圈，人们称之为"圈"，又称"赵堡架"，是陈氏新架的代表。陈氏新架太极拳形成后，老架中的一些拳套便逐渐消失。

### 2. 杨氏太极拳

杨氏太极拳为清代杨福魁所创，其孙杨澄甫修改定型。杨福魁字露禅，别号禄禅，河北永年人。早年至陈家沟师从陈长兴学艺，学得陈氏老架太极拳。拳技以"柔中寓刚，绵里藏针"著称。19世纪50年代，任京师旗人武术教习，在向政治文化界人士传授太极拳过程中，逐步改变动作，自成一派。他的儿子杨鉴、杨钰，也是当时的太极拳名家。杨福魁逝世后，所遗拳路经其孙杨澄甫（兆清）修改定型为杨氏太极拳。杨氏太极拳以架式舒展端正、均匀柔和见长。杨氏门人著述颇丰，有《太极拳术》《太极拳使用法》《太极拳体用全书》《太极拳术十要》《太极拳之练习谈》等专著。1947年，杨氏太极拳门人田兆麟的弟子陈炎林，与两位著名翻译大家、复旦大学的陈遽教授和葛传椝教授，一起翻译了第一本英文太极专著《Tai-Chi Chuan: the effects and practical application》，由上海别发书馆（Kelly & Walsh Limited）出版发行。70多年来，先后出多家出版社出版17次②，对太极拳的国际传播影响力无可估量。

### 3. 武氏太极拳

武氏太极拳为清代武禹襄所创，发展至今近200年。武禹襄为河北永年人，幼习洪拳。最初师从杨福魁，后去河南温县跟陈青萍学陈氏新架太极拳，再从吴全佑学吴氏太极拳，然后融会贯通，自成一派，后经李亦畬、郝为真修改定型，所以也称"郝氏太极拳"。其特点为架式紧凑简洁、动作舒展、步法严格、虚实分明。武禹襄学理验证，以《王宗岳太极拳论》

① 康戈武，《文化瑰宝 健身益友》（副标题为《太极拳发展概略》）[N]. 北京：《人民日报》，2001年2月10日第四版、14日第八版、16日第八版.

② 金艳. 1947年版《太极拳》英文本考论 [J]. 成都体育学院学报. 2019，45（6）：74-81.

潜心研练，总结出《十三势行功要解》《太极拳解》《十三势说略》《四字秘诀》《打手撒放》等名篇，从拳理、拳法到刀杆运用，形成了一个完整的太极拳学派。

### 4. 吴氏太极拳

吴氏太极拳是由清代满族人吴全佑及其子吴鉴泉从杨氏太极拳演化而成。吴全佑师从杨福魁父子，为清咸丰、同治年间的太极拳高手，继承杨氏小架拳式并有所演化。其子吴鉴泉在继承父亲拳技基础上，进一步增益修订，使套路精纯，形成了吴氏太极拳流派。其特点是架式小巧规矩，动作细腻柔和，体态松静自然。吴氏太极拳发源于北京，兴盛于上海、广州和香港等大城市。

### 5. 孙氏太极拳

孙氏太极拳由清末民初孙福全所创。孙福全字禄堂，河北定县人。早年师从形意拳大师郭云深练拳 8 载、又师从八卦拳传承人程庭华大师 2 年，后从郝为真学武氏太极拳，其拳技精纯，融合太极、形意、八卦三家之长，独树一帜而成孙氏太极拳。孙氏太极拳以架高步活、转换轻盈为特点。孙氏太极拳从创立至今百余年，成拳较晚。因步法进退相随，运转开合相接，所以也称"开合活步太极拳"。孙禄堂著有《形意拳学》《八卦掌学》《太极拳学》《八卦剑学》。

## （三）太极拳内容与分类

### 1. 套路运动

套路就是精心系统设计的整套的动作。太极拳套路演练的基本要素包括：身体姿势、练习轨迹、练习时间、练习速度、练习速率、练习力量、练习节奏、攻防意识等 8 个部分。各个流派的代表传承人精心设计了套路，确保传承有据。教练套路不仅提升了初学者兴趣，而且也保证了常年修炼者入规中距。国家体委（国家体育总局）自 1955 年起，即组织武术家整理出版了《简化太极拳（24 式）》，1962 年修订了 88 式太极拳套路，1979 年创编了 48 式太极拳竞赛套路，此后各式太极拳竞赛套路先后面世。

套路运动是以技击攻防为主线，综合了各种身法、腿法和手法，以攻守进退、动静疾徐、刚柔虚实等矛盾运动的变化规律编成的整套练习形式。套路运动按演练形式又可分为单练、对练和集体演练三种类型。

单练包括徒手的拳术与器械，比如简化太极拳、陈氏老架、杨氏太极拳 108 式、太极剑、太极刀等套路。

对练包括徒手的对练、器械对练、徒手与器械对练，比如太极拳对练、三杆对练等。

集体演练包括徒手的拳术、器械或徒手与器械等形式。

### 2. 搏斗运动

搏斗运动是在一定条件下两人或多人，按照一定的规则进行斗智、斗技的对抗实战式。搏斗运动的目的是检验技术性攻防实用性。慢学套路为练功、快悉搏击在应用。套路运动和搏击运动相辅相成，互为验证。搏击运动的攻防要求，与引导套路运动练习过程中身法、腿法和手法等准确到点到位，都是为了把握"过犹不及"的原则不偏不倚。

太极拳中的推手被列入到武术竞赛项目。推手是两人按照一定的规则，使用掤、捋、挤、按、采、挒、肘、靠等手法，双方粘连黏随，通过肌肉的灵敏感觉来判断对方的用劲，然后借劲发劲将对手推出，以此决定胜负的竞技项目。

### 3. 功法运动[①]

功法运动是为掌握和提高武术套路和格斗技术，围绕提高身体某一运动素质或者改善身体的某些机能和功能，又或锻炼某一特殊技能而编组的专门练习。

太极拳中的功法内容主要以内功功法为主，比如无极桩、混元桩、开合桩、升降桩、定步桩等；是采用以意领气、以气运身、以身发力为基本锻炼手段的一种内外兼修的方法。其目的在于人体运动时意、气、劲、形一动俱动，一到俱到，一至俱至的能力。通过内功锻炼，可以获得内状外勇、内外合一及激发人体潜能的效果。

## 第二节　太极拳的八维度特征与功能

### 一、太极拳的八维度特征

不同流派的太极拳名家对太极拳特点有着精妙的总结。冯志强先生从广义尺度总结为：综合性、适应性、功能性、经济性、安全性、科学性、哲理性、艺术性；王善德先生总结武氏太极拳的特点为：结构严谨、缜密入微、化发守中、圆点互根，强调身法、合乎丹道，形势混元，内含一气，二气交感、行气贴背，步如临渊、劲若抽丝，神聚气歙、五音开合，包获周匝、合力共震；沈家桢先生总结的陈氏太极拳特点为：意气运动、弹性运动、虚实运动、节节贯穿运动、一气呵成运动、刚柔相济运动及快慢相间运动；杨澄甫先生总结为：虚灵顶劲、含胸拔背、松腰、分虚实、沉肩坠肘、用意不用力、上下相随、内外相合、相连不断、动中求静。各家总结就习拳而言大同小异。

任何事物特点的征象、标志，即其特征。同样太极拳有其自身特征，准确地讲有其维度特征，所谓维度特征，是指两两特征存在相互影响和相互作用。用维度特征来描述太极拳的特点或特征，更能符合太极拳的理论要求和应用修炼。太极拳教学中强调师傅的口传心授，其根本原因在于特征之间的相互影响和相互作用。因此，太极拳名家吴图南先生称太极拳为"太极拳，口授之学也"[②]。用维度特征表述，有利于习练者在没有老师耳提面命口授之下，实习自我对照提升。八个维度特征如下：心静体松、立身中正、以意导动（用意不用力）、周身掤劲、圆活连贯、虚实分明、上下相随、刚柔相济。（图1-2-1）

#### 1. 心静体松

练太极拳要求思想集中，全神贯注于动作，做到"神聚、心静、意专、体松"。

"心静"是练太极拳的重要原则。心静即要求专心，在练拳时，思想要集中，意识不断地引导动作，并且灵活变换，使任何动作都有一定的指向，不顾此失彼。且要有耐心，不可焦躁或心猿意马，否则动作方向、姿势不正确，就难以把太极拳学好、练好。

"体松"是和心静同样重要的一个原则，是贯彻"用意不用力"的重要措施。运动时，在心静的前提下用意引导肢体内外各个器官、关节和肌肉的放松，逐步做到全身不该用力处毫不用力，尤其不用拙劲，内外各部分无一处不松，尽量使身体自然舒展而不僵硬。按照规

---

① 邱丕相. 中国武术导论 [M]. 北京：高等教育出版社，2010.7.

② 吴图南. 吴图南太极拳精髓 [M]. 北京：人民体育出版社，1991.1：7

矩用劲，以意贯注于动作过程之中，按照动作的虚实变化适度地完成动作。

### 2. 立身中正

太极拳练习过程中自始至终强调立身中正，保持身体直立，整体上要求做到头顶悬、虚灵顶劲，沉肩坠肘，含胸拔背，脊柱放松，松腰圆裆，提胯敛臀，屈膝微坐。习练者可以反复用武术谚语警示：低头猫腰学艺不高。立身中正有利于提起精神，使注意力集中。在技击中，有助于准确判断、及时反应和灵活应对。清代陈氏太极拳主要传承人陈长兴，立身中正，不偏不倚，人称"牌位先生"。其他拳种，比如象形中的醉拳、鹰抓拳、地躺拳等都没有像太极拳那样刻意强调立身中正。拳师甚至要求太极拳的习练者在日常行为举止中，也要做到立身中正。

### 3. 以意导动

人体的任何动作（除反射性的动作外），包括各种体育锻炼的动作，都需要经过意识的指挥。练习太极拳的全部过程也要求用意识（指想象力）引导动作，把注意力贯注到动作中去。强调用意不用力，用意念引领动作，不用僵硬之力、肌肉紧张之力。做到拳论所要求的"神为主帅，身为驱使""以意行气，以气运身"，意动身随就是这个意思。一举一动均用意不用力，先意动而后形动，逐步做到意到气到，气到劲到。

### 4. 周身掤劲

掤劲是太极拳的独有特点，为一个最基本技法，即肢体放长，全身一体的轻灵弹性劲。源于意识引导下，由无极态产生的内气充盈状态下，劲力混元向外，圆满而具张力。内气腾然末梢，掤劲节节贯通，周身灵敏，动作轻灵。甚至有人称太极拳为掤劲拳。掤劲需要依靠口授，搭手听劲。练习掤劲，体悟到松而不懈，克服松而懈的弊病。

### 5. 圆活连贯

练太极拳要求"一动无有不动""由脚而腿而腰，总需完整一气"，要求做到上下相随、节节贯串地连贯圆活。动作要圆活，即动作要圆满、灵活，在一连贯的弧形动作中圆满地不凹不凸，无有缺陷，不起棱角，变动又非常轻灵活泼。圆满灵活运用到动作上，要求达到中正不偏、不越界限、不被压扁、走化粘依、不丢不顶、处处圆满灵活。

习练者每一势如何起、如何落，要仔细揣摩，到定式时必须意识贯注，似停非停，这种势与势之间的承接，就称作连贯。连贯就是要求上一动作和下一动作折叠地衔接起来，转接处微微贯动，不僵不滞，不能有停顿断续之处。

### 6. 虚实分明[①]

太极拳对虚实的要求是很严格的，虚实诀中说："练拳不谙虚实理，枉费功夫终无成。"因此，太极拳以虚实为第一义。虚实分为整体和局部两个方面，从整体动作来说，动作达到终点为"实"，动作的转变过程为"虚"；从局部动作来说，主要支撑体重的腿为"实"，辅助支撑或移动换步的腿为"虚"。例如身体重心在右腿上，则右腿为实，左腿为虚，这样虚实就分清了，做起动作来也就转动轻灵，毫不费力。如不能分虚实，则迈步重滞，自立不稳。分虚实主要是避免动作不分主次、平均用力和双重、呆滞的毛病。

初练者首先要注意两腿转换的虚实，使动作平稳舒展，不偏不倚，演练动作时重心要稳定。待局部虚实分清后，再体会与把握整体的虚实。最后达到在太极拳的演练中"虚中有实，

---

① 吴忠农著. 简化太极拳练势与运气 [M]. 北京：北京体育大学出版社，1993.

实中有虚"的境界。

### 7. 上下相随[1]

练习太极拳，周身运动必须协调一致，如《拳论》中所说："一动无有不动。"在完成任何动作时，整个身体，每一个部位，都要协调地动起来。决不可做成手动脚不动、脚动手不动，而是要使每一个动作"由脚而腿而腰总要完成一气"，使上、下肢和躯干的运动协调地配合。演练时，步随身换，手领神随，姿势既协调又优美，才是太极拳"上下相随"的技术。

### 8. 刚柔相济[2]

刚柔相济是太极拳的突出特点，是太极阴阳学说的明显体现，是太极拳的精髓。

太极拳的"刚"，是以腰为轴，利用太极拳的缠丝劲，牵动丹田之气，在瞬间发出的爆发力，亦称弹簧劲。不是日常提重物或推举重物使用的那种蛮力、拙力。

太极拳的"柔"，是由放松得到的轻柔和柔和，是身体去掉僵劲后的手足屈伸圆润自如和动作的自然协调，是一种轻灵而又沉着，并且含有弹性和韧性的感觉。柔由松来，求柔必先求松。做到身体放松，一要掌握好虚灵顶劲、沉肩坠肘的要领，同时要把周身关节处处松开；二要能做到"用意不用力"。"不用力"是指不用拙力，且用力要自然，要适度。

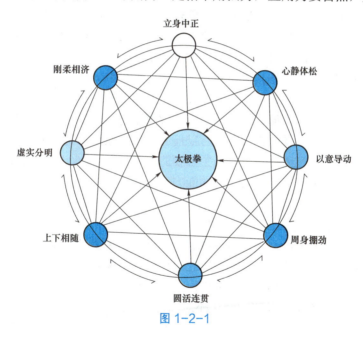

图 1-2-1

## 二、太极拳的功能

### （一）太极拳的健身功能

太极拳健身功能的显著特点是其终身性，包括伴随人生命活动的全过程，即太极拳健身

① 吴忠农著. 简化太极拳练势与运气［M］. 北京：北京体育大学出版社，1993.
② 郭振兴. 杨式太极拳英汉双语基础教程［M］. 北京：北京理工大学出版社，2015.1.

可以伴随人一辈子，人们可以在不同年龄段选择太极拳作为健身运动。

中国人重视生命虚静，强调身心意放松，注重养生之道，平衡身理、调节心理、稳定情绪。练习者在进行套路的练习过程中，同步实现了调身、调心、调意，从而增进健康功能处于最佳状态。即使是在以武术作为技击手段的古代，人们也没有忽略它的健身价值，王宗岳在《十三势歌》中说："详推用意终何在？益寿延年不老春。"说明到清代武术的社会功能已在明显转变，习拳的终极目的已在于"益寿延年"，武术的健身价值更是日益突显出来了。

作为武术运动项目之一的太极拳，更是突出其独特的健身价值。由于太极拳在发展的过程中受到了中国传统医学、中国养生导引之术的影响、渗透，在主动防御疾病方面具有积极的作用。因此，轻柔缓慢的太极拳，以其独特的运动方式受到海内外人群的青睐。松静自然、气沉丹田、中等强度的运动，不仅对心血管、呼吸系统有良好的影响，而且有利于调节神经系统、陶冶性情、缓解压力等，对当代大健康社会的建立有着更为重要的意义。

### （二）太极拳的防身功能

太极拳作为一个拳种，其最本质的特征就是技击性。太极拳的一招一式同时兼备健身和防身功效。通过练习太极拳，一方面可以全面地提高人的身体素质；另一方面也可以学会一些攻防技击技术，直接提高练习者进行技击对抗的水平。

由于太极拳本身就具有攻防技击特点，所以通过太极拳训练可以使练习者了解、熟悉、掌握一些攻防技击技术。虽然有些动作是经过加工、改造的，已不完全等同于原来在生死搏斗中所运用的攻防实战技术，但这些技术中仍包含着原来实战技术的核心要点，所以在掌握了这些技术以后，再经过必要的训练，是可以使之还原成原来的生死搏斗中的实战技术。同时在其训练的过程中，练习者也随之提高了必要的专项身体素质，这也更有利于练习者准确掌握和运用这些技术，进一步提高其自卫的能力。

### （三）太极拳的修身功能[①]

在中国传统文化熏陶下的武术，对习武者的伦理、道德要求很高，"未曾习武先习德"，将道德放在一个非常重要的地位。长期习练武术可以将道德内化为人的自觉意识和行为，因而武术的道德修养塑造功能必然有利于人健康成长，有利于社会的和谐发展。

太极拳被称为"哲拳"，习练者以自强不息精神为动力，以厚德载物品质为保障，以"修身、齐家、治国、平天下"为己任，达到修身养性、陶冶情操的目的。尤其在现代信息化快节奏的生活中，安逸、恬静的田园式生活态度可以有效地消除和缓解高压力、快节奏给人带来的种种伤害，有张有弛才能帮助人们健康地工作和生活。以强身健体、修身养性、艺术鉴赏为目的的太极拳练习，能够提高人们的生活能力和质量，帮助人们抵御和消除学习、工作、生活压力导致的焦虑，提高社会适应能力和人们的道德修养。

---

① 邱丕相. 中国武术导论［M］. 北京：高等教育出版社，2010.7.40-41.

## 第三节　太极拳与其他学科

### 一、太极拳与中国武术

#### （一）太极拳拳理基础[①]

太极拳作为武术项目中的一个拳种，符合武术运动原理，具有技击性。也就是太极拳动作本身符合攻防规律，具有攻防含义，能够产生一定的攻防实效，这也是太极拳动作与体操、舞蹈、导引等其他运动的基本区别，也是本质区别之一。

太极拳在创造过程中，广泛吸收了其他武术拳种动作，精心组编而成。根据史料记载，太极拳吸收了明朝戚继光的拳法，戚继光的拳法也是在吸收了众多民间武术基础上形成的，把戚继光的《拳经三十二势》和陈氏太极拳的图诀加以比较，可以发现不仅动作名称相似，而且架势也十分相近。在《陈氏拳械谱》上也有"红拳"的记载。即使从现在广泛流传的太极拳中，也不难看出与其他拳种相似的动作，如杨式太极拳的"搬拦捶"与八极拳的"落砸捶""栽捶"，与少林拳小红拳的"下栽捶"外形动作几乎一致，这些都说明太极拳动作主要取材于其他武术拳种，并保留了武术动作固有的技击性。同样的弓步，作为太极拳由于技击性的要求，上步时前脚要求微内扣，有套索对方脚跟的含义，而作为体操化的弓步并无此意；同样的冲拳，作为舞蹈化的表演则无须做到"手背与小臂齐平"，而太极拳的冲拳就必须如此，否则违反了攻防原理，不能产生攻防实效，也就不符合武术运动原理。

太极拳拳谱、拳论中充满技击内容，也反映了太极拳具有技击性。在现有的文献中，可以清楚地看到有关太极拳技击思想、战术、方法、训练的论述，被尊称为太极拳经典的《太极拳论》中讲到"人刚我柔谓之走，我顺人背谓之粘，动急则急应，动缓则缓随……"，通篇讲技击思想，策略方法也唯武事论。其他如《打手歌》《十三势歌》《四字密诀》等，也都讲的是技击内容，说明太极拳具有技击性。

不管太极拳的技击功能是否在衰退，不能否认的是，从动作属性上来看，太极拳是以练习技击动作为手段，来实现健身技击等多重功能的拳种，即太极拳动作具有技击性，这种技击性必须保留在套路里，体现在动作中，这是太极拳区别于其他运动的本质特点，也是衡量太极拳动作准确与否必不可少的一条重要原则。换句话讲就是太极拳动作必须符合武术运动理论，这也正是太极拳之所以称为"拳"的道理所在。如海底针、白猿献果、翻花舞袖、玉女穿梭、上步七星等，不少太极拳的拳式名称中本身就暗含了极强的技击性。比如海底针，海底即暗指会阴穴位，练习海底针，即瞄准会阴方向攻击对手小腹。

#### （二）中国传统武德

所谓武德，就是经过武术拳种习练活动的人，在社会活动中所应遵循的道德规范和所应具有的道德品质、道德操守。简而言之，就是武术道德。武德作为一种美德，一种社会意识

---

① 冯志强.太极拳全书［M］.北京：学苑出版社，2000.1.

形态，指导人们共同的武术生活及其行为的准则、规范，并渗透在习武者的思想和言行中。为了培养高尚的品德，武林的各拳种流派都订有自己的"门规""戒律""戒约"，并有"三不传""五不传""十不传"以及"八戒律""十要诀"等作为武德的标准。各门各派也都认定："功夫有限，仁者无敌"，所以在遇到冲突时，要做到"尚德不尚力，重守不重攻"。习武者首先要以德服人、以德慑人，行不通时才可以施展武艺，制服对方，而不应单凭武力，先发制人。弘扬和倡导是会而不用、点到即止、以和为贵的风尚，杜绝好狠斗勇、冥顽戾气。

太极拳作为武术中的一个流派，同样也有着相关的内容。主要包括：尊师重道、礼貌文明、爱国爱家、知晓大义、明辨是非，存仁义之心、与人为善、助人为乐、惩恶扬善、见义勇为，能吃苦耐劳，有坚忍不拔之志，诚心、专心、诚信、守法、守约、勇气、认真、坚持、自信、自强、自尊等，这些都是需要传承下去的宝贵精神财富。修炼太极拳本质上是一个传承中华传统优秀文化的过程，通过对身心的全方位修炼来不断地完善自己，验证和体悟中国传统健身哲学，尤其是太极拳论的一个渐次修炼过程，做一个具有高尚道德、完美人格的人。

## 二、太极拳与中国传统哲学

太极拳理论充满中国传统哲学思想，但更多的不是研讨哲学思想，而是如何应用传统哲学指导太极拳的修炼。太极拳受传统哲学渗透影响，具有哲理性，充满辩证思想。从哲学角度来看，太极拳被誉为"哲拳"，这不仅由于太极拳的称谓带有浓厚的哲学意味，也不仅由于太极拳动作要领蕴含着深刻的哲学意味，而是由于传统哲学思想对太极拳的全面渗透，形成了独特的运动思想、特别的技术要求、突出的价值功能。正如杨澄甫先生所言"中国之拳术，虽派别繁多，要知皆寓有哲理之技术，……太极拳，乃柔中寓刚，绵里藏针之艺术，于技术上、生理上、力学上，有相当之哲理存也。"如果说古典哲学对各门拳术都有影响，那么对太极拳的影响则是最全面、最系统、最深刻的，恐怕没有哪一门拳术能与之相媲美。从古老的《周易》到宋明理学，都对太极拳有不同程度的影响。

对太极拳术产生影响的古典哲学包括以下几个方面：

### 1. 老子学说

老子通过不断前进的生产现象与生活实践，看到"天下莫柔于水，而攻坚疆者莫之能胜"，意即看上去柔弱的水却能冲决一切坚强障碍。以草为例，"万物草木之生也柔脆，其死也枯槁"，"故坚强者死之徒，柔弱者生之徒"，由此通过大量的生动事物变化现象，终于概括出一般的道理"天下之至柔，驰骋天下之至坚"，上升到哲学层次形成"贵柔""守雌""反者道之动，弱者道之用"的思想。在太极拳中形成"以小胜大""以弱胜强""以柔克刚"的"反者"技击思想，这是太极拳的一个重要特征。此外，老子的一些具体思想对太极拳的技术要求都产生了深刻影响，如"致虚极，守静笃"追求虚静的修道思想，影响了太极拳的"心静""神敛"要求的形成；"道"的"周行不殆"的循环思想影响并形成了太极拳"圆"的运动特征；"道法自然""无为而治"，促成了太极拳"松静自然""舍己从人"的技术要求；"虚其心，实其腹"的修道状态，直接指导了太极拳"含胸拔背""气沉丹田"的形成，等等。

### 2. 阴阳学说

在《周易·系辞》中，"易有太极，是生两仪，两仪生四象，四象生八卦"，提出"一阴一阳谓之道"，"刚柔相摩，八卦相荡"。北宋周敦颐著《太极图说》，创立以太极为中心的世界构成说，认为一动一静产生阴阳构成世界。后经历代哲学家的发展，形成了运用阴阳对立统一运动说明事物发展变化规律的古典阴阳学说，对太极拳的影响巨大。不仅太极拳称谓反映了这一点，更重要的是拳理阐释、拳架组成、运动规律、技术要求、攻守原则等无不包含阴阳哲理。《太极拳论》开宗明义："太极者，无极而生，阴阳之母，动之则分，静之则合"，"一阴一阳谓之拳"，太极拳就是由阴阳两大范畴构成的运动。比照太极图来看，太极拳中动静、刚柔、虚实、开合等对立统一状态，与太极图的阴阳消长、转化规律是一致的。太极拳的动作圆活，招招不离弧形，式式都像圆形，使整套动作圆转连贯、一气呵成。太极图也是置于平面圆形中，而且双鱼环绕，恰如练习太极推手时两人双搭手的形态。练习中双方臂膀组成环状不断变化，你进我退，粘边黏随，正符合彼阴吾阳、相互消长、交替变化的规律。

太极拳家认为，太极是一切的原动力，宇宙既有太极，人身也有太极，而且人身的腹部就是太极，所以《太极十三式歌》中说："命意源头在腰隙，刻刻留心在腰间。"

### 3. 中国武术的哲学境界——天人合一

中国古典哲学的根本观念是"天人合一"。这种"天人合一"的思想体现到武术中，表现为习武者追求人与自然的统一。清代杨氏传抄《太极拳谱》中记载："乾坤为一大天地，人为一小天地也。"所以在练习的过程中，人们总是在追求人体与大自然的和谐相通，使人顺乎自然，其运动也要服从大自然的变化规律，以此来求得物我、内外的平衡，达到阴阳平和。

太极拳也是以自然现象阐发拳理。如王宗岳说太极拳是"长拳者，如长江大海，滔滔不绝也"，不仅说明了太极拳的技术特点，也表明了演练时还要注意养成"腹内松静气腾然"的内心活动，皆是以江海之势喻拳势。

任何文化的交融结合都有它的载体和途径，古典哲学对太极拳的渗透也同样，并非无稽之谈。传统哲学对太极拳的渗透载体主要有两类：一类是有文化的太极大师，如《太极拳论》的作者王宗岳，"少时自经史而外，黄帝老子之书及兵家言无书不读"，以及道士出身的张三丰，后来的陈鑫、武禹镶、李亦畬、孙禄堂等，他们著书立说，大大促进了太极拳对传统哲学的吸收。另一类是太极拳的实践者，他们虽然不像前者那样通晓经书哲学，也许目不识丁，但是他们间接地受古书的影响很大，而且更重要的是，他们在练拳实践中体悟到了哲理。他们的体悟虽然是朴素的思想，却也很好地继承了传统哲学内含。传统哲学对太极拳渗透的途径主要有两种：一是用哲理说拳理，指导练拳，如《太极拳论》就像一篇哲学散文，解说拳理。二是通过吸收其他艺术，间接吸收哲理，如传统医学、兵学等。正像"传统的中医学并不是现代意义的科学，而是自然哲学"一样，太极拳在创造之初，是建构在传统哲学基础之上，也就是说传统哲学不仅宏观指导太极拳的形成，而且具体到技术要求，几乎每一个动作，从外形到内涵都有一定的哲学意味，这构成了太极拳又一个特征，也是衡量动作对否的法则。

## 三、太极拳与中国医学

"拳起于《易》，而理成于医"，这句古语说明了武术与中医学的关系。中国古拳法心意蕴藏着极其深奥的人体生命学的基本原理，明清以来兴起的形意、八卦、太极等内家拳术，在创编过程中也无一不受到中医学、气功学、经络学的影响。

太极拳同样吸收了传统医学的经络、俞穴、气血、导引、藏象等理论，具有健身性。陈鑫在《太极图说》中详细收录了穴位歌诀，指引修炼行功导气。

吐纳之术被太极拳直接吸收。《黄帝内经》中记载："中央者，其地平以湿，天地所以生万物也重，其民食杂而不劳，故其病多痿厥寒热，其治宜导引按乔。"所谓"导引，谓摇筋骨动肢节。按，谓抑按皮肉。乔，谓捷举手足"。庄子描述导引说："吹嘘呼吸，吐故纳新，熊经鸟伸，为寿而已矣。"晋代李颐注谓："导气令和，引体令柔。"说明导引实际上是呼吸配合动作，活动全身，疏通经络的健身运动，包括引体、导气、按摩、存想等内容。太极拳正是吸收了这一特点，要求呼吸与动作配合，所谓"拳式呼吸"，但是这种配合又不完全等同于导引动作，有太极拳自身的特点。中医认为，经络是布满人体的气血通道，发源于脏腑，布流于四肢百骸，脏腑经络气血失和，而疾病生，和则健身益寿。太极拳与之结合，要求"以气运身""以窍运身""气遍身躯"；通过以腰为轴，带动四肢，旋腰转脊，螺旋缠绕，意想劲力传递，循经而动，劲贯窍穴，布流周身，通任、督练带和冲脉，促进气血运行，疏通经络，起到健身作用。"形与神俱，不可分离"，"独立守神，肌肉若一"的医理，被太极拳吸收为"形神皆备""内外皆修""以意导动"的要求。《素问·上古天真论》中写道："故能形与神俱，而尽天年。"形即外形身体，神为精神心理。"精神内守，病安从来"，太极拳理根于此，讲求"意在蓄神"，"形诸神明"，重"意""神"，以及内在的练习与外形的统一，所谓"内不动，外不发"，合中医健身之理，"故能寿蔽天地，无有终时"，太极十三势歌言"详推用意终何在，益寿延年不老春"。太极拳的健身性理根于传统医理，又符合现代科学（后述），每一个动作都有其特殊的健身功能，构成了太极拳的重要特征。

## 四、太极拳与美学

姿态自然美。培根曾说过："论起美来，状貌之美，胜于颜色之美，而适宜并优雅的动作之美又胜于状貌之美。""流美者，人也！"太极拳之美充分说明了这一点。太极拳作为一项人体运动，属于人体文化，在中华文化的长期熏陶下，它不仅仅是一门实用的技击艺术，而且表现出了武术运功绚丽多姿的形式。太极拳练习过程中的形、神、意、气、势、态、韵、律，无处不展现太极之美。

韵律美、节奏美，太极拳和舞蹈在表现的审美功能上具有相同的特点如结构、形式和内蕴美。以太极拳的套路来看，太极拳具有内外合一、行拳流畅、形神兼备、刚柔相济、节奏分明的运动特色。虽然套路中的动作是以格斗为基础，但经过提炼、组合后，演练中除了攻防含义，还有意识、呼吸、动作的有机配合，使它动则快速有力，静则稳如磐石，动静有韵味。太极拳和舞蹈运动规律一致，要求"欲前先后，欲左先右，欲上先下"，遵循"道者反之动"的原则，使动作与动作的衔接产生出一种圆、流转的空间动态。太极拳运动讲究以动而求静、外动而内静、动静相生。静则稳如磐石，动则快如闪电。在套路演练中充满节奏的美妙，使力与美、气与势、神与精灌输其间。

神韵气质美。太极拳自始至终保持身体直立，整体上要求做到头顶悬、虚灵顶劲，沉肩坠肘，含胸拔背，目光内敛深邃，器宇轩昂，威仪庄严。太极拳尤重神韵，而在太极拳套路的演练中，神随形转，形随意动，使整个套路协调而富有生气，演练时如行云流水般一气呵成，周身一体，身手放长，构成浑然天成的神韵气质美。太极拳中的"劲"起于脚跟，发于腿，主宰于腰间，形于手指，发于脊骨，由脚而腿而腰，一气呵成；发劲时则要求劲整，所谓"周身合下成千斤"。太极拳运动意欲向上，必先寓下，意欲向左，必先右去，前后左右，内外相合，且刚柔相济。同时武术的"精、气、神"也体现出英武、阳刚之美，使人感到一种勇往直前、势不可挡的气势。

太极拳作为传统武术的一个项目，植根于中华民族源远流长的传统文化。它要求练习者在锻炼中调养自己的眼、耳、心三性，使眼光锐利、耳目灵通、心性灵勇。所谓"眼耳有闻，心必随之，心性灵勇，气血况至"。潜移默化地陶冶自己的情趣，培养坚定、果敢、刚毅不屈、勇猛无畏的性格，给予人们美的享受。通过学习太极拳，人们可以知美、识美、懂美、爱美，可以享受德与美的交融，可以领略"德美以动心，神美以修性，形美以怡情"，并可以达到调气息、壮筋骨、除疾病的功效。

## 五、太极拳与力学

太极拳作为身体运动，其中包含着较为丰富的力学知识，如牛顿定律、动量定理、力的叠加以及力量传递等，都在太极拳中有所应用，这些知识的应用使太极拳有了自己的特点。太极拳讲究借力打力，能够做到"四两拨千斤"，这些都与力学知识有着密不可分的关系。练习者掌握好相应的力学知识，可以很好地理解太极拳的运动原理，也能更好地掌握以柔克刚、以静制动的动作原理，进而提高自身的太极拳水平。下面我们主要从太极拳拳架和技法两个方面认识太极拳与力学的关系。

### （一）太极拳拳架的力学原理

#### 1. 立身中正——人体动态平衡

平衡力学是研究物体在外力的作用下，处于平衡状态的性质和行为的力学分支。在太极拳十三势中的"定"也说明了平衡在太极拳运动中的重要作用，尤其太极拳的缓慢柔和阶段，虽然路线都是弧线，但由于角速度较小，可以认为近似于一个动态平衡。

从人体受力来看，"立身中正"承受了三方面力的作用，包括：人受到重力的作用；地面对人的支持力；地面和脚的摩擦力。人体力学平衡的条件包括以下几方面。

（1）身体四肢为杠杆：两脚开立，身体中正安舒，成为不规则的人体杠杆。符合"杠杆可曲可直，没有固定的形状，只要是能绕固定点转动，且不发生形变的物体，都可称为杠杆"的原理。

（2）腰顶为转动轴：人体腰顶上下一条线，即是人体的重心，支点又是旋转的中轴。

（3）动力与阻力：使杠杆转动的力称为动力；阻碍杠杆转动的力称为阻力。

（4）力臂：从支点到力的作用线的距离叫力臂（即支点到力点之间的距离）。动力臂是指支点到动力作用线的距离；阻力臂是指支点到阻力作用线的距离。

（5）人体杠杆的平衡条件，即"动力与动力臂的乘积等于阻力与阻力臂的乘积"。

人体重心的垂线在两脚围成的面积之间，这是人体保持平衡的最重要的条件，因此，保持人体平衡的最好方法是让人体重心的垂线保持在脚底的支撑面内（脚所围成的面积），并且尽量靠近支撑面的中心位置。太极拳拳理要求练习者保持立身中正，发力时以腰部为枢纽，上下左右要确保进退灵活，从而形成轮圆之势，这样一切动作都可以将腰部作为支点，手脚自由挥洒，形成一个杠杆模型[①]。这样能更好地控制上体的重心保持在中心位置。

### 2. 动力来源——支持力和肌张力

太极拳的动力分为内力和外力，以来源于人体肌肉收缩的肌张力为源动力，是内力；以来源于两脚虚实变换过程中脚踏地的反作用力为主动力，是外力。张昌亨主编的《运动生物力学》中说道："肌肉与人体的其他软组织不同，在神经的控制下，它能使化学能在常温下转换成机械能，通过自身的主动收缩而造成人体各关节的机械运动。""肌肉收缩时的最大功率就是身体所具有的最大爆发力。这种能力不仅使身体运动，更重要的是加速运动。"牛顿第三定律中说道："当甲物体对乙物体有作用时，则乙物体对甲物体有反作用力，而物体的作用力与反作用力总是等大、共线、反向的。""作用力与反作用力必定是同一性质的力。如果作用力是摩擦力，反作用力也是摩擦力；如果作用力是弹性力，那么反作用力亦是弹性力。"

用"运动生物力学"和"机械运动力学"的原理剖析和解读太极拳动力，即大脑通过中枢神经控制主动支配腰部骨骼肌收缩产生肌肉张力为源动力（内力），驱动两腿虚实变换对地面产生反作用力为主动力（外力），这样进一步明确了太极拳动力产生的真正原因和依据。

### 3. 周身一家——人体整体协调运动

周身一家是太极拳中对身法的要求，是指在打拳和推手当中，人体应该尽量保持整体的运动，手上的每一动作和身体的每一运动都由脚带动起来，双肩和两胯要在一个平面运动，而且手脚要同时同步，一动俱动，一停俱停。

周身一家所带来的第一个好处是质量 $m$ 的增大。根据牛顿的惯性定律可知，质量 $m$ 越大，则物体的惯性越大，相应地要改变其运动状态所需要的力也就越大。这意味着，当练习者用周身一家的方法行拳或推手时，对手想干涉或改变这种运动就更加困难。

周身一家所带来的第二个好处是力的传导效率的提高。我们知道摩擦力从脚底产生，要利用好摩擦力，必须能够把摩擦力最大限度地传导到手上。在摩擦力从脚底传导到手的过程中，摩擦而无法传导到手上。做到周身一家可以改善这些问题，从而提高力的传导效率。

## （二）太极拳技法的力学原理

### 1. 牛顿定律

惯性定律认为，物体有保持其运动状态的特性。太极拳技击理论要求"闪开正中，定横中"，较形象地说明了技击对抗中如何应用惯性定律。当对方直线进攻己方胸部时，对方具有一定向前移动的速度，如果此时出乎对方意料，己方用闪空法躲过对方的进攻，对方就会由于惯性而失去平衡，向前跌倒；或者在闪空的同时从对方后背沿对方运动方向加一力，如

---

① 孙运红. 太极拳运动中的力学原理分析［J］. 中学物理教学参考. 2017，（12）：77-78.

此效果会比前一种更明显，这就是所谓的"顺水推舟"。[①]

太极拳的"引进落空""弧线运动"说明了物体的加速度与它所受的合力成正比，与它的质量成反比。任何运动的物质的路线都是直线，如果你想以一个角度控制来势的力量，改变它的方向，破坏掉对手进攻的重心位置，最好的方法是采用弧形运动。它不仅中和了来势的力量，而且可以为自己所用；因为在很小的反击力量的帮助下，能取得显著的效果。这是中和后的攻击方式。如果避开了进攻力量，跟随对手撤退方向的回击也会非常有力。

太极拳的发力应用的主要是牛顿第三定律。牛顿第三定律阐明了力作用的相互性，即两个物体之间的作用力与反作用力总是大小相等、方向相反，且作用在同一条直线上。在太极拳运动中，练习者无论是出拳还是出腿都要配合着蹬地的动作，其脚部蹬地的动作有多大，则地面就会提供等大的反作用力，这样才能有效提升相关动作的作用力。这也是太极拳拳谱中所说的"其根在脚，发于腿，主宰于腰，发于脊背，达于肩臂，形于手指"。在太极推手中，当对方对己方施加作用力时，己方则用力蹬地，借助地面的反作用力，进一步将力量作用于对方的身上。在上述过程中，人蹬地的力量越大，则人将获得的反作用力就越大。

### 2. 动量定理

动量定理运用于武术运动中，主要表现在加大打击力和减小缓冲力两方面。本书中主要说明动量定理在太极拳运动中减小缓冲力方面的知识。

太极拳的"以柔克刚""以弱胜强""以慢制快"即是在对方来攻击时利用皮肤和肌肉灵敏的感觉，延长对方力的作用时间，使打击力的效果得不到发挥。之所以看起来"以慢制快"，是因为太极拳用较长的时间缓冲，而实际上太极拳动作的起动速度、进行速度、反应速度并不慢。而"以弱胜强"则是因为太极拳处处走弧线，力的作用时间长，做功距离长，而 $Ft = mv_1 + mv_0$，力的作用取决于力 $F$ 的大小与力的作用时间 $t$ 的乘积。太极拳走弧线，延长了力的作用时间，所以只需很小的力就可以起到较大的作用效果，因而可以"以弱胜强"。[②]

### 3. 杠杆原理

前面讲到人体杠杆的平衡，就杠杆模型来讲，支点、动力作用点和阻力作用点是它的三个重要参数，支点距离阻力点越近，距离动力点越远，则杠杆越省力；反之，支点距离阻力作用点越远，距离动力作用点越近，则杠杆就越费力。因此，太极拳运动中选择合适的支点以及动力作用点非常关键。例如太极拳中的野马分鬃式，其动作要求左手下插，然后向前上方挑、托、掤，并且用右手做出下采和捌的动作，形成下扣上翻的摔法技巧；同时，右手在挑、掤之际又合左肩靠，并将下盘作为支点构成一个由外向前的推力。

### 4. "力偶"走圆转动

一圆是太极拳的主要特征。一圆是由力学"力偶"（图 1-3-1）原理产生的，当大脑神经支配腰骨骼肌收缩的肌张力（腰隙的抽换），带动两腿屈伸虚实变化，产生对地反作用力的同时产生偏心力矩，驱动四肢屈伸运动。因一腿渐虚，另一腿同时渐实，开裆、圆裆产生人

① 马文海著. 武术运动生物力学［M］. 开封：河南大学出版社，2010，71-72.

② 马文海著. 武术运动生物力学［M］. 开封：河南大学出版社，2010，81.

体圆转运动，即"力偶"的作用，即符合"两个力大小相等、方向相反，而不在一条直线上的力。'力偶'能使物体转动"的原理，也有克服双重的道理。所以太极拳每一势，或者左旋右转，或者迈步进退，都是三维的立体的圆转运动。例如太极拳中的单鞭动作，练习者的双臂必须伸展为一条拉直的鞭子，甩出去时务必要做到柔中有刚。在技击方面单鞭动作有化守为攻、连消带打的作用。如果对方用左手向己方攻来，己方可以采用右手勾手向右侧架开来手，同时用左腿插在对方两腿之间，并配合着用右手攻击对方的胸部，由此产生让对方倒地的力矩，破坏对方的平衡。

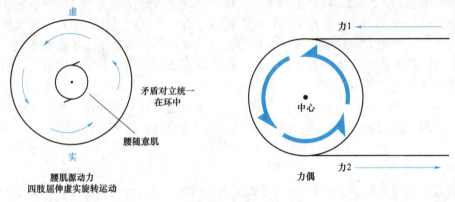

图 1-3-1　力偶

在外力的作用下，被动顺随，用意不用力，内部产生"力矩""力偶"的机理，外部形成螺旋转动，这是太极拳运动的基石。为什么太极拳是用意而不是用力？这是因为被动顺随，用意是为了产生力偶，使身肢杠杆螺旋转动，使自身自然形成"四两拨千斤"的功能。这是太极拳用意不用力的科学规律。用力是双重，不能产生力偶，不能形成"四两拨千斤"的功能，自然就滑到拼力的道路上去了。

# Chapter 1　Overview of Tai-chi Chuan

## Section 1　Brief History of Tai-chi Chuan

### 1. Concept of Tai-chi Chuan

#### (1) Tai-chi

To understand the word *Tai-chi* or the Grande Terminus, we must first perceive what *Tai* and *Chi* are. *Tai* means very, extremely, tremendously and supremely; *Chi* means the apex, the paramount, the principle of neutrality and reaching the maximum limit. Tai and Chi combined form the compound word *Tai-chi*, meaning the highest, the ultimate, the absolute, the only and the neutral. The word *Tai-chi* is originated from *Zhouyi* (*The Book of Changes) — Xici (The Great Appendix)*. It says, "Where there is Tai-chi, there is peace and harmony between the positive and the negative, which produce four emblematic symbols, which again produce the eight trigrams." Tai-chi is the origin of life, and the movement of Qi (vital force) is divided into Yin and Yang, which engender four seasons, and hence sky, earth, wind, thunder, water, fire, mountains and marsh appear as eight forms of natural phenomena, giving birth to all matters in the universe. According to *the Chinese Etymology Dictionary* (*Ciyuan*), Tai-chi refers to the primitive vital force of the original chaos of the universe. The principle of Tai-chi is that Yin and Yang are opposed to each other, unified with each other and transformed into each other. By Song Dynasty (960—1279), a complete Tai-chi doctrine had been well established, represented by scholars ZHOU Dunyi and ZHU Xi, where ZHOU Dunyi wrote T*he Essay of Tai-chi Diagram* and ZHU Xi argued that Tai-chi is the natural law governing all things in heaven and on earth, based on which Tai-chi Chuan is able to decipher movement mechanism.

#### (2) The Origin of the name of Tai-chi Chuan

"*Chuan* (fist)"means pugilism or boxing. It's a martial art of unarmed combat. According to stone relief of Han Dynasty(202 B.C.—220), pugilism was born back in pre-Qin Dynasty (Palaeolithic period—221 B.C.). The pugilism named as Tai-chi, and the pugilism guided and interpreted by Tai-chi theory, are called *Tai-chi Chuan*. Tai-chi Chuan is one of the most eminent

Chinese martial art forms. In its early days, it was called Long Boxing or "Mian (soft) Boxing" because of the fluidity of its movements resembling the incessant flow of the Yangtze River; it's also known as *Thirteen Stances* as it encompasses eight gates techniques (wardoff, rollback, press, push, pull, split, elbow and shoulder) and five steps (step forward, step back, look left, look right and central equilibrium). During QIAN Long period in Qing Dynasty (1636—1912), WANG Zongyue from Shanxi province was the first to interpret Tai-chi philosophy systematically, and wrote *On Tai-chi Chuan*. This is the earliest literature record of the name of Tai-chi Chuan, which has been commonly used ever since.[1]

## 2. The Formation and Development of Tai-chi Chuan

### (1) The origin of Tai-chi Chuan

Experts and scholars have divergent views on the origin of Tai-chi Chuan. We believe that Tai-chi Chuan can be divided into ancient Tai-chi Chuan and modern Tai-chi Chuan, referenced from the available key historical literature. According to the conclusions made by Mr. WU Tunan in *The Essence of Tai-chi Chuan by Wu Tunan*, there was CHENG Lingxi, a native from Xiuning county, Huizhou prefecture during the time of Emperor Wu of Liang Dynasty (464-549), who refined Tai-chi Chuan. His teacher HAN Gongyue created *Fifteen Stances*. In Tang Dynasty (618—907), XU Xuanping from Huizhou prefecture and LI Daozi from Anqing prefecture practiced Tai-chi Chuan to nurture body and mind. XU Xuanping created *Thirty-Seven-Stance Tai-chi Chuan* and the Tai-chi Chuan LI Daozi created was called *Innate Boxing* (Xiantian Chuan), or *Long Boxing* (Chang Chuan). In Yuan (1271-1368) and Ming Dynasty(1368-1644), ZHANG Sanfeng (1247-appx.1412), a Taoist master with phenomenal martial art technique, invented Tai-chi Chuan named as *Thirteen Stances*, also known as *Long Boxing*[2]. WANG Zongyue, a native from Shanxi province during the period of Emperor KANG Xi and Emperor QIAN Long in Qing Dynasty (1636-1912), taught Tai-chi Chuan in his martial art institute in Luo Yang and Kai Feng city while dedicating to studying Tai-chi Chuan theory and practicing technique. His book *Tai-chi Chuan Diagram* is also named as *The Manual of Tai-chi Chuan,* involving the sections of *The Theory of Thirteen Stances, The Theory of Tai-chi Chuan, Interpretation of Tai-chi Chuan, Song of Thirteen Stances, Song of Sparring, Understanding How to Practice Thirteen Stances* and *Names of Thirteen Stances*. Up to date there's no complete lineage of ancient Tai-chi Chuan to be found given the limited historical archive, and thus myths and speculations about the origin of Tai-chi Chuan have been many.

In addition, according to TANG Hao, a historian on Chinese martial art, Tai-chi Chuan was first practiced by the Chen family in Chen Jiagou village, Wen prefecture in Henan province.

---

① YU Cui-lan, *Simplified Tai-chi Chuan* [M]. Nanjing: Phoenix Science Press, 2006.2 (1).

② *The Essence Tai-chi Chuan by Wu Tunan*, p. 265.

CHEN Wangting created it. He was a martial art master and a scholar of *HUANG-LAO* (the Yellow Emperor and LAO Zi) Taoism, who invented Tai-chi Chuan, Tai-chi weapon forms and Tai-chi competition routines. To create Tai-chi Chuan, he drew inspirations and essence from ancient Chinese guided breathing exercise, Yin-Yang theory under the *Yi-jing* (*The Book of Changes*) philosophy, the theory of meridians of traditional Chinese medicine, QI Jiguang's Thirty-Two-Stance Long Boxing and many other schools of boxing art in Ming Dynasty. Over the past three centuries of inheritance and evolution, various schools of Tai-chi Chuan have risen[①]. From our perspective, the Tai-chi Chuan Mr. TANG Hao studied should be deemed as modern Tai-chi Chuan, which has a clear and continuous lineage.

The late Ming Dynasty and early Qing Dynasty saw the incremental formation of Tai-chi Chuan. The Chen family relocated from Hongdong prefecture, Shanxi province to Chen Jiagou village, Henan province in the 7th year of Emperor HONG Wu(1368-1398) of Ming Dynasty. They were expert practitioners of martial art. Between the period of Emperor CHONG Zhen of Ming Dynasty and the period of KANG Xi of Qing Dynasty, CHEN Wangting (1600-1680) of the ninth generation, who's accomplished culturally and in martial art, created the preliminary framework of Tai-chi Chuan by taking the best of different schools of martial art, on top of his integration of popular folk and military pugilism. The Tai-chi Chuan frame of CHEN Wangting emphasizes coordination between movements and breathing. The guided breathing technique of Tai-chi Chuan initially is mainly derived from *Huangting Classic* of Taoism, as indicated in CHEN Wangting's writing as "*Huangting* has been my best companion reading" . In mid-Qing Dynasty, Tai-chi Chuan was no more nascent but mature. Its representatives during this period included CHEN Changxing (1771-1853) from the 14th generation of the Chen family , YANG Luchan (1799-1872) from Yongnian prefecture, and WU Yuxiang (1812-1880) who was taught by YANG Luchan and CHEN Qingping.

In the first half of the 20th century, Tai-chi Chuan was booming in Beijing, with ample schools, stories and deepening study of Tai-chi theory. On Tai-chi Chuan's techniques, the *Mian (soft) Chuan Frame* created by YANG Luchan was refined by his son YANG Jianhou (1839-1917) and his grandson YANG Chengfu (1883-1936), and later became the popular YANG-style Tai-chi Chuan routine. In the early period of the Republic of China, HAO Weizhen (1849-1920), the disciple of LI Yishe from Yongnian prefecture, moved to the capital Beijing to teach WU-Style Tai-chi Chuan created by WU Yuxiang. SUN Lutang (1861-1932) from Wan prefecture of Hubei province learned under him and created SUN-style Tai-chi Chuan, by incorporating *Xing Yi Chuan* (Form-and-will Boxing) and *Eight-Trigram Palms*. WU Jianquan (1870-1942) from Daxing prefecture, Hebei province, was hired to teach Tai-chi Chuan at Beijing Sports Research Institute. He learned YANG-style Tai-chi pugilism frame from his father WU Quanyou (1834-1902), and later created WU-style Tai-chi Chuan by simplifying the original frame and highlighting the

---

① Chinese Martial Arts Pugilism and Weapon Form Compilation Group, *Chinese Martial Arts Pugilism and Weapon Form Book* [M]. People's Sports Publishing House, 1993, (132).

lightness and flexibility. And hence we witnessed the rapid growth and development of various schools of Tai-chi Chuan①. Over the past century, the recent schools of Tai-chi Chuan including LI-style, HE-style and WANG Qihe style have also arisen, referenced from classic Tai-chi theory and Tai-chi diagram.

### (2) Traditional Schools of Tai-chi Chuan

① CHEN-Style Tai-chi Chuan

CHEN-style Tai-chi Chuan is an essential school which is the most widespread in Tai-chi Chuan's history. Its lineage indicates that CHEN-style Tai-chi Chuan lays the foundation for other schools, of which YANG-style, SUN-style, WU-style (吴式) and WU-style (武式) are derived. CHEN-style Tai-chi Chuan includes the old frame and the new frame, with a clear lineage.

The old frame of CHEN-style Tai-chi Chuan was created by CHEN Wangting in late Ming Dynasty. According to *CHEN-Style Tai-chi Chuan Diagram* written by his descendants, CHEN Wangting created totaled five routines of Tai-chi Chuan. But only the routine of Thirteen Stances, and the routine of Cannon Punch are preserved to date, while the others have been lost. The so-called Thirteen Stances, or CHEN-style Old Frame is the earliest form of Tai-chi Chuan with 108 movements in total, featuring the wide and low frame, spiral and winding movements, underscoring the transition from being loose into being soft, transforming the softness to the firmness, the firmness restored to the softness, intertwined with accelerating force, jumping and stamping movements. CHEN Xin, the Tai-chi Chuan inheritor of the eighth generation of the Chen Family, epitomized the thoughts in Tai-chi theory and wrote classic works including *CHEN-Style Tai-chi Chuan Diagram Explained*, *Introduction to Tai-chi Chuan*, *The Three-Three-Six Tai-chi Chuan Diagram* and *Genealogy of Chen Family*.

CHEN-style New Frame of Tai-chi Chuan was created by CHEN Changxing, Tai-chi master from Chen Jiagou village in Henan province in Qing Dynasty. He smoothed out the old frame movements by removing the explosive jumping movements while loyally preserving the main content and the wide and low frame feature of the old frame, making it more suitable for the elderly and the physically weak to practice, so people call it as "the simplified version". Later, his sibling CHEN Qingping created a more compact form, adding incremental circles into the frame. The frame is also called *ZHAO-BAO Frame*, one of the representatives of CHEN-style New Frame. After CHEN-style New Frame is formed, some routines of the old frame have been obsolete over time.

② YANG-Style Tai-chi Chuan

It was invented by YANG Fukui from Yongnian prefecture, in Hebei province in Qing Dynasty. His grandson YANG Chengfu modified and finalized it. YANG Fukui, courtesy name Lu

---

① KANG Gewu, *Cultural Treasures, Fitness and Beneficial Friends"* (subtitled *"An Overview of Tai-chi Chuan Development* [N]. Beijing: *People's Daily*, February 10th, 2001, page 4, 14th, page 8, 16th, page 8.

Chan, was from Yongnian prefecture, Hebei province. In his early days, he learned CHEN-style Tai-chi Old Frame, Tai-chi Chuan from CHEN Changxing in Chen Jiagou village. He was famous for his Tai-chi technique of the firmness conceived in the softness like a needle hidden in silk gloss. In 1850s, he became a martial art instructor for Manchu bannermen in the capital, teaching Tai-chi Chuan to cultural and political elites and establishing his own school of Tai-chi Chuan by gradually modifying the movements. His sons YANG Jian and YANG Yu were also renowned Tai-chi masters of the time. After YANG Fukui passed away, his legacy Tai-chi routines were modified and finalized as YANG-style Tai-chi Chuan by his grandson YANG Chengfu (Zhaoqing). YANG-style Tai-chi Chuan features extended and upright frame as well as even and gentle movements. There are proliferate writings by the Yang family and their disciples, such as *Tai-chi Chuan Technique*, *The Manual of Tai-chi Chuan*, *The Encyclopedia of Tai-chi Chuan*, *Ten Keys of Tai-chi Chuan Technique* and *On Tai-chi Chuan Practice*. In 1947, CHEN Yanlin, disciple of TIAN Zhaolin of YANG-style Tai-chi Chuan school, collaborated with two distinguished translators, i.e., professor CHEN Kui and professor GE Chuangui from Fudan University, and translated the first work on Tai-chi Chuan into English, *Tai-Chi Chuan: The Effects and Practical Application*, published by Kelly & Walsh Limited. The book has been reprinted for 17 times subsequently by numbers of publishing houses over the past seven decades[1], with profound impact on the international communication of Tai-chi Chuan.

③ WU-Style Tai-chi Chuan (武氏)

Created by WU Yuxiang in Qing Dynasty, it has gone through around 200 years of development. WU Yuxiang was from Yongnian prefecture, Hebei province, practicing *Hong Chuan* (HONG Boxing). He firstly learned Tai-chi Chuan from YANG Fukui, and later went to learn CHEN-style Tai-chi New Frame from CHEN Qingping in Wen prefecture in Henan province, then learned WU-style Tai-chi Chuan from WU Quanyou. He then integrated the essence of those schools and formed his own. LI Yishe and HAO Weizhen modified and finalized the whole version, so it's also called HAO-style Tai-chi Chuan. It features compact and succinct frame, extended movements, strict footwork and stark contrast between substantiality and insubstantiality. WU Yuxiang validified his Tai-chi system with his in-depth study on various schools of Tai-chi Chuan. He was dedicated to studying WANG Zongyue's *Theory of Tai-chi Chuan*. Based on his interpretation and summary of those thoughts, he wrote master pieces about Tai-chi Chuan including *Interpretation of Thirteen Stances*, *Interpretation of Tai-chi Chuan*, *Thirteen Stances Explained*, *The Four-Word Keys to Tai-chi Chuan* and *Playing Hands Releasings*, establishing a complete Tai-chi Chuan school comprising the theory, the technique and the maneuver of Tai-chi saber and long pole.

④ WU-Style Tai-chi Chuan (吴氏)

WU Quanyou, a Manchu in Qing Dynasty, and his son WU Jianquan, further developed YANG-style Tai-chi Chuan and created WU-style Tai-chi Chuan, which is originated in Beijing.

---

① Jin Yan, Instisute Newspaper 2019 (Vol. 45) No.6 p.74-81.

WU Quanyou was a Tai-chi Chuan master during the period of Emperor XIAN Feng and Emperor TONG Zhi in Qing Dynasty, who studied Tai-chi Chuan under YANG Fukui and his son, and, inherited YANG-style small-frame Tai-chi Chuan which evolved later. His son WU Jianquan further modified his father's pugilism technique, optimizing the whole Tai-chi Chuan routine and thus establishing WU-style Tai-chi Chuan school. It features exquisite and disciplined frame, as well as, delicate and gentle movements with loose and natural postures. WU-style Tai-chi Chuan was originated in Beijing and flourished in such big cities as Shanghai, Guangzhou and Hong Kong.

⑤ SUN-Style Tai-chi Chuan

It was invented by SUN Fuquan in late Qing Dynasty and early period of Republic of China. SUN Fuquan, courtesy name Lutang, from Ding prefecture, Hebei province. Early on, he studied under Xing Yi Chuan (Form-and-will Boxing) master GUO Yunshen for eight years, then studied Eight- Trigram Boxing under inherited master CHENG Tinghua for 2 years, later studied WU-style Tai-chi Chuan under HAO Weizhen. He possessed outstanding techniques, integrating the essence of Tai-chi, Xing Yi Chuan (Form-and-will Boxing), and Eight-Trigram Boxing, and thus creating the unique SUN-style Tai-chi Chuan. It features elevated frame, nimble footwork and lively transitions. SUN-style Tai-chi Chuan has more than 100 years of history but it's regarded as a late form. Because of its each footwork technique containing a corresponding stepping action, and its emphasis on opening and closing, it's also called *Opening and Closing Active-Step Tai-chi Chuan*. SUN Lutang wrote *Theory of* Xing Yi Chuan *(Form-and-will Boxing)*, *Theory on Eight-Trigram Palms*, *Theory on Tai-chi Chuan* and *Theory on Eight-Trigram Sword*.

## (3) Tai-chi Chuan's Content and Classification

① Routines

A routine is a choreographed set of systematic movements. The elementary elements of Tai-chi Chuan routine include body postures, training trajectory, training time, training speed, training velocity, training force, training pace, and the awareness of offence and defense. Represented inheritors of each Tai-chi Chuan school carefully design routines to assure a well-documented heritage. Teaching Tai-chi Chuan routines can not only enhance beginners' interest but also ensure regular practitioners to be disciplined. China's National Sports Commission (General Administration of Sports of China) has organized martial art masters to compile and publish *Simplified Tai-chi Chuan (24 Stances)* since 1955, revised the 88-Stance Tai-chi Chuan routine in 1962, created the 48-Stance Tai-chi Chuan competition routine, and other Tai-chi Chuan competition routines have been subsequently published.

The Tai-chi Chuan routine is centered around technical offence and defense, combining different body postures, leg movements and hand movements. Following the rules of offence and defense, advance and retreat, movement and stillness, fast and slow, firmness and softness, substantiality and insubstantiality, the whole routine form is defined. The practice forms of routines include single practice, paired practice and group practice.

The single practice includes unarmed pugilism and weapon form, such as simplified Tai-chi Chuan, CHEN-style Tai-chi Chuan Old Frame Routine, the 108-Stance YANG-style Tai-chi Chuan, Tai-chi sword and Tai-chi saber.

The paired practice includes unarmed paired practice, weapon-paired practice, unarmed and weapon-paired practice, such as Tai-chi Chuan paired practice and three-pole paired practice.

Group practice includes unarmed pugilism, weapon form or unarmed and weapon form.

② Combat

Combat is a fight form conducted by two or more people under certain conditions who follow certain rules to compete in wits and technique. The goal of combat is testing the feasibility of technical offence and defense. Learning the routine slowly is for practicing skills, and grasping the combat form fast is for application. The routine exercise and combat are supplementing to each other as mutual verification. The requirements of offence and defense in combat and the precise pointing and positioning of the body postures, leg movements and hand movements used during the guided routine exercise, are aiming at mastering the "neither excessive nor deficient" principle.

Pushing Hands of Tai-chi Chuan has been listed as a martial art competition program. Pushing Hands is a two-person competition where one senses the magnitude and the direction of the opponent's force, and yield the force or redirect the force to the opponent, by sticking and adhering to each other, using hand movements of "ward off, roll back, press, push , pull, split, elbow and shoulder".

③ Practicing Methods[1]

Practicing methods are specialty exercises designed to strengthen a certain athletic ability, to improve a certain physical function or to train for a specific skill, in order to master and enhance martial art routine and combat technique.

The practicing methods of Tai-chi Chuan are mainly internal skill practicing methods, such as infinite stance, primordial stance, opening and closing stance, Yin Yang stance and static stance. It's a practicing method to cultivate the intrinsic and extrinsic energy by doing basic exercises of using the spirit to lead the Qi (vital force) , driving the vital force to move the whole body, and using the whole body to exert the force. The goal is to move with intention, vital force, strength and form, to achieve unity of all movements, the precision of pointing and positioning all at once. Through internal skill practicing methods, one can attain power inside out, the harmony of heaven and man, and the unlocked human potential.

① QIU Pixiang. *Introduction to Chinese Martial Arts* [M]. Beijing: Higher Education Press, 2010.7.

# Section 2   8–Dimension Features and Functions of Tai–chi Chuan

## 1. 8–Dimension Features of Tai–chi Chuan

Various masters from different schools of Tai-chi Chuan epitomized the features of Tai-chi Chuan brilliantly. Mr. FENG Zhiqiang summed it up from a broad sense. It's comprehensive, adaptive, functional, economical, safe, scientific, philosophical and artistic; Mr. WANG Shande formulated the features as follows: meticulously-structured, exquisite, neutralizing and transforming attacks while keeping the gravitational center, circles and points being rooted in each other, emphasizing on body postures, being aligned with Dan-Taoism, releasing primordial energy, preserving the intrinsic Qi (vital force), Yin interacting with Yang, keeping Qi (vital force) flowing by sticking it to the back, stepping like approaching the abyss, exerting force like spinning, refining the spirit and accumulating energy, controlled opening and closing of the vital force among organs and channels, surrounding the opponent with the vital force to contain him/her like patching up wounds, achieving resonance and synergy; Mr. SHEN Jiazhen viewed CHEN-style Tai-chi Chuan as the movement between the spirit and the vital force, the exercise with flexibility, the movement containing substantiality and insubstantiality, the exercise linking up all the joints, the exercise with continuous breathing, the movement with balanced firmness and softness, and the movement with alternating fast and slow pace; Mr. YANG Chengfu systematized the features as straightening the head and body, hollowing the chest and raising the back, loosening the waist, distinguishing the substantiality and insubstantiality, lowering the shoulders and elbows, using the intent instead of the force, the upper and lower body following each other, the harmony between the internal and the external, continuity without intermission, and pursuing inactivity out of activity. Hence, from the perspective of Tai-chi Chuan practicing, those masters share a great deal of commonality as regards Tai-chi Chuan's features.

Everything has its own features, which are symbols of its characteristics, so does Tai-chi Chuan. Precisely speaking, it has distinctive dimensional features, meaning there are paired features impacting each other and interacting with each other. Using dimensional features to describe Tai-chi Chuan is more appropriate to facilitate comprehension, in line with the theoretical requirements of Tai-chi Chuan and application. The mutually-impacting and interacting features are the primary reason for underscoring oral teaching by mentors on Tai-chi Chuan, from which it inspires true understanding on Tai-chi Chuan. Based on that, eminent Tai-chi Chuan master Mr. WU Tunan said, "Tai-chi Chuan should be learned through oral teaching"[1]. Therefore, using dimensional features for Tai-chi Chuan description is beneficial for practitioners to conduct comparative study and attain self-improvement in Tai-chi Chuan, when oral teaching by mentors is not available. The eight dimensional features include being concentrated and relaxed, keeping upright body postures, using the intent to guide the movement, exerting the overall ward-off force, movements being coherent, circular and agile, distinguished substantiality and insubstantiality, the upper and lower body following each other, and balanced firmness and softness.

### 1. Being concentrated and relaxed

Practicing Tai-chi Chuan requires full concentration on the movements, with accumulated energy, an empty mind, a sole focus and a relaxed body.

Being concentrated is an essential principle of Tai-chi Chuan practice. It requires an undistracted focus on using the intent to incessantly guide the movements and to make swift changes, so that every movement is with its intended direction with no neglect of any. Being concentrated requires patience and an empty mind erasing all anxieties and distractions, otherwise the movement's direction and posture would be astray, hindering practitioner's learning and mastery of Tai-chi Chuan.

Being relaxed adheres to the same principle of being concentrated. It's a key measure of "using the intent instead of the force". In movements, the prerequisite to being concentrated is using the intent to guide all organs, joints and muscles inside and outside the limbs to relax. Bit by bit practitioners are trained to relax the whole body without wasting any force, the so-called awkward force in particular. The body should be set loose inside out, making the body naturally be expanded without stiffness. Exert forces as guided, use the intent throughout the movement and complete the movement with moderate corresponding substantiality and insubstantiality.

### 2. Keeping upright body postures

Holding the body posture upright is a consistent emphasis over the course of Tai-chi Chuan exercise. The general requirements are raising the head, straightening the head and body, lowering the shoulders and elbows, hollowing the chest and rais the back, relaxing the spine, loosening the waist and rounding the crotch area, lifting the hip and sinking the sacrum, and bending knees like slightly sitting. Keeping in mind a common martial art proverb would help one maintain the correct posture, "skills won't grow if you bow and drop your chin low". Keeping an upright body posture refreshes practitioners' mind and enhances concentration. In the attack, it helps practitioners make the right calls, and respond timely and neatly. CHEN Changxing, the main inheritor of CHEN-style Tai-chi Chuan in Qing Dynasty, was well known for keeping upright body posture with elegant balance. People call him "Mr. Lofty". Upright body posture is an underscored critical requirement in Tai-chi Chuan while other pugilisms such as Drunken Brawler, Eagle-Claw Boxing and Ground Tumbling Boxing do not emphasize it as much.

---

① WU Tunan, *The Essence of Tai-chi Chuan by Wu Tunan* [M], People's Sports Publishing House, 1991.1, p. 7.

Tai-chi Chuan coaches even command Tai-chi Chuan practitioners to maintain the upright body posture in their daily conducts.

### 3. Using the intent to guide the movement

Any bodily movements (except reflective movements), including various movements in sports, need to be guided with the intent. The whole process of practicing Tai-chi Chuan requires using the intent (meaning imagination) to guide the movement, and setting the focus solely on the movement. The emphasis is laid on using the intent instead of the force, using the intent to guide movements without using the rigid or stiff force of the muscles. The keys to meeting the requirements set by the Tai-chi Chuan theory are "the intent is the commander, and the body is the soldier", "using the intent to channel Qi (the vital force), using the vital force to move the body" and "the body moves along with the move of the intent". Every action is led by the intent instead of the force. The intent prevails and the movement follows. Gradually the practitioner shall achieve that the vital force goes wherever the intent goes, and the strength arrives at wherever the vital force arrives.

### 4. Exerting the overall ward-off force

The ward-off force is a unique feature of Tai-chi Chuan. It's the most basic technique. The force is light and elastic generated by thoroughly expanding the body. It's originated in the guidance of the intent. When the intrinsic energy is ample at the infinite state, the primordial force is being outward, round and elastic. The intrinsic energy reaches the end of every nerve of the practitioner, and the ward-off force is going through every joint, making him/her agile and light. Some even claim Tai-chi Chuan as Ward-off Chuan. Mastering the ward-off force relies on oral teaching by the coach, and listening to the force through touches of hands. To practice exerting the ward-off force, one should learn to be relaxed without being slack and overcome the flaw of being relaxed and slack.

### 5. Coherent, circular and agile movements

In Tai-chi Chuan, "one movement links up with all others" and "connecting every movement with the breathing flowing from feet to legs to waist". The upper and lower body follows each other, and the movement is completed by linking the joints one after another. Movements being circular and agile, means the movement shall be completed in a coherent arc with neither concave nor convex surfaces, nor defects and nor angles. The changes should be light and lively. When the principle is correctly applied, the movements will be in the central equilibrium neutralizing the coming attacks in circles, without overstepping, flattening, sticking, losing the opponent or direct attacking.

Every rise and fall of each movement need to be studied discreetly. For fixed-step movements, they should be fully intended and the boundary of stop and start is intangible. Such a transition between each movement is described as "coherent". Being coherent refers to incessant link-up of the prior and the next movement with no rigidity nor stiffness, no breaks nor pauses.

### 6. Distinguished substantiality and insubstantiality[①]

Tai-chi Chuan poses strict requirements on substantiality and insubstantiality. As said in the poem on substantiality and insubstantiality, "Had you not understood the truth of substantiality and insubstantiality for Tai-chi Chuan practice, you would've wasted your energy and failed". Therefore, Tai-chi Chuan prioritizes substantiality and insubstantiality. It's divided into the overall and local aspects. For overall movements, the movement reaching the end point is substantiality, and the transition of the movement is insubstantiality. If the center of gravity is on the right leg, then the right leg is substantiality and the left leg is insubstantiality. With the two clearly defined, the movements aligned with this rule would look effortless with light and agile transitions. Otherwise, the steps would be heavy and clumsy with no stable foundation. Distinguishing substantiality and insubstantiality is to prevent failing prioritizing movements, exerting force evenly, and movements being clumsy and rigid.

Beginners should first focus on the substantiality and insubstantiality of the transition between both legs, making movements smooth and expanded while maintaining the center of gravity, without leaning nor slanting. When one can distinguish the local substantiality and insubstantiality clearly, he then should try to understand its correlation with the overall substantiality and insubstantiality. Ultimately, the status of "substantiality is conceived in insubstantiality, and vice versa" would be achieved.

### 7. The upper and lower body following each other[②]

When practicing Tai-chi Chuan, the movements of the whole body shall be coordinated. As *Theory of Pugilism* says, "one movement links up with all others". To complete any movement, every part of the body should be mobilized and coordinated. Do not make disconnected movements such as hands moving while feet are standing still, or feet moving and hands not. To succeed in "connecting every movement with the breathing flowing from the feet to the legs to the waist", the upper and lower limbs and the trunk need to coordinate together. In practice, the steps shall change along with the body posture, and the intent arises when the hands are raised. Postures are both coordinated and graceful, embodying the technique of "the upper and lower body following each other".

### 8. Balanced firmness and softness[③]

Balanced firmness and softness is an outstanding feature of Tai-chi Chuan. It's the essence of Tai-chi Chuan, an embodiment of the theory of Yin and Yang of Tai-chi.

The firmness of Tai-chi Chuan is generated from the waist as an axis, using the spiral force of Tai-chi Chuan and the Qi (vital force) of Dantian (the navel psychic center) to exert the instantaneous explosive force. It's also known as spring force. It's a force opposite to the awkward force, or clumsy force used for lifting or pushing up heavy items in our daily life.

① WU Zhongnong. *Simplified Tai-chi Chuan Movements and Breathing Exercise* [M]. Beijing: Beijing Sport University Press. 1993.

② WU Zhongnong. *Simplified Tai-chi Chuan Movements and Breathing Exercise* [M]. Beijing: Beijing Sport University Press. 1993.

③ Guo Zhenxing. *Basic Textbook of Yang Style Tai-chi Chuan in English and Chinese* [M]. Beijing: Beijing Institute of Technology Press, 2015.1.

The softness of Tai-chi Chuan refers to the softness and gentleness gained from relaxation. It's the lightness of limbs and natural coordination of movements attained by removing the rigid force of the body. It's light and collected, elastic and resilient. The softness comes from relaxation, and thus relaxation is imperative to gaining softness. To properly relax the body, straighten the head and body while lowering the shoulders and elbows; meanwhile all joints need to be relaxed. Moreover, one should learn "using the intent instead of the force". The force to be avoided refers to the awkward force in this context. And when the right force needs to be exerted, it should be natural and moderate.

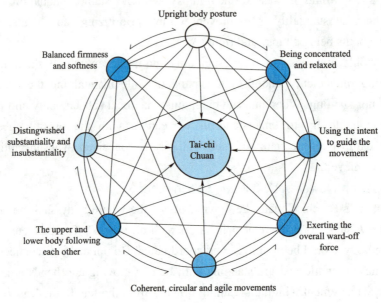

Figure 1-2-1

## 2. Functions of Tai-chi Chuan

### (1) The function of fitness of Tai-chi Chuan

Tai-chi Chuan is known as a lifelong exercise for fitness, a companion throughout all life activities for practitioners. People can choose practicing Tai-chi Chuan for fitness across different ages.

Chinese people value the tranquility and peace in life, underpinning the ease of body and mind, and paying attention to wellness through balanced lifestyle, stable psychological health and calmness. Practitioners can gain remarkable benefits of balancing body and mind during the practice, hence reaching their optimal state of health. The predecessors of Tai-chi Chuan in ancient time, also valued its fitness attribute in spite of using it mainly as an attack measure. WANG

Zongyue says in his *The Song of Thirteen Stances*, "What's the reason for studying Tai-chi Chuan strenuously? It's for prolonging life and gaining vitality". It indicates that the social function of martial art in Qing Dynasty had been changed. The ultimate goal of practicing pugilism was already about strengthening longevity and vitality. The fitness value of martial art had become more notable.

Tai-chi Chuan as one of the key martial art programs in China has its prominent and unique fitness value. During the course of its development, Tai-chi Chuan has been significantly influenced by traditional Chinese medicine, and traditional Chinese breathing exercises for wellness. It plays an active role in preventing disease infection. Therefore, Tai-chi Chuan is widely favored by people home and abroad for its gentleness and slow pace. As an exercise, it emphasizes being relaxed and natural, sinking the breath to the navel psychic-center, and its intensity is moderate. Not only does it strengthen the cardiovascular and respiratory systems, but also it helps regulate the nerve system, soothing mind and dissolving pressure. In the big-health-care society nowadays, Tai-chi Chuan has its own profound stance.

### (2) The function of self-defense of Tai-chi Chuan

Tai-chi Chuan is a kind of pugilism with technical attack in nature. Each movement of Tai-chi Chuan has the efficacy of both fitness and self-defense. As a kind of technical attack, it improves people's physique and thus enhances practitioners' combat abilities; on the other hand, practitioners can also learn some offence and defense techniques to strengthen their combat quality.

Offence and defense tactics are innate in Tai-chi Chuan. One can learn and master such through practicing Tai-chi Chuan. Though some movements have been modified, not exactly the same as the original ones used in life-and-death battles, they still possess the core of the tactics used in actual battles. Harnessing them combined with the training needed, one will be able to grasp the authentic actual tactics used in cruel battles, during which the practitioner will also strengthen his specialty physical ability.

### (3) The function of self-cultivation of Tai-chi Chuan[1]

The martial art nurtured by traditional Chinese culture, sets a high bar on ethics and morality. As quoted, "Be moral, before practicing martial art". Morality is an indispensable critical part. Regular martial art practitioners are able to internalize their self-awareness and behaviors, nurturing their physical and mental health, and contributing to social harmony.

Tai-chi Chuan is deemed to be pugilism of philosophy. Practitioners are motivated by striving along to be a better self, and backed by ample social commitment and discipline. By taking the responsibility of "cultivating the moral self, managing the family, governing the state and safeguarding peace under Heaven ", one gets to be nurtured in character and temperament. The

---

[1] QIU Pixiang. *Introduction to Chinese Martial Arts* [M]. Beijing: Higher Education Press, 2010.7.40-41.

serene idyllic life attitude advocated in Tai-chi Chuan helps dissolve the harms of stress and speed caused by modern life with information explosion. Only by keeping the right pace of life with moderate intensity and relaxation can one work healthily. When Tai-chi Chuan is practiced for fitness, self-cultivation and art appreciation, it uplifts people's overall capabilities and life quality, safeguarding people from anxiety caused by study, work and life pressures. The moral character and social adaptability of practitioners would thus be entrenched.

# Section 3   Tai-chi Chuan and Other Disciplines

## 1. Tai-chi Chuan and Chinese Martial Art

### (1) The foundation of Tai-chi Chuan Theory[①]

Tai-chi Chuan, as one kind of pugilism in martial art, follows martial art exercise principles, with the art of attack as its prominent feature. Its art of offence and defense is effective, which, in nature, differs from gymnastics, dance and breathing exercise.

During the evolution of Tai-chi Chuan, it has been widely internalizing other martial art movements and delicately choreographed its own. On which, according to historical records, the pugilism method of QI Jiguang in Ming Dynasty is an essential reference for Tai-chi Chuan. This method itself was built upon various folk martial arts. If we compare *Thirty-Two Stances of Pugilism Theory* by QI Jiguang with CHEN-style Tai-chi Chuan diagram. We'll find much similarity in movements' names and frames between the two. Also the recording about Hong pugilism is found in *CHEN-Style Tai-chi Chuan Weapon-Form Diagram;* The outer form of "deflect downward, parry and push" in CHEN-style Tai-chi Chuan is quite similar to that of "smashing punch" and "punch downward" in Baji Boxing, and "down punching" of Xiao Hong Boxing. It shows that Tai-chi Chuan movements are mainly derived from other folk music art genres, and their inherent technical attack attributes are preserved in Tai-chi Chuan. The bow stance in Tai-chi Chuan for instance, the front foot is slightly buckled when stepping forward, as required for this technical attack to lock the opponent's heel, while the gymnastics bow stance doesn't have that requirement. Likewise, the fist punching in Tai-chi Chuan is imperative to "level the back of hand and the forearm" to realize the effect of attack, while this movement in dance doesn't need to.

There's proliferate writing on technical attacks stated in Tai-chi Chuan's diagrams and the theory on Tai-chi Chuan, indicating that Tai-chi Chuan stresses art of attack. We can find a plenty of art-of-attack-related philosophy, tactics methods and the training of attack in existing Tai-chi Chuan literature. In *the Theory of Tai-chi Chuan*, a Tai-chi Chuan classic, it says, "When the opponent's force is firm, mine should be soft to transform the incoming attack. This is called

---

① Feng Zhiqiang. *Pandect of Tai-chi Chuan* [M]. Beijing: Xueyuan Publishing House. 2000.1.

following; when the opponent is moving and you adhere to him while following in the same direction, it is called "sticking". When your opponent moves fast, you should response fast; when he moves slowly, you should follow more slowly..." The thoughts on the art of attack are a consistent theme throughout the piece. The stated tactics and methods are all centered around martialism. Such as *Song of Sparring*, *Song of Thirteen Stances*, *Four-Word Secrets* also dwell on art of attack, illustrating that as an essential Tai-chi Chuan feature.

Regardless of the art of attack of Tai-chi Chuan being regressing or not, Tai-chi Chuan does use technical attack movements to achieve multiple functions of fitness, combat and so forth. Thus, such an art of attack would be naturally preserved in Tai-chi Chuan's routines, exemplified in movements, as an innate feature differing Tai-chi Chuan from other sports. It's also an indispensable principle measuring the accuracy of Tai-chi Chuan movements. In other words, Tai-chi Chuan movements must comport with martial art theories. That's why Tai-chi Chuan is categorized as a kind of Chuan. A number of Tai-chi Chuan movements such as Needle at Sea Bottom, White Ape Offering Fruit, Overturning Flowers and Wavering Sleeves, Fair Lady Weaving at the Shuttle and Stepping up to Seven Stars, imply a strong element of art of attack as named. For instance, on the movement Needle at Sea Bottom, "Sea Bottom" refers to the *huiyin* (perineum) point. Aiming at the direction of huiyin to attack the lower abdomen of the opponent is the key to practicing this movement.

### (2) Traditional Chinese ethics of martial art

Ethics of martial art is the sum of all ethical qualities and moral discipline abided by martial art practitioners in social activities. In a word, its ethics are lied in martial art. Ethics of martial art is a virtue, a principle of social awareness that guides people's martial art and other activities, implemented in martial art practitioners' thinking and conducts. To cultivate noble ethics, various pugilism schools establish their own code of conduct, discipline and commandments. The rules of "Three Don'ts for Inheritance", "Five Don'ts for Inheritance", "Ten Don'ts for Inheritance" and "Eight Commandments" and "Ten Keys" are benchmark for ethics of martial art. All schools agree that "Kung Fu has its limit, but a person with kindness doesn't". Therefore, when conflicts arise, one should put ethics before force, focusing on defense instead of offence". Martial art practitioners should first win others' trust with his ethics, and deter others with his ethics. Attack in martial art should be practitioners' last resort to contain the opponent, after all other means have been exhausted. Simply using force only to contain others is digressed from the ethics principles. What's advocated is that "harnessing it but not using it", "peace comes first", "solving the conflict with the art of attack but no overdoing". Violent aggression and stubbornness are strictly prohibited.

Tai-chi Chuan, as a school in martial art, carries such similar elements, including "respect teachers and principles", "be polite and well behaved", "love your family and country", "embrace the greater good", "act on clear ethical standards", "be kind and righteous", "be kind to others", "offer help to others", " advocate kindness and suppress evil", "be bold to fight for justice", "work hard", "be tenacious", "be focused", "owning integrity", "abide by laws and deeds", "courage", "be strenuous", "be persevering", "be confident", "strive to be a better self", and "self-respect". All such are virtue treasures that shall be passed down to offspring. Practicing Tai-chi Chuan, in essence, is a process of inheriting the brilliant traditional Chinese culture. By training the body and mind in an all-rounded manner to be a better self, from which one will self-verify and comprehend the traditional Chinese philosophy of fitness. The gradual and progressive learning and practicing of the theory of Tai-chi Chuan, in particular, would underpin that, so that one would be nourished to become a noble person with an outstanding character.

## 2. Tai-chi Chuan and Traditional Chinese Philosophy

The theory of Tai-chi Chuan is rich in traditional Chinese philosophical thoughts, not for purely philosophical discussion purpose, but about how to apply traditional philosophy to guide Tai-chi Chuan practice. Tai-chi Chuan is heavily influenced by traditional philosophy filled with dialectics. From philosophy stand point, Tai-chi Chuan is acclaimed as pugilism of philosophy, not simply because of its profound philosophical connotation in name, nor its movements encompassing visceral philosophical meaning, but because of the overarching influence traditional philosophical thoughts have posed on Tai-chi Chuan. It helps Tai-chi Chuan form its unique movement vision, specific technical requirements and excellent values and functions. As commented by YANG Chengfu, "Pugilisms in China have their own techniques with deep philosophical meanings despite of the large number of schools…Tai-chi Chuan is an art with firmness concealed in softness, like a needle hidden in cotton. It has its own system on technique, physiology and mechanics." Classical philosophy impacts on various schools of pugilism, and its impact on Tai-chi Chuan is deepest, widest and most systematic among others. From ancient philosophy classic *Zhouyi (Book of Changes)* to Confucian school of idealist philosophy in Ming and Qing Dynasty, they both have influenced Tai-chi Chuan, to varying degrees.

The classical philosophies influencing Tai-chi Chuan include:

### (1) LAO theory

By observing evolving matters in life and production, Laozi had an epiphany that "in the world there is nothing more submissive and weaker than water. Yet for attacking that which is hard and strong, nothing can surpass it", meaning that the seemingly submissive and weak water can defeat all hard barriers. Take grasses as another example, "Grasses and trees are pliant and fragile when living, but dried and shriveled when dead." "Thus, the hard and the strong are the comrades of death; the supple and the weak are the comrades of life." Vast live matters and changes are boiled down to the universal truth of "the supplest can go through the hardest in the world". It's elevated to the philosophical level and it forms the thoughts of "value peace", "keep humility", "to reverse is how Tao works; the power of Tao resides in weakness". Correspondingly, in Tai-chi Chuan's thoughts on the art of attack, there are concepts of "underdogs battling giants", "the weak beating the strong", "softness conquering firmness". Such reversed truths are a vital feature of

Tai-chi Chuan. Moreover, some concrete ideas of Laozi profoundly impacted the technical requirements of Tai-chi Chuan. The concept of "approaching the utmost emptiness by staying with peace and calmness" by Laozi engendered the ideas of "being concentrated" and "accumulating intrinsic energy" in Tai-chi Chuan. The cyclical idea of "eternally revolving without failing" stated in Laozi's "Tao" also catalyzed the formation of "circling" as a movement feature in Tai-chi Chuan. Laozi's "Tao models itself after nature", "to govern by doing nothing against nature" engenders Tai-chi Chuan's technical requirements of "be relaxed, focused and natural" and "let the opponent in and follow him". The monasticism state of "keeping an empty mind and the navel center solid" by Laozi is a guidance to form Tai-chi Chuan's concepts of "hollowing the chest and rais the back" and "sinking Qi (vital force) to the navel psychic-center".

### (2) The theory of Yin and Yang

According to *Zhouyi (The Book of Changes) — Xici (The Great Appendix)*, "Where there is Tai-chi, there is peace and harmony between the positive and the negative, which produce four emblematic symbols, which again produce the eight trigrams." It argues that "Tao consists of one Yin and one Yang", "softness and firmness dispatch each other, and eight trigrams succeed one after another". In the *Essay of Tai-chi Diagram* written by ZHOU Dunyi, in Northern Song Dynasty, it established the world view centered around Tai-chi, where activity and inactivity produce Yin and Yang to form the world. With the development made by generations of philosophers, the classical theory on Yin and Yang has been matured to interpret the patterns of changes and development of matters, by using the law of unity of oppositeness of Yin and Yang. It impacts Tai-chi Chuan tremendously. Not only is it named after that, but more importantly, the Yin and Yang philosophy is ingrained in its theory, the structure of the frame, movement patterns, technical requirements and the principle of offence and defense. As stated in the opening of *The Theory of Tai-chi Chuan*, "Tai-chi was born from the Grand Terminus; it's the mother of Yin and Yang; Activity is divisible while inactivity is combinable." "Chuan consists of one Yin and one Yang." Tai-chi Chuan is a sport comprising Yin and Yang. In the Tai-chi diagram, activity and inactivity, firmness and softness, substantiality and insubstantiality, opening and closing are all status of unity of opposites, in line with the law of Yin and Yang transformation and "wane and wax between each other". The movements of Tai-chi Chuan are circular and agile, each movement is circling with a trajectory of arc, making the whole routine coherent, round and complete. The Tai-chi diagram is placed within a circle with the double-fish symbol, resembling the status of pushing hands where two practitioners' hands are joined. During the practice, both arms form a constantly changing circle. The tactics of "You advance, I retreat", "let the attacker in and follow him" comport with the law of Yin and Yang, being waning and waxing between each other and being transformed to each other.

Tai-chi Chuan masters see Tai-chi as the primordial force of all. In the universe lies Tai-chi, so does in the human body, and the human's abdomen is Tai-chi. Hence, as written in *The Song of Thirteen Stances*, "the source of life comes from the waist, so one should keep the awareness within the waist."

### (3) Harmony of Nature and man, the philosophical ground of Chinese martial art

The underlying concept of Chinese classical philosophy is "harmony of Nature and man". Such thought in martial art is embraced in that practitioners pursue the unity of human and nature. As noted in the Yang's family's copy of Tai-chi Chuan diagrams in Qing Dynasty, "Heaven and earth is a grand universe, and a human is a small universe, too." During the practice therefore, people have been incessantly pursuing the harmony and connection between the human body and nature. The practice helps people follow nature and make their movements aligned with the law of changes in nature, so as to realize the balance between the external world and self, between the external and the internal, and eventually the harmony of Yin and Yang.

Tai-chi Chuan explains and interprets its theory by using examples of mother nature. For instance, WANG Zongyue said "Long Boxing is like a long river or ocean flowing on and on ceaselessly". It not only explains the technical features of Tai-chi Chuan, but also reveals that practitioners should attention to maintaining the habit of "keeping relaxed and collected inside so that Qi (vital force) would rise up like steam". Natural phenomena such as the momentum and forms of ocean and rivers are common metaphors to describe stances of Tai-chi Chuan.

The exchange and integration of any culture needs its own medium and channels. The Chinese classical philosophy's influence on Tai-chi Chuan also has such, mainly in two ways. On one hand, Tai-chi Chuan masters with deep cultural prowess significantly facilitate Tai-chi Chuan's inclusion of the essence of Chinese classical philosophy. WANG Zongyue, for example, author of *The Theory of Tai-chi Chuan*, "had been well-versed from the Tao of Huang-Lao (the Yellow Emperor and Laozi), classical philosophy, history and martialism". In addition, eminent Taoist ZHANG Sanfeng, and CHEN Xin, WU Yuxiang, LI Yishe, SUN Lutang and others, also wrote books explaining the theory with their profound insights and vision of Tai-chi Chuan. On the other hand, substantial practitioners of Tai-chi Chuan, heavily influenced by the aforementioned Tai-chi Chuan classics, have been sharing their experience and thoughts with others. Though they may not be as well-versed as those predecessors and they may be even illiterate, their shared thoughts are simple but with well-inherited connotations of traditional Chinese philosophy. And there are two channels of spreading traditional Chinese philosophy to Tai-chi Chuan. First, using philosophy as practice guidance to interpret the theory of Tai-chi Chuan. For instance, *The Theory of Tai-chi Chuan* is like a philosophical prose explaining the pugilism theory. Second, Tai-chi Chuan assimilates the essence of other disciplines such as traditional Chinese medicine and martialism, in this way it indirectly absorbs philosophical thoughts into its own. Just as "Traditional Chinese medicine is not built upon modern science but philosophy of nature", Tai-chi Chuan is framed based on classical Chinese philosophy at its birth. In other words, classical Chinese philosophy broadly navigates the formation of Tai-chi Chuan. When it comes down to specific technical requirements, almost every movement of Tai-chi Chuan contains a certain philosophical connotation from the outer form to the inner core, which acts as a feature of Tai-chi Chuan, and a metric to evaluate movements' accuracy.

# 3. Tai-chi Chuan and Traditional Chinese Medicine

"Chuan is originated from *Yi* (*Book of Changes*) and its theory is developed upon traditional Chinese medicine", this ancient saying scientifically illustrates the relation between martial art and traditional Chinese medicine. Ancient Chinese pugilism methods encapsulate abstruse mechanisms of human life science. The "internal pugilisms" emerged since Ming and Qing Dynasty, such as Xing Yi (mind and body) Chuan, Eight-Trigram Boxing, and Tai-chi Chuan, have all been influenced and shaped by traditional Chinese medicine, Qigong (breathing technique therapy) and the theory of meridians.

Likewise, Tai-chi Chuan has also integrated the theories of traditional Chinese medicine spanned from meridians and collaterals, acupuncture point, Qi (vital force) and blood, Daoyin (guided breathing exercise) and visceral outward manifestation, to establish its own function of fitness. *The Essay of Tai-chi Chuan Diagram* by CHEN Xin entails *Song of Acupuncture Points* to advise the guided breathing when practicing Tai-chi Chuan.

The art of inhalation and exhalation is right encompassed in Tai-chi Chuan. As noted in *Huangdi Neijing (The Yellow Emperor's Inner Classic)*, "The middle land is flat and humid, with many creations appearing in heaven and earth. Their people eat anything yet not moving their body, and hence they succumb to disease, paralyses and weakness invaded by chills and fever. Daoyin (guided breathing exercise) and massage are the cure." This sentence is explained by another scholar as, "Daoyin, is about loosening ligaments and bones, moving limbs; massage is about massaging skin and muscles; stamping is about stretching limbs." As depicted by Zhuangzi on Daoyin, "Blowing and breathing with the open mouth; inhaling and exhaling the breath; expelling the old breath and taking in the new; passing their time like the (dormant) bar, and stretching and twisting (the neck) like a bird. All such simply show the desire for longevity". LI Yi in Jin Dyansty noted, "Guide breathing to become peaceful; lead the body to become supple." It indicates that Daoyin is in fact a physical exercise complimented with breathing, an exercise for the whole body and for dredging meridians, including body movements, guided breathing, massaging and meditation. Tai-chi Chuan encapsulates all such factors, requiring the coordination between breathing and movements in the way of "pugilism breathing". But such a coordination doesn't equal to guided movements only. It has the unique Tai-chi Chuan features. Traditional Chinese medicine thinks that meridians and collaterals are channels of Qi and blood distributed throughout the body. Originated in organs, they spread and extend to bones and limbs. Diseases arise when Qi and blood are insufficient; and when they're ample, the health is strong and the life is long. So, it's required that "use Qi to move the whole body", "focus on a selected acupuncture spot to move the body accordingly", "spread Qi to the whole body"; using the waist as an axis to move the limbs, turning the waist and rotating the spine spirally, using the intent to transmit the force, moving by following meridians, the force reaching acupuncture spots, the force going through the whole body, being connected with Ren, Du and Chong meridians. It enhances one's fitness by stimulating the circulation of Qi and blood and dredging meridians. The principles in medicine "the outer form and intrinsic energy are inseparable" and "preserving the intrinsic energy and the body as a whole" are translated into Tai-chi Chuan's requirements of "own both the outer form and the intrinsic energy", "conduct internal and external practice", "use the intent to guide movements". In *Huangdi Neijing (The Yellow Emperor's Inner Classic)*: *Plain Questions: On the State of Heavenly Genuineness in Remote Antiquity,* it says "keep the outer form and the intrinsic energy together to live out your heavenly years". The outer form refers to human body, and the intrinsic energy refers to one's mental state. As quoted, "preserve your intrinsic energy inside and ailment will never follow", the theory of Tai-chi Chuan is rooted in that. First and foremost is the intent, underscoring that "keep the intent of accumulating intrinsic energy", "the outer form reveals your intrinsic energy state" and "use the intent to guide movements". Practicing uniting the intrinsic energy and the outer form is a key to Tai-chi Chuan. "Don't move when the inner core remains still". It fits the fitness principle according to traditional Chinese medicine. "In this way your longevity will be endless." In *Song of Thirteen Stances*, it says "What's the reason for studying Tai-chi Chuan strenuously? It's for prolonging life and gaining vitality". Traditional Chinese medicine lays the foundation for Tai-chi Chuan to build its fitness function also in line with modern science. Every movement of Tai-chi Chuan has its specific fitness functions, which is a vital feature of Tai-chi Chuan.

## 4. Tai–chi Chuan and Aesthetics

Elegance of postures is a beauty of nature. Francis Bacon once said, "In beauty, that of favor, is more than that of color; and that of decent and gracious motion, more than that of favor". "It's the person who uses his intent that creates beauty!". And the beauty of Tai-chi Chuan fully illustrates that. Tai-chi Chuan as an exercise for humans, to some extent, is a form of human body culture. Long nourished by Chinese culture, not only is it a practical art of attack, but also a form of brilliance and versatility of martial art. During the practice of Tai-chi Chuan, its outer form, the intrinsic energy, the intent, Qi (vital force), stances, postures, tempos and rhythms are all presenting the beauty of Tai-chi Chuan.

On the beauty of rhythms, Tai-chi Chuan has the beauty of "structure, form and the inner core", similar to dance in terms of aesthetics. A Tai-chi Chuan's routine features the unity of the internal and the external, the fluidity of movements, the ownership of the outer form and the intrinsic energy, balanced softness and firmness and clear-cut rhythms. Despite that the movements are based on combat, but they're refined in the way that they can be swift and powerful when moving, and steady and still like a rock. It has its own grace either moving or static. Tai-chi Chuan, like dance, also has its movement rhythms. By embracing the principle of "to reverse is how Tao works", Tai-chi Chuan requires "to advance, retreat first", "to go left, go right first", "to go up, go down first", so that the transition of movements produces a round, fluid and dynamic space. Tai-chi Chuan highlights pursuing inactivity out of activity, maintaining the inter peace while moving externally, activity and inactivity are being the cause of each other. It can be as quiet and steady as a rock, and as rapid as the lightning. It carries its own pace and rhythm, when either moving or static. The beauty and charm of the rhythm of Tai-chi Chuan routines entrench power, presence, momentum, intrinsic energy within.

Tai-chi Chuan is elegant. The body should be held upright. The overall requirement is that raising the head, straightening the head and body, lowering the shoulders and elbows, hollowing the chest and stretching the back, eyes being deep and collected, being poised and lofty, carrying a grand presence. Elegance in Tai-chi Chuan is essential. When practicing Tai-chi Chuan's routines, the intent moves along with the outer form, and the outer form moves when the intent rises, making the whole routine coordinated and lively. Like floating clouds and flowing water, it's coherent as an integrated piece where the practitioner's body and limbs are expanded, forming a kind of grace that's natural and effortless. The force exerted in Tai-chi Chuan is rooted in heels, generated from legs, controlled within the waist, reaching fingers, and going through the spine. It transmits from feet to legs to the waist as a whole; when the force is exerted, it requires the force to be a complete one, in the way that "the whole body coordinates to generate this force of a thousand catties". In Tai-chi Chuan, if one intends to move up, he should move down first. Likewise, go right first if you want to go left. The internal and external are combined, back and forth, left and right. Balanced firmness and softness is another key. The elements of "essence, Qi (vital force) and intrinsic energy" embody the beauty of masculinity and magnificence, with the indomitable momentum of going forward.

As a traditional martial art program, Tai-chi Chuan is rooted in the long and glorious traditional Chinese culture. It requires practitioners to train his eyes, ears and heart during practice, honing his agility and sensitivity of auditivity, listening, and spirituality. As quoted, "whatever his eyes see and his ears hear, his heart will follow; he's decisive and agile while his Qi and blood are ample". Over time it cultivates practitioners' temperament, nurturing their decisiveness, courage, perseverance and fearlessness in character, rendering beauty to people to savor. Through studying Tai-chi Chuan, they connect with beauty, comprehend beauty, appreciate beauty and adore beauty. They enjoy the integration of ethics and beauty, and appreciate "The beauty of ethics touches one's heart; the beauty of intrinsic energy strengthens one's will, and the beauty of forms brings joy." The efficacy of regulating breathing, strengthening bones and ligaments and curing diseases, can also be attained through Tai-chi Chuan.

## 5. Tai-chi Chuan and Mechanics

Tai-chi Chuan as a physical exercise sees wide application of mechanics including Newton's Laws of Motion, Law of Conservation of Momentum, superposition of forces and force transmission. Such application constitutes Tai-chi Chuan's uniqueness. Tai-chi Chuan is particular about employing the opponent's own strength to beat him, and "moving a thousand catties with four taels". Such skills are closely correlated to the corresponding dynamics knowledge. By mastering such knowledge, practitioners can well comprehend Tai-chi Chuan's movement mechanism and better mastering the movement principles of "use softness to conquer firmness" and "use inactivity to contain activity", so that his Tai-chi Chuan will be improved. As follows, the relation between Tai-chi Chuan and dynamics will be elaborated in regards to the frame of Tai-chi Chuan and its techniques.

## (1) Mechanic principles applied in the frame of Tai-chi Chuan

### 1. Keeping upright body posture – maintaining dynamic balance of a human body

Equilibrium mechanics is a branch of mechanics that studies the nature and behavior of objects in equilibrium under the action of external forces. The Chinese character "定"("Ding", stillness) stressed in the Tai-chi Chuan routine also indicates that balance plays a vital role in Tai-chi Chuan. During the slow and gentle session in particular, it can be deemed as a dynamic balance due to a small angular speed despite of all routes being arcs.

On the human body forces: the person is subject to gravity; the ground's support force on the person; the friction force between the ground and feet. Conditions of human mechanical equilibrium include:

(1) limbs are the lever: spread two feet and keep the upright posture, forming an irregular human lever, following the principle of "the lever can be bent or straight without a fixed shape. Any objects that can rotate around a fixed point with no deformation can be called "levers".

(2) the waist top as a rotating axis: and the next line below the waist top is the center of gravity, and the fulcrum is the middle axis of rotation.

(3) Dynamics and resistance: the force that makes the lever rotate is called dynamics; the force that prevents the lever from rotating is called resistance.

(4) Force arm: the distance from the fulcrum to the line of force (i. e., the distance between the fulcrum and the force point). Resistance arm: the distance between the fulcrum and the line of resistance arm.

(5) The human body lever balance conditions: "the product of dynamics and force arm equals to the product of resistance and resistance arm".

The vertical line of the human body's center of gravity is in the middle of the area circled by two feet, which is a critical condition for maintaining the body's balance. Therefore, the best method to maintain the body's balance is placing the vertical line within the supporting surface between two feet (the area circled by feet), and trying to approach the center of the supporting surface. Tai-chi Chuan's theory requires practitioners to keep upright postures, employing the waist as hub, forming circles to ensure flexible advancing and retreating in four directions, up, down, left and right. In this way, the fulcrum of all movements is the waist while hands and feet are moving freely, creating a lever model[1].

---

① SUN Yunhong. Analysis of Mechanics Principle in Taijiquan Movement [J]. Physics Teaching Reference of Middle School, 2017, (12) : 77-78.

### 2. Source of power – support force and muscle tone

The power of Tai-chi Chuan includes: the source power from muscle tone generated by muscle contraction, an inner force. And the main power is the counter force coming from the process of switching substantiality and insubstantiality of two feet, an outer force. In *Biomechanics of Sports* edited by ZHANG Changheng, it says, "muscles differ from other soft tissues of the human body. Under the control of nerves, it converts chemical energy to mechanical energy at room temperature. Its active contraction enables mechanical movements of all joints". "When muscles are contacted, the biggest power is the most explosive force the body has. This ability not only makes the body move but also accelerates the movement." According Newton's Third Law of Motion, "When object A acts on object B, then object B has its reacting force on object A. And the acting force and the reacting force are constantly equal, collinear and the two directions inverse to each other." It also says, "the acting force and reacting force must be the forces of the same nature. If the acting force is friction force, so is the reacting force; if the reacting force is elastic force, so is the reacting force."

Employing principles of biomechanics of sports and mechanics to analyze and interpret the power of Tai-chi Chuan can further clarify the root cause and its supporting evidence of the power generated by Tai-chi Chuan, which includes the source power (inner force) coming from muscle tone by muscle contraction from skeletal muscles controlled the central nervous system, and the reacting force coming from the process of switching substantiality and insubstantiality of two feet.

### 3. Keeping the body as a whole – overall coordinated physical exercise

Keeping the body as a whole is the requirement on body postures in Tai-chi Chuan, meaning that when throwing fists and pushing hands, one should keep the body as a whole during the movement. Each movement of hands and of the body should be triggered by feet, and both shoulders and hips should move within the same plane. Hands and fee need to be synchronized. When one moves, the others move; when one stops, the others stop.

An advantage of keeping the body as a whole is increasing the mass (m). It's known that the bigger the m is, the bigger the inertia of the object is, according to Newton's Law of Inertia. Consequently, the force required to change the motion state is bigger. That makes it more difficult if the opponent wants to interfere with or to change such a movement, when Tai-chi Chuan practitioners employ this method to play Tai-chi Chuan or push hands.

Another advantage of this method is its force transmission rate is increased. We know that friction force is generated from the bottom of feet. To well utilize friction force, one must maximize the friction force to transmit it to hands. Keeping the body as a whole can solve difficulties in transmitting friction force from the bottom of feet to hands, so as to enhance force transmission rate.

## (2) Theories of mechanics in Tai-chi Chuan's techniques

### 1. Newton's Laws of Motion

The Law of Inertia states that objects have the characteristic of keeping their own motion state. The theory on art of attack in Tai-chi Chuan requires practitioners to "dodge the center of the vertical plane and focus on the center of the horizontal plane. It vividly illustrates how the Law of Inertia is applied in combat. When the opponent attacks me towards my chest in a straight line, the opponent has a certain speed of forward motion. If at that moment, I dodge him to avoid his attack, the opponent would lose his balance due to inertia and would be liable to fall over; or while I'm dodging him, I exert the force to the back of the opponent following the direction of his movement. This counter attack would be even more effective than the former one, called "pushing the boat along with the current". [1]

The "attract to emptiness and discharge" and "arc movement" indicate that the acceleration of an object is proportional to the combined force it is subjected to, and is inversely proportional to its mass. Any moving object's trajectory is linear. If you want to use an angle to control the incoming force, you need to change its direction and shift the gravitational center the opponent aims at attacking. The best way of it is using arc motion, which not only neutralizes the incoming force, but also uses it and forces back. With a very small counter force, it can already yield great results. This is the attack method to adopt after neutralizing the incoming force. If the incoming force is dodged, the counter attack following the opponent's retreating direction would also be very powerful.

Newton's Third Law of Motion is applied in force exertion of Tai-chi Chuan. The law illustrates the reciprocity of forces, meaning that the acting force and the reacting force between two objects are constantly equal in magnitude, two directions inverse to each other and collinear. Either throwing out the fist or kicking needs the supporting move of the feet thrusting against the ground. When a foot thrusts against the ground, an equal reacting force is generated by the ground, enhancing the acting force of the movement. This is in line with the principle stated in some Tai-chi Chuan diagrams: "The force exerted in Tai-chi Chuan is rooted in heels, generated from legs, controlled within the waist, reaching shoulders and arms, going through the spine and formed in fingers." In Tai-chi pushing hands practice, when one exerts a force to the opponent, the opponent would use his feet to thrust against the ground to generate the reacting force, further countering back the force to the other, during which the bigger the thrusting force is against the ground, the bigger the reacting force the practitioner receives.

### 2. Law of Momentum

Law of Momentum applied in martial art in terms of increasing hitting force and reducing buffer force. In this book it mainly illustrates the effect of reducing buffer force by employing Law of Momentum in Tai-chi Chuan.

The techniques of "using softness to conquer firmness", "underdogs battling giants"and "playing slow to beat the fast" in Tai-chi Chuan are about prolonging the force acting time of the opponent, and disabling the effect of hitting force. That it looks like "playing slow to beat the fast" is because Tai-chi Chuan takes a relatively long buffer time but in fact the initial speed, propagation speed, the ongoing speed and the reaction speed are not low; "Underdogs battling giants" is about using arc lines of Tai-chi Chuan to prolong force acting time. With the arc lines, the force acting

---

① MA Wenhai. *Biomechanics of Martial Arts* [M]. Kaifeng: Henan University Press, 2010, 71-72.

time and work distance are both longer. According to mechanics, $Ft = mv_1 + mv_0$, the effect of force is determined by the magnitude of $F$ and its product with $t$, force acting time. Therefore, one can employ a small amount of force to yield a much bigger resultant force.[1]

### 3. Law of Leverage

In terms of the lever model, the fulcrum, power point and resistance point are its three key parameters in the model of lever. The closer the fulcrum is to the resistance force point, the farther it is from the power point, then the more effort the lever will save. In contrast, the farther the fulcrum is from the resistance point, the closer it is to the power point, then the more effort the level will exert. Therefore, it's essential to select the right fulcrum and power point in Tai-chi Chuan. Take the movement, "Partition of Wild Horse's Mane", as an example, it requires the left hand to plunge down, then to raise the hand while picking, holding and warding off subsequently; meanwhile the right hand should more downward to pull and split, exercising the hand technique of "turning upward while buckling downward". At the same time, the right hand is leaning towards the left shoulder while it's picking and warding off, and the lower body is acting as a fulcrum, constituting a pushing force outward and forward.

### 4. The "force couple" circles and rotates

One circle is Tai-chi, a main feature of Tai-chi Chuan. One circle is produced by the force couple mechanics. The muscle tone (alternating tension and relaxation within the lumbar region) from skeletal muscle contraction in the waist controlled by the central nervous system, lead the changes of substantiality and insubstantiality, flexion and extension between both feet. The reacting force against the ground meanwhile generates eccentric torque, driving limbs to flex and extend. With one foot gradually being insubstantial and the other foot gradually being substantial, rounding the crotch area initiates rotation of the human body, which is actually the effect of "force couple", following the principle of "both forces are equal in magnitude, two directions inverse to each other, but not on the same line. Force couple makes objects rotate." It's the principle of overcoming redundant force. Thus, every movement of Tai-chi Chuan, either rotating to the left or to the right, stepping up or backward, is all three-dimensional rotational motion. (Figure) For instance, for the "Single Whip" movement of Tai-chi Chuan, one should extend both arms like pulling a whip straight, and he should do the throw-out move in the way that firmness is concealed by softness. In the art of attack, Single Whip can transform defense to offence, neutralize the incoming attack and follow up with a stronger hit. If the opponent uses the left hand to attack me, I should use the right-hand hook to counter him on the right; meanwhile using the left leg thrusting between both legs of the opponent, using the right hand to attack his chest, in this way the torque that makes the opponent fall is generated to destroy the opponent's balance.

Under the external force, one should be submissive and follow the opponent, using the intent instead of the force, in this way torque and force couple would be generated inside and the spiral rotation is formed outside. This aforementioned process is the cornerstone of Tai-chi Chuan. Why

---

① MA Wenhai. *Biomechanics of Martial Arts* [M]. Kaifeng: Henan University Press, 2010, 81.

does Tai-chi Chuan use the intent instead of the force. The purpose of being submissive and following is all for generating force couple, making the levers of the body and limbs spirally rotate, naturally realizing the function of "moving a thousand catties with four taels". This is the science of using the intent instead of the force. "Using the force" would cause redundant force rather than generating force couple. Those who do that would fail to "move a thousand catties with four taels", and would be trapped to fight with their physical strength only.

# 第二章　太极拳技术原理

## 第一节　太极拳基本技法[①]

### 一、虚灵顶劲

虚灵顶劲即"顶头悬"。练拳时讲究头部的头正、顶平、项直、颌收，要求头顶的百会穴处要向上轻轻顶起，同时又须保持头顶的平正。要使头正、顶平，就必须使颈项竖直、下颌里收。顶劲不可过分用力，要有自然虚灵之意。做到虚灵顶劲，精神才提得起来，动作才能沉稳、扎实。

### 二、气沉丹田

气沉丹田，是身法端正，宽胸实腹，"意注丹田"，意识引导呼吸，将气徐徐送到腹部脐下。太极拳在运动时，一般都是采用腹式呼吸，同时"意注丹田"，这样能达到太极拳"身动、心静、气敛、神舒"的境地。

用腹式呼吸来加深气息的深长，应自然、匀细、徐徐吞吐，要与动作自然配合，不能用强制的方法。要求整套动作都要与一呼一吸结合得非常密切，应根据动作的开合、屈伸、起落、进退、虚实等变化，自然地去配合。一般地说，呼吸总是与胸廓的张缩、肩胛的活动自然结合着。在一个动作里，往往就伴随着一呼一吸，而不是一个动作固定为一吸或是一呼。这种与动作自然配合的方法运用得当，可以使动作更加协调、圆活、轻灵、沉稳。

### 三、含胸拔背

含胸是胸廓略向内涵虚，使胸部有舒宽的感觉。这样有利于做好腹式呼吸，能在肩锁关节放松、两肩微含、两肋微敛的姿势下，通过动作使胸腔上下径放长，横隔肌有下降舒展的机会。它既能使重心下降，又使脏腑、横膈肌活动加强。

拔背与含胸是相互联系的，要含胸就势必拔背。拔背是在胸部略向内涵虚时背部肌肉向下松沉，两肩中间颈下第三脊骨鼓起上提，并略向后上方拉起，不能单纯地往后拉。这样背

---

① 全国体育学院教材委员会审定. 武术［M］. 北京：人民体育出版社，1991.6.

部肌肉就会有一定的张力、弹力，皮肤有绷紧的感觉。

含胸拔背，胸背肌肉须松沉，不能故意做作。

## 四、松腰敛臀

太极拳要求含胸、沉气，因此在含胸时就必须松腰。松腰不仅帮助沉气和下肢的稳固，更主要的是它对动作的进退旋转、用躯干带动四肢的活动及动作的完整性，起着主导作用。

敛臀则是在含胸拔背和松腰的基础上使臀部稍作内收。敛臀时，可尽量放松臀、腰部肌肉，使臀部肌肉向外下方舒展，然后轻轻向前、向里收敛，像用臀部把小腹托起来似的。

## 五、圆裆松胯

裆，即会阴部位。头顶百会穴的"虚灵顶劲"要与会阴穴上下相应，这是保持身法端正、气贯上下的锻炼方法。

裆部要圆，又要实。胯撑开，两膝微向里扣，裆自圆。会阴处上提，裆部自会实；加上腰部的松沉、臀部的收敛，自然产生裆劲。

太极拳讲究"迈步如猫行"，要求步法轻灵稳健，两腿弯屈轮换支持身体进行活动。因此髋部关节须放松，膝关节须灵活，才能保证上体旋转自如，踢腿、换步灵便。

## 六、沉肩坠肘

太极拳在松肩的前提下要求"沉肩坠肘"，两臂由于肩、肘的下坠会有一种沉重的内劲感觉，这就是上肢内在的遒劲。两肩除沉之外，还要有些微向前合抱的意思，这能使胸部完全涵虚，使脊背团成圆形。两肘下坠之外，也要有一些微向里的裹劲。这样的沉肩坠肘，才能使劲力贯串到上肢手臂。

## 七、舒指坐腕

舒指是掌指自然伸展，坐腕是腕关节向手背、虎口的一侧自然屈起。手掌的动作是整体动作的一部分，许多掌法都是与全身动作连成一气的，因此舒指坐腕，实际是将周身劲力通过"其根在脚，发于腿，主宰于腰，形于手指"，完整一气。

## 八、尾闾中正

尾闾中正是关系身躯和动作姿势"中正安舒""支撑八面"的准星。因此在进行太极拳运动时极重视尾闾中正，不论是直的或是斜的动作姿势，都必须保持尾闾与脊椎成直线，处于中正状态。更重要的是，尾闾中正还影响着下盘的稳固。所以尾闾中正同样是和以上七点连贯统一的。能够统一地做到这八点，就可以使躯干、上肢、下肢的内在劲力达到完整如一的状态。

## 九、内宜鼓荡，外示安逸

鼓荡是对内在精神所提的要求，是精神振奋的意思。内宜鼓荡是指内在的精神要振奋，然而这种振奋是沉着的、"神宜内敛"的，并不流于形色，表现是安逸的。

## 十、运动如抽丝，迈步如猫行

太极拳运动要像抽丝那样既缓又匀、又稳又静，迈步要像猫那样轻起轻落，提步、落步都要有轻灵的感觉。静是太极拳特点之一，练太极拳首要的条件就是要做到心理安静，排除杂念，使精神完全集中到运动上来。心静，才能"用意不用力"，使运动像抽丝那样安静。太极拳讲究"用意识引导动作"，是一种"会意"的运动。"缓以会意"，只有徐缓的活动才能会意，因此它要求运动像抽丝那样徐缓不躁。太极拳又讲究速度均匀，要求保持适当的等速运动，又需像抽丝那样均匀地抽拉。其步法必须像猫迈步那样轻灵。

## 第二节　太极拳技术要求[①]

### 一、身形技术

#### 1. 头部

练习太极拳时，对头部姿势的要求是自然上顶，避免颈部肌肉硬直，不要东偏西歪或自由摇晃。头颈动作应随着身体位置和方向的变换，与躯干的旋转上下连贯协调一致。面部要自然，下颌向里收回，用鼻呼吸。口自然合闭。

眼神要随着身体的转动，注视前手（个别时候看后手）或平视前方，神态力求自然，注意力一定要集中，否则会影响锻炼效果。

#### 2. 躯干部

（1）胸背部：太极拳要领中指出要"含胸拔背"，或者"含蓄在胸，运动在两肩"，意思是说在锻炼过程中要避免胸部外挺，但也不要过分内缩，应顺其自然。"含胸拔背"是互相联系的，背部肌肉随着两臂伸展动作，尽量地舒展开，同时注意胸部肌肉要自然放松，不可使其紧张，这样胸部就有了"含"的意思，背也有"拔"的形式，从而也可免除胸肋间的紧张，呼吸调节也自然了。

（2）腰脊：练习太极拳，要求身体端正安舒。要做到这点，腰部有着很重要的作用。在流传的说法中有"腰脊为第一主宰""刻刻留心在腰间""腰为车轴"等，都说明了腰是身体转动的关键，对全身动作的变化，调整和稳定重心，起着非常重要的作用。练习时，无论进退或旋转，凡是由虚而逐渐落实的动作，腰部都要有意识地向下松垂，以助气下沉。腰部下垂时，注意要端正安舒，腰腹部不可前挺或后屈，以免影响转换时的灵活性。腰部向下，松

① 体育系通用教材. 武术 [M]. 北京：人民体育出版社，1978.9.

垂，可以增加两腿力量，稳固底盘，使动作圆活、完整。

（3）臀部：练习太极拳时要求"敛臀"，保持自然状态，避免臀部凸出或左右扭动。要松腰、正脊以维持躯干的正直。

### 3. 腿部

在练习太极拳的过程中，对于步法的进退变换和周身的稳定程度，两腿起着决定性作用。因此要求腿部动作要正确、灵活、稳当。在练习时，要特别注意重心移动。脚放的位置，腿弯屈的程度，重心的移动和两腿的虚实变化都与整个套路动作的前后衔接密切相关。

腿部活动时，总的要求是松胯、屈膝、两脚轻起轻落，使下肢动作轻、稳，进退灵便。迈步时，一腿支撑体里，稳定重心；然后另一腿缓缓迈出。脚的起落，要轻巧灵活。前进时，脚跟先着地；后退时，脚掌先着地，然后慢慢踏实。横步时，侧出腿先落脚尖，然后脚掌、脚跟依次落地。跟步、垫步都是先落脚尖或脚掌。

步型和步法都要求腿部动作虚实分明，除"起势""收势"外，避免体重同时落在两腿上（双重）。右腿支撑大部体重时，则右腿为实，左腿为虚；左腿支撑大部体重时，则左腿为实，右腿为虚。为了维持身体平衡，虚脚起着一个支点作用（如虚步的前脚和弓步的后脚）。蹬脚、分脚的动作，宜慢不宜快（个别动作除外），应保持身体平衡稳定。摆腿动作（摆莲腿）或拍脚动作不可紧张。

### 4. 臂部

练习太极拳总的要求是沉肩垂肘，使肩、肘两个相关联的关节放松。运动时，注意肩关节松沉，并有意识地向外引伸，使手臂有回旋的余地。

太极拳的手臂一伸一屈都不可平出平入、直来直往，应把腕部和前臂的旋转动作确切地表现出来。对手的动作要求是：凡是收掌动作，手掌应微微含蓄，但不可软化、飘浮。当手掌前推时，除了注意沉肩垂肘之外，要徐徐内旋，同时手腕微向下塌。手法的屈伸翻转，要力求轻松灵活。出掌要自然，手指要舒展。拳要松握，不要太用力。

手和肩的动作是完整一致的。如果手过度向前引伸，就容易把臂伸直，达不到"沉肩垂肘"的要求；而过分地沉肩垂肘，忽略了手的向前引伸，又容易使臂部过于弯屈。总之，动作时，臂部始终要保持一定的弧度，推掌、收掌动作都不要突然断劲，这样才能做到既有节律，又连绵不断，轻而不浮，沉而不僵，灵活自然。

## 二、运动方法

练习太极拳，除了要求头部、躯干和四肢的基本姿势正确，动作合乎要领外，还要特别注意运动方法，这样才能体现出太极拳的独特风格，更好地提高锻炼效果和技术水平。

### 1. 心静体松

"心静"和"体松"是练好太极拳的两个基本方法，它对于其他方法的运用和掌握，起到一种保证作用。

所谓"心静"，就是在练拳时，思想上尽量排除一切杂念。无论动作简单或复杂，姿势高或低，心理上始终保持安静状态，使精神能贯注到每个细小的动作中去，做到专心练拳。从预备式开始，就要求思想集中，全部精神用到动作上，引导着动作，作到"意到身随"。比如，两手前按时，就要先有向前按的想象；同样，如意欲沉气，就要有使气下沉的想象，意不停，动作也随之不停。

在动作中，如果能做到排除杂念、思想集中，会有以下几点作用：首先，把动作想得细致周到，并能把动作做得柔和连续而有节律，这种有节律的动作有利于调节大脑皮质和中枢神经系统的机能状态，和增强身体其他各部器官功能。其次，可使大脑的其他部分处于抑制的休息状态，消除思维和其他局部单一工作所引起的疲劳，避免过度兴奋和无谓的紧张，调整大脑的平衡作用。最后，能保证"用意不用力"的运用和用意识引导动作，从而调整呼吸，使意识、动作和呼吸三者密切结合，达到全身上下、内外全面锻炼的效果。

所谓"体松"，就是要求练拳时，要保持全身的肌肉、关节、韧带和内脏都处于自然、舒展的状态，使其不受任何拘束或压迫。太极拳要求的"松"是"舒松"，不是松软无力或松懈疲怠，而是在身体自然活动或稳定情况下，使某些可能放松的肌肉和关节尽力放松。在练习中要求人体的脊柱按自然形态直立起来，使头、躯干、四肢等部分进行舒松自然的活动。具体来说，就是要避免造成一切不该用力的部位，避免无谓的紧张。而用力的部位也要保持自然开展的状态，按照动作的要求，使姿势正确，进退稳健。如维持平衡时，腿部要支持住重心，使进退变转轻灵自如；两臂该圆的要做到圆满，腿该屈的要屈到所要求的度数，肌肉不可表现僵滞，不能用生硬造作的拙力（即僵劲）。

"松"是完成姿势正确、周身协调、动作舒展、变转圆活的基础和保证。有人练起拳来浑身僵硬，动作呆板。尽管他们手脚的部位摆对了，头颈也放正了，看起来就是不舒服、不自然，主要是没掌握"松"的要领。也有些人打拳时，手脚动作不够开展，如提手上式的前臂（右臂）本应保持自然微屈，腕部前引，肘部下垂，肩向下松沉，整个手臂在舒松中带有沉着的劲，但往往因弯屈过大，上臂前臂之间成了直角，结果势必造成肩部耸起，肘关节、肱二头肌也随之紧张。太极拳的一招一式、伸腿打拳都要自然舒展，肌肉的一张一弛也是相互交替进行，所以掌握了要领之后，在适当的速度下打上半小时太极拳，身体各部并不酸疼，反而感到轻松舒适、"气不涌出、面不改色"。如果不是遵循这条原则，打起拳来必然容易疲劳，心跳气喘，不能持久。

有些人把"松"体会成软绵无力，如手向前按时，腕部不塌、指尖不挑，掌心也不前撑（即展指舒掌），手腕过于软化无力；或做成摇荡飘浮、上下异动，这都是不正确的。

### 2. 连贯圆活

所谓连贯，是指在各个拳式之间或者各个动作之间，都要前后衔接，不可在衔接处有显著的停顿或者露出断续的痕迹（在无形中用意识表示虚实轻重者不在此限），务必使全部动作节节贯串，绵绵不绝，一气呵成。这一特点主要在于要使各个姿势的和谐动作连接起来，中间既有节分，又要连贯不停，形成一种自然的节奏，来提高动作的效果。拳论中所说"如长江大海滔滔不绝"，就是这个意思。另外，这种有节奏的连续运动，动作异常细致，前一个动作的完成，恰好是下一个过渡动作的开始，好像是把所有的定式和过渡动作变成很多珠子，用线穿起来一样，组成一个完整的拳套。比如"揽雀尾"动作，初学时可以把掤、捋、挤、按分成四个局部动作，独立开来；熟练之后，就要把这四个动作衔接在一起，动作中间虽然仍要保持一定的节奏感，即一个动作做完了，微微一沉，似停非停就立刻接下一个动作，整个过程精神贯注，意识集中，不可松懈间断。简化太极拳的二十四个姿势动作、第二套太极拳四十八个姿势动作之间的节奏感，都应这样处理。

所谓圆活，是指练习起来要灵活自然，衔接合顺。有分、抱、云、架、按、挑、搂、推、穿、插等掌法变化；臂部的本身不仅永久保持自然弯屈的状态，而且运行的路线也都按不同的曲线反复变转。下肢也是随时保持自然弯屈的状态，重心稳定，姿势似展似未展，曲中求直。认识和掌握这一规律，就能自觉地避免动作直来直往和转死弯、拐直角的现象，使动作圆活不滞。在动作要领上，要特别注意运用腰脊带动四肢进行活动，体会转腕旋臂（不要故意缠绕）、松肩垂肘、屈膝松胯等要领。虽然强调走弧形、曲线，但要转动自如，做到变转圆活，轻灵顺遂。

### 3. 柔缓均匀

太极拳是以慢动作为主，所以"柔""缓"是太极拳的动作特征。

"运劲如抽丝"这一要求，说明在用劲时要同抽丝一样绵绵不绝，用力不僵不拘，速度不忽快忽慢，使动作柔缓均匀（发力动作除外）。但动作缓慢也不是越慢越好，因为过慢则气势散漫，要以气势连贯、呼吸自然、动作不停为度。打一套"简化太极拳"，正常速度以4～6分钟为宜。

练习太极拳时，在连续不断当中要保持一定的匀度（等速运动）。要使运动速度大体平均，必须使身体重心虚实变换得当。如果不能保持身体的平衡稳定，也难做到动作均匀。另外在动作的匀度上，可把整个套路的过程比作一条虚线的结构。这些点比喻套路中的各个动作；均匀的空隙比喻动作与动作之间的连接速度。这样就能使动作在无形中按照虚线所示规律进行速度的分配，逐渐使身体动作能够在柔和缓慢的运动过程中掌握好均匀的运动速度。

### 4. 上下相随

有人说，打太极拳时，全身"动无有不动"，又说，练拳时全身"由脚而腿而腰总须完成一气"，这些都是形容"上下相随、周身协调"的要求。

初学太极拳的人，虽然在理论上知道许多动作要以腰部为轴，由躯干带动四肢来进行活动，但因为意识与肢体动作还不能密切配合，想做到周身协调也是有困难的。最好先通过单式练习（如单练"起势""云手"等），以求得躯干与四肢动作的协调，同时也要练习步法（如站虚步、弓步及移动重心、变换步法等），以锻炼下肢的支撑力量和熟练地掌握步法要领。然后再通过全部动作的连贯练习，使步法的进退转换与躯干的旋转、手法的变化相互配合，逐渐地达到全身既协调而又完整，从而使身体各个部位都得到均衡的锻炼与发展。

一般来说，上下肢和躯干之间的配合、这一动作和下一动作之间的密切联系，为外部协调；意识、呼吸与动作之间的配合，则为内部协调。要做到外部协调，在肢体的配合上，就要做到"上下相随"。不是摆好了手再摆腿，而是使躯干和四肢相应地进行活动。因此，必须以腰作轴，用躯干带动四肢，并与手、脚动作和眼神的变化相互配合，随着方向和位置的改变，使全身各部不停地运动着，一直到拳术套路结束为止。

### 5. 虚实分明

运动本身就是矛盾。在太极拳练习中，常常把矛盾转换概括称作虚实变化。太极拳从整体动作来分，除个别情况外，动作达到终点定式为"实"，动作变转过程为"虚"。从动作局部来分，主要支撑体重的腿为实，辅助支撑或移动换步腿为虚；体现动作主要内容的手臂为实，辅助、配合的手臂为虚。分清了动作的虚实，我们用力的时候，就要有张有弛，区别对待。实的动作和部位，用力要求沉着、充实；虚的动作和部位，要求轻灵、含蓄。例如动作达到定式或趋于完成时，腰脊和关节要注意松沉、稳定。动作变转运动时，全身各关节要注意舒松、活泼。上肢动作由虚而实时，前臂要沉着，手掌逐渐展指舒掌、塌腕（也称坐腕），握拳要由松而紧；由实而虚时，前臂运转要轻灵，手掌略微含蓄，握拳由紧而松。这样，结合动作的虚实变化，打起拳来就能做到既轻灵又沉着，避免了不分主次、平均用力和双重、呆滞的毛病。

明白了虚和实、刚和柔的对立后，还要掌握二者的统一。太极拳所有动作，都是矛盾双方共处在一个统一体的运动转化过程（两手、两腿大多是一虚一实相互交替），就是动作做到终点时，也要求各部位关节、肌肉保持少许伸缩转化余地，过去称为"虚中有实、实中有虚"。这就要求在用力上不能绝对化，既要明确矛盾的主要方面，也要注意矛盾的次要方面，做到柔中寓刚，刚中寓柔，避免僵化、软化现象。太极拳每个动作、每个瞬间，都是处在几种相反相成的力量作用下，在相互牵制和对抗中进行的。比如手臂前推时，掌根向前用力，同时肘部向下沉，肩窝向后缩，上体尽力放松，这样力量的运用就能做到沉而不僵。手臂后收时，肩部放松并向后带，肘部外（内）引，手腕也微微放松，使前臂自然而圆活地旋转，既不要突然断劲，又不要故意缠绕摇摆，使动作轻而不浮，活而不散。

动作的虚实和身体重心的转移关系密切。因为一个姿势与另一个姿势连接，位置和方向的改变，处处都贯穿着步法的变换和转移重心的活动。在锻炼中也要注意身法和手法的运用，由虚到实，或由实到虚，既要分明，又要连贯不停，一气呵成。如果虚实变化不清，进退变化就一定不灵，容易发生动作迟滞、重心不稳和左右歪斜的问题。"迈步如猫行，运劲如抽丝"，就是形容练习太极拳应当注意脚步轻灵和动作均匀。

太极拳的动作，无论怎样复杂，首先要把自己安排得舒适，这是太极拳"中正安舒"的基本要求。凡是旋转的动作，应先把身体稳住再提腿换步；进退的动作，先落脚而后再慢慢地改变重心。同时，躯体做到了沉肩、松腰、松胯及手法上的虚实，也会帮助重心的稳定。这样，无论动作快慢，就不会产生左右摇摆、上重下轻和稳定不住的问题。

### 6. 意识、动作、呼吸三者结合

练习太极拳时，肢体配合协调、动作之间连贯，仅仅是"协调完整"的一部分，而意识、动作和呼吸三者密切结合，才是达到全身上下内外统一和谐、完整一体的最后关键。

所谓意识、动作和呼吸三者密切结合，其实就是在意识的主导下，使动作和呼吸紧密结合起来。意识活动和呼吸过程都要配合动作的要求，反过来又要促进动作的完善。而意识在太极拳中始终起着主导作用。所以，太极拳要求"以意导体，以体导气"，意思就是意识引导动作、动作结合呼吸。

意识引导动作就是把想象和动作结合起来，随想随作，使想象引导着动作运行。当然，引导不是不分主次地绝对平均，而是把意识用在动作虚实转换中的主要部位。比如"云手"，眼睛虽然注视着右手不停地随着腰部转动，但对于左手的摆动、重心的左右移动，也没有放松不管，只是重点注意右手而已；等到左手转到上边时，注意力又转移到左手上去。意识就是在这种不停的活动中，起着引导和调节的作用。

关于太极拳意识引导动作，特别要注意以下几个要点。

第一，意识集中不是情绪紧张、动作呆板。意识活动要与劲力虚实、张弛相一致，形成有节奏有变化的运动。意识活动和劲力运用，是统一运动的两个方面，都要体现"沉而不僵，轻而不浮"的特点。

第二，练拳时要注意情绪饱满，精神贯注（包括眼神运用），这是意识活动的重要体现。

练习太极拳既不能精神表现紧张，也不能显得疲疲沓沓、毫无生气，而应在外示安逸的过程中，精神饱满，自然生动，富有生气。

第三，意识、劲力、动作三者是统一的，但它们的相互关系则有主有从。

意识引导劲力，劲力产生运动。所以太极拳要求"先在心，后在身"，势换劲连，劲换意连。但是这种主从关系，不能理解为脱节、割裂。意识的变化要表现在劲力和动作上。练太极拳不能片面追求"虚静"，追求"有圈之意，无圈之形"，这样就会把意识活动割裂架空，使人莫测高深，无所适从。

那么动作怎样结合呼吸呢？太极拳要求呼吸深长细匀，通顺自然。初学时只要求自然呼吸。动作熟练以后，可以根据个人锻炼的体会和需要，在合乎自然的原则下，有意识地引导呼吸，使其更好地适应劲力与动作的要求，这种呼吸叫"拳势呼吸"。比如，太极拳动作接近完成时，大多数要求劲力沉着充实，动作稳定，要求沉肩、虚胸、实腹，这时就应该有意识地呼气，推动腹肌和膈肌运动。太极拳的动作转变过程，情况比较复杂，一般来说，凡是用力含蓄轻灵、肩胛开放、胸腔舒张时，应该有意识地吸气；而用力沉稳坚实、肩胛内合、胸腔收缩时，应该呼气。身体上起时一定要吸气，下蹲时一定要呼气；举手时吸气，臂下落时必定要呼气。而拳势呼吸，就是要使这种自发的配合变成自觉的引导过程。也可以适当地运用逆腹式呼吸方法，以加大腹肌和膈肌的活动范围，使呼吸更为加深加长，动作更为沉稳、轻灵。

## 第三节　太极拳呼吸方法[①]

### 一、自然呼吸法

自然呼吸法是指人们按照原来的呼吸频率和呼吸方法呼吸，只是更为柔和。要求顺乎自然，柔和均匀，丝毫不用力，不加意念支配，采用鼻吸鼻呼、鼻吸口呼均可。

### 二、腹式呼吸法

#### 1. 顺腹式呼吸法
吸气时腹肌放松，横膈肌随之下降，腹部隆起，呼气时腹部缓慢回收。

#### 2. 逆腹式呼吸法
吸气时腹肌收缩，横膈肌随之下降，腹壁内凹；呼气时腹肌放松，腹壁放松隆起。

腹式呼吸是通过横膈肌的运动来完成的呼吸，增强了膈肌运动，使胸腔容积增大，气体进出量增加。它可以使呼吸完全，功能残气减少，尤其是使双肺下部的通气功能得到改善，所以对呼吸系统疾病有较好的疗效。由于增强了腹肌的收缩和放松，对腹腔内脏直接起了一定的按摩作用，有助于改善消化系统功能。

---

① 汪长芳等. 传统养生体育教程 [M]. 北京：北京体育大学出版社，2014.04.

## 三、拳势呼吸法

拳势呼吸法是指按照一呼一吸的呼吸规律与动作完全配合，是在动作相当熟练时采用的方法。在练习时，要注意调整呼吸的深度、频率。在练习太极拳时，当做到开、起、升、屈等动作时，就要有意识地深吸气，同时要有轻灵向上提的意识，如"白鹤亮翅""如封似闭"动作中，手向上提和双手回收的动作，就属于深吸气。相反的，做到合、落、降、伸等动作时，就要有意识地、均匀地深呼气，同时要有充实和下沉的意识，像"海底针""揽雀尾"动作中的下蹲和向前挤、按的动作，是属于深呼气的。总之，一般由实转虚的动作，应当吸气，同时要注意轻灵自然；由虚转实的动作，应当呼气，同时要注意沉着稳定，慢慢就自然了。

有些动作开合不明显，或两臂一上一下、一前一后，屈伸兼有，这时要分清主次，以主要动作为准，结合呼吸，同时还要和两腿的进退虚实结合起来。如"海底针"接"闪通臂"动作，右手提起开始上举时，身体和手都要向上运动，应该吸气，等到左脚迈出向前弓腿和左手向前推的时候，虽然右臂仍在继续上举，但要以左手前推和左腿落实前弓为主，结合深呼气来完成动作。"拳势呼吸"的运用不是绝对的，因为太极拳套路的结构，动作的编排，都是考虑前后衔接连贯、全面锻炼的需要，在编排上不是仅从呼吸的节拍出发。不仅不同的太极拳路，练起来时呼吸的次数、深度各有不同，就是同一套路，不同体质的人和以不同速度练习时，呼吸也无法强求一律。可以这样说，练拳时只能要求在主要动作和胸肩开合较明显的动作上，做到"拳势呼吸"。在练一些过渡动作，以及个人感到呼吸难以结合的动作时，仍需要进行自然呼吸，或采用辅助呼吸（短暂呼吸）加以过渡调节。所以练太极拳无论什么时候，无论技术如何熟练，总要"拳势呼吸"和"自然呼吸"结合使用，才能保证呼吸与动作的结合顺畅妥善，符合太极拳"气以直养而无害"的原则要求。不要简单地开列"呼吸程序表"，使呼吸机械绝对，强求统一。尤其是病员或体质较弱的人练太极拳，更应因人制宜，保持呼吸的自然顺遂，不能以力使气，生硬勉强，违背呼吸的自然规律，以免有伤身体。

# Chapter 2 Technical Principles of Tai-chi Chuan

## Section 1 Basic Techniques of Tai-chi Chuan[①]

### 1. Straightening the Head and Body

Straighten the Head and Body, i. e. suspending the head and relaxing the neck. When practicing Tai-chi Chuan, the head should be upright, the top of the head should be level, the neck should be straight and the chin should be tucked in. *Baihui Point (The junction between the midline of the head and the 2-ear-tip line)* on the top of head should push up while maintaining the levelness of the top. If practitioners want to ensure the uprightness of head and levelness of top, they should keep the neck straight and chin tucked in. The force of lifting should be moderate to make the head lifted by a hidden energy. As long as the technique is practiced, the spirit can be lifted up to ensure stable and solid movements Figure 2-1-1 Leftmost: Straighten the head and body.

### 2. Sinking the Breath to the *Dantian*

Sinking the breath to the *Dantian* makes the body upright, broadens the chest and makes the abdomen solid. "Bringing mind down to the *Dantian*" means guiding breath with mind and send the *qi* to the lower belly. When practicing Tai-chi Chuan, abdominal breathing is always used. Meanwhile, it is also necessary to bring mind down to the *Dantian*, thus achieving the required status of practicing Tai-chi Chuan, i. e. "moving body, peaceful mind, sinking *qi* and relaxed spirit".

The application of abdominal breathing aims to deepen the depth of breath. The aspiration should be natural, uniform and slow as well as cooperating with the movement naturally. Forced breathing is not allowed. It is required that the whole set of movements should coordinate with each

---

① Approved by the National Sports Institute Textbook Committee. *Martial Arts*[M]. Beijing: People's Sports Publishing House, 1991.6

breath according to the opening and closing, flexion and extension, lifting and descending, advancing and receding, substantiality and insubstantiality of the movements. Generally speaking, breathing always naturally coordinates with the expansion and contraction of the thorax and the movement of the shoulder blades. A movement is often accompanied by both the inhaling and exhaling rather than a separate inhaling or exhaling. If this method coordinates with the movement naturally, the movement can be more coordinated, flexible, light and stable.

## 3. Hollowing the Chest and Raising the Back

Hollowing the chest is to make the chest slightly inward with a comfortable and expanded feeling. This is conducive to abdominal breathing, and can expand the chest vertically through the movement while relaxing the acromioclavicular joint, slightly containing the shoulders and slightly sinking the ribs. It enables the diaphragm muscle to fall and stretch, lowering the center of gravity and strengthening the activities of viscera and diaphragm muscle.

Raising the back and hollowing the chest are interrelated. While hollowing the chest, practitioners will raise back naturally. Raising the back refers to that when the chest is slightly contained, the back muscles will relax downward, and the third chine under the neck in the middle of the shoulders is bulging and lifted up, and it can not be simply pulled back. In this way, the back muscles will have a certain tension and elasticity, and the skin will feel tight.

When hollowing the chest and raising the back, the chest and the back muscles must relax downward in a natural way.

## 4. Relaxing the Waist and Making Buttocks Tucked in

When practicing Tai-chi Chuan, people should contain the chest and sink *qi*. When containing the chest, practitioners must relax waist. Relaxing the waist not only contributes to sinking *qi* and stabilizing the lower limbs, but also plays a leading role in forward and backward movements, rotation, the movement of limbs driven by the trunk and the integrity of movements.

As for making buttocks tucked in, it refers to slightly retracting the buttocks on the basis of hollowing the chest, raising the neck and relaxing the waist. When making buttocks tucked in, relax the buttocks and waist muscles as much as possible to stretch the buttocks outward and downward. Then gently retract the buttocks forward and inward, as if holding the lower abdomen with the buttocks.

## 5. Rounding the Crotch and Relaxing the Hip

The crotch is the perineum area. Straightening the head and body made by Baihui point on the top of head should correspond to Huiyin Point. And this is the method to practice maintaining the upright posture and making *qi* pass through the top and bottom of the body.

The crotch should be round and solid. Keep the crotch open, slightly make the knees inward,

and the crotch will be round. Lift up the perineum, and the crotch will be solid. Relax the waist and make the buttocks tucked in will produce crotch strength.

In Tai-chi Chuan, practitioners should "walk like a cat". It requires light and steady footwork. Practitioners should bend the legs to alternatively support body movement. Therefore, they must relax the hip and keep the knee joint flexible to ensure the free rotation of the upper body and the flexibility of kicking and step changing.

## 6. Lowering the Shoulders and Elbows

In Tai-chi Chuan, on the condition of relaxing the shoulders, it is also required to sink the shoulders and bend down the elbows, making the arms having a feeling of internal strength and generating the internal power of upper limbs. While sinking the shoulders, practitioners should also hold the shoulders slightly forward to fully contain the chest, making a round back. While lowering the shoulders and elbows, the strength should be generated inward to make the strength reach the upper limbs.

## 7. Relaxing the Fingers and Settling the Wrists

Relaxing the fingers refers to stretching fingers naturally. Settling the wrists refers to bend the wrists to the back of the hands or the web between the thumb and the index fingers. The movement of the palm is a part of the whole set of the movement. Many palm movements are made along with the whole body movements. Therefore, the key of this technique lies in that "The strength of the whole body roots at the feet, then transfers through the legs and is controlled from the waist, moving eventually through the back to the arms and fingertips".

## 8. Keeping the Coccyx Centrally Aligned

Keeping the coccyx centrally aligned will ensure the upright and comfortable body and full support of movement and posture. Tai-chi Chuan gives top priority to keeping the coccyx centrally aligned. No matter practitioners are practicing straight or oblique movements or postures, they should keep the coccyx and spline centrally aligned. More important, the steadiness of lower limbs also lies in this technique. Therefore, this technique is connected to and coherent with the above seven techniques. As long as practitioners can practice these eight techniques well, they can make unite strength through the body, upper limbs and lower limbs.

## 9. Raising up the Inner Spirit and Displaying the Calmness and Peace

Raising up the inner spirit is the requirement for the spirit. At the same time the inner spirit should also be aplomb. And the "raising up" should not be displayed. Rather, calmness and peace should be displayed.

## 10. Moving Gently and Steadily and Walking like a Cat

The movement in practicing Tai-chi Chuan should be slow, even, stable and quiet which is just like reeling off raw silk from cocoons. And practitioners should walk like a cat with light steps. Calmness is one of the characteristics of Tai-chi Chuan. The very requirement for practicing Tai-chi is to have a clam mind and concentrate on the movements without distractions. As long as having a peaceful mind, practitioners can "use mind rather the force" and make the movement peaceful as reeling off raw silk from cocoons. Tai-chi Chuan is a perception sport, and aims to "guiding the movement with consciousness". "Being slow to perceive" refers to that only slow movement can facilitate the perception. Therefore, the movement should be slow and clam as reeling off raw silk from cocoons. In Tai-chi Chuan practicing, an even speed is also important. Therefore, the movement should be at an appropriate constant and even speed which is like that of reeling off raw silk from cocoons. The footwork should be as light as the cat's walking.

## Section 2   Technical Requirements for Tai-chi Chuan[①]

## 1. Body Shape Techniques

### 1.1  Head

When practicing Tai-chi Chuan, the head should lift naturally without stiffness of neck or slanting or shaking. The movement of head and neck changes along with the variation of body position and direction to be coherent with the rotation of trunk. The face should be in a natural state. Tuck in the chin and breathe with the nose. Close the mouth naturally.

The eyes move along with the rotation of the body. Practitioners should gaze at the front hand (sometimes the rear hand) or gaze forward evenly. Practitioners must be natural as much as possible and concentrate mind to ensure the effect of practice.

### 1.2  Trunk

(1) Chest and back: The essentials of practicing Tai-chi Chuan requires "hollowing the chest and raising the back" or "containing the chest and moving with the shoulders". In other words, rather than protruding or exceedingly retracting the chest, practitioners should do everything naturally during the practice. "Containing the chest and raising the back" is correlated and the muscles of the back will stretch along with the extension of arms. Meanwhile, relax the muscle of the chest naturally to avoid tension. Therefore, the chest will be contained and the back will be

---

① *General Textbook for Department of Physical Education: Martial Arts*[M]. Beijing: People's Sports Publishing House. 1978.9.

raised, eliminating the tension between the ribs and regulating the breath naturally.

(2) Waist and spine: When practicing Tai-chi Chuan, the body should be upright and calm. To this end, the waist is very important. As a saying goes, "Waist and spine are the dominating part", "You should always pay attention to the waist" and "You should take the waist as the axis", we can see that waist is the key for body rotation and it plays an important role in changes in body movements and adjustment and stabilization of the center of gravity. During the practice, whether it is a forward or backward step or rotation, as long as there is a shift of center of gravity, the waist should relax consciously to facilitate *qi* to sink. When practitioners sink waist, they should make it upright and calm without leaning forward or backward to ensure the flexible transition. Sinking the waist will deliver the strength to legs and stabilize the lower limbs to make the movements flexible and complete.

(3) Buttocks: When practicing Tai-chi Chuan, the buttocks should be tucked in naturally. Keep the buttocks no protruding or twisting. Relax the waist and keep the spine centrally aligned to maintain the upright trunk.

### 1.3  Leg

During the practicing of Tai-chi Chuan, legs are playing a decisive role in the changes in footwork and stability of the whole body. Therefore, the leg movement should be accurate, flexible and stable. Special attention should also be paid to the shift of the center of gravity during the practice. The smoothness and coherence of the whole set of movement lies in the position of the feet, the flexion of legs, the shift of the center of cavity and the transition of substantiality and insubstantiality.

As for the leg movement, the general requirements are relaxing the hip, bending the knees and lifting up and putting down the feet gently. In this way, the movements of the lower limbs will be gentle, stable and flexible in moving forward and backward. When practitioners step forward, they should step on the heel first; when steping backward, they should step on the sole first and step on the whole foot gradually. When practitioners make a side walk, they should step on the tip of the foot of the moving leg first and make the sole and heel reach the ground gradually. When practitioners make a following step and skipping step, they should step on the tip or sole of the foot first.

Both stance and footwork require that the leg movement should feature distinguished substantiality and insubstantiality. Except the "commencement form" and "closing of Tai-chi", practitioners should avoid the legs bear weight at the same time (double). When the right leg bears most of the weight, the right leg is solid and the left leg is empty; when the left leg bears most of the weight, the left leg is solid and the right leg is empty. In order to maintain body balance, the empty foot acts as a fulcrum (such as the front foot of the empty stance and the rear foot of the bow stance). The action of kick and parting kick should be slow rather than fast (except for individual actions), and the body should be balanced and stable. Do not be nervous in leg kick (lotus kick leg) or single slap kick.

### 1.4   Buttocks

The general requirement is to lower the sholders and elbows, relaxing the two associated joints. When exercising, practitioners should pay attention to the relaxation and solidness of the shoulder joints, and consciously extend outward to ensure enough space for arm rotation.

When practicing Tai-chi Chuan, don't stretch or bend arms straightly. In fact, practitioners should rotate the wrists and forearms. The requirements for hand movement are as follows: when retracting palms, the palm should be slightly contained without collapsing or shaking; when pushing forward palms, practitioners should bend down the elbows, rotate them inward slowly, and relax the wrists slightly downward at the same time. The flexion, extension and rotation of the hands should be easy and flexible. When stretching palms, it should be natural and fingers should be stretched. When making a fist, it should be loose without exceeding tension.

The movements of hands and shoulders are complete and consistent. If the hand is excessively extended forward, it is easy to straighten the arm, failing to "lower the shoulders and elbows". If practitioners sink the shoulders excessively without stretching forward the hands, that will lead to the excessive flexion of arms. In short, during the movement, the arm should always maintain slightly curved. When practitioners push forward and retract palms, do not stop suddenly. Only in this way, can they make movements segmental and continuous, light but not floating, solid but not stiff, flexible and natural.

## 2. Practice Methods

When practicing Tai-chi Chuan, practitioners should maintain the correct basic postures of the head, trunk and limbs and the movements. Moreover, they should also pay special attention to the practice methods to reflect the unique style of Tai-chi Chuan and better improve the practice effect and skills.

### 2.1   Being concentrated and relaxed

The two basic methods to practice Tai-chi Chuan well is "being concerntrated" (psychological calmness) and "being relaxed". They play a decisive role in the application and mastery of other methods.

As for "being concentrated", it refers to eliminate all distractions when practicing Tai-chi. No matter the movement is simple or complex, the posture is high or low, always keep calm psychologically to concentrate on each tiny movement and the whole practice. From the preparation form, concentrate all the minds on the movement and lead the movement with mind to achieve "body movement driven by intention". For example, if practitioners push forward their hands, they must first have the imagination of pushing forward; Similarly, if they want to sink $qi$, they must have the imagination of sinking $qi$. If the intention continues, the movement will also keep on. As making a movement, if practitioners can eliminate distractions and concentrate on it, they can think carefully about the movement, and make the movement soft, continuous and rhythmic. This rhythmic movement is conducive to regulating the functional state of cerebral

cortex and central nervous system and enhancing the function of other organs. Meanwhile, it can inhibit other parts of the brain from being active, eliminate the fatigue caused by thinking and other local single function, and avoid excessive excitement and unnecessary tension to adjust the balance of the brain. In addition, if practitioners can use their mind rather the force and guide the movement with the mind, they can adjust the breath, and coordinate mind, movement and breath, achieving comprehensive exercise from head to bottom, and inside to outside.

As for "being relaxed", it requires that the muscles, joints, ligaments and internal organs of the whole body should be in a natural and relaxed state without any restraint or oppression during practicing Tai-chi. In Tai-chi Chuan,, the "relaxing" refers to "relaxation" rather than weakness or fatigue. It aims to relax the muscles and joints as much as possible under the natural activity or stability of the body. In practice, keep the spine upright naturally, making the head, trunk, limbs and other parts move in a relaxed way. Specifically, practitioners should avoid making unnecessary strength or tension. The parts exerting force should also maintain a natural state, make the correct posture according to the requirements for the movement and advance and retreat steadily. For example, when maintaining balance, the legs should support the center of gravity to make the transition of forward and backward moving light and flexible; the round arms should be in a full round state, and the bent legs should bend to the required degree. The muscles should not be stiff, and the clumsy force (i. e. stiff force) is prohibited.

"Relaxation" is the basis and guarantee for correct posture, body coordination, movement and smooth transition. Some people are stiff when they practice Tai-chi. Although their hands and feet are in a correct position and their heads and necks are upright, they look uncomfortable and unnatural. The cause of their stiffness lies in that they don't get the essentials of "relaxation". When some people practice Tai-chi, they cannot extend their hands and feet to an enough extent. For example, when lifting a hand, keep the forearm (right arm) bent slightly in a natural way flexion, lead the wrist forward, bend down the elbow, relax the shoulder downward and make the arm have calm strength in a relaxed state. However, excessive bending will result in a right angle between the upper arm and forearm, causing the rising of shoulders and the tension of elbow joint and biceps brachii. Every movement in Tai-chi Chuan should be made naturally and muscles should alternate tension with relaxation. As mastering the essentials, if practitioners practice Tai-chi for half an hour at an appropriate speed, they will not feel any sour or hurt. In fact, they will feel relaxed and comfortable, as "*qi* does not flow out and they can remain calm". If practitioners fail to follow this principle, it is inevitably that they will feel fatigue when practicing Tai-chi. The practice will not last for a long time as heart beats faster and people feels out of breath.

Some people regard "relaxation" as softness and weakness. As they push the hand forward, they don't relax their wrist the hand, raise their fingertips or support their palms forward (that is, stretch the fingers and relax the palm), making the wrist too soft and weak. Some of them also shake or float their hand up and down, which is not correct.

## 2.2　Coherence and flexibility

Coherence refers to the connection between each style or movement, showing no significant pause or interruption at the connection (except for those who virtually use mind to express the substantiality and insubstantiality). All movements should be continuous and completed at one go. This feature is mainly to connect the harmonious movements of various postures which are segmental and continuous, forming a natural rhythm to improve the effect of movements. As a saying goes, "the movements of Tai-chi Chuan is like the restless water of Yangtze River and the sea". In addition, this rhythmic continuous movement is extremely meticulous. The completion of the previous movement is just the beginning of the next transition movement. It seems that all the set patterns and transition movements are the beads which are threaded together to form a complete set. For example, for the movement of "grasping bird's tail", at first, the four movements (warding off, pulling down, pressing and pushing) can be practiced independently. After becoming proficient, practitioners should connect these four movements together. They still need to maintain a certain sense of rhythm in the transition of movements. In other words, as finishing one movement, practitioners should sink slightly as they are not making a pause to start the following movement. Practitioners should focus during the whole process without any interruptions. For the postures and movements of 24 Stances of Simplified Tai-chi Chuan and the 48 stances of the second set of Tai-chi Chuan, the practicing should feature the rhythm.

Flexibility refers to that the practice should be flexible and natural in a coherent way. The changes in such palm forms as extending, holding, waving hands like cloud, blocking palm, pushing, raising, brushing, pushing forward, threading, and thrusting should be flexible and coherent. The arms should always bend naturally and their movement will change repeatedly according to different curves. The lower limbs should always bend naturally with stable center of gravity and extend in a way that it seems they are not extended to create a sense of straightness in the curved legs. With understanding and mastering of this rule, practitioners can consciously avoid the rigid movements and dead turns to make the movements flexible and smooth. In terms of movement essentials, the upper and lower limbs movement should be driven by waist and spine. In addition, they should turn the wrists and rotate the arms (do not wrap it intentionally), relax the shoulders and bend down elbows, and bend the knees and relax the crotch. Although it is emphasized to walk in an arc and curve, it is necessary to rotate freely to make the movement flexible, light and smooth.

## 2.3   Slow yet smooth and continuous movement

Most of the movements in Tai-chi Chuan are quite slow. Therefore, the movement features softness and slowness.

The requirement of "mobilizing the *Jin* (strength) like drawing/pulling silk" indicates that the strength should be as continuous as drawing the silk. The strength should be free from stiffness or rigidness in a moderate speed to make the movement slow yet smooth and continuous (except the movement exerting strength). However, the movement should not be too slow or the vigour will be sluggish. It is necessary to have a consistent vigour and breathe naturally to keep the movement going on. Normally, a set of "Simplified Tai-chi Chuan"will be finished in 4 to 6 minutes.

When practicing Tai-chi, keep a certain degree of uniformity (constant speed movement) in a continuous process. In order to ensure a constant speed, you should transit the center of gravity in an appropriate way. If practitioners fail to keep the balance and stability of the body, it's difficult to move at a constant movement. In terms of motion uniformity, the whole routine can be compared to a dotted line structure (...), which is connected by many dots. We can regard these points as the movements in the routine and the uniform gap as speed of movement transition. In this way, the movement can be invisibly distributed according to the law shown by the dotted line. Gradually practitioners can ensure the constant speed as they practice Tai-chi in a slow and gentle manner.

## 2.4　The upper and lower body following each other

According to some people, when practicing Tai-chi Chuan, we should "move the whole body together". According to other people, when practicing Tai-chi Chuan, we should ensure that "from the feet, to the legs, then to the waist, there always must be complete integration into one *qi*". These are the requirements of "upper and lower parts of the body moving as an integrated whole in a coordinated way".

For the beginners of Tai-chi Chuan, although they know the theory that many movements should take the waist as the axis and the limbs movements should be driven by the trunk, it is difficult for them to achieve overall coordination as they cannot coordinate the mind and limbs movements. Therefore, it is recommended to practice single exercise (such as "commencement form" and "waving hands like clouds") first to obtain the coordination of trunk and limb movements. At the same time, it is recommended to practice footwork (such as empty stance, bow stance, shift of center of gravity, footwork change, etc.) to exercise the support strength of lower limbs and master the essentials of footwork. Then, through the consistent practice of all movements, the forward and backward conversion of footwork, the rotation of trunk and the change of hand movements can coordinate with each other, gradually achieving the coordination and integrity of the whole body movements and exercising all parts of the body in a balanced way.

Generally speaking, the coordination between the limbs and the trunk and the close relationship between current movement and the next movement are called external coordination; the coordination between mind, breath and movement is called internal coordination. To achieve external coordination, under the condition of limbs cooperation, we should ensure that "upper and lower parts of the body move as an integrated whole". Instead of moving legs after moving hands, practitioners should make the trunk and limbs move coordinately. Therefore, taking the waist as the axis, they should make limbs movement driven by the trunk. At the same time, the movement should coordinate with the changes of hand and footwork and eyes. With the change of direction and position, all parts of the whole body move continuously until the end of the routine.

## 2.5　Distinguishing substantiality and insubstantiality

Movement itself is a contradiction. In Tai-chi Chuan, the transformation of contradiction is often concluded as the change of distinguished substantiality and insubstantiality. From the perspective of overall movement, except for individual cases, the fixed end form of the movement is "substantiality", and the change process of the movement is "insubstantiality". From the perspective of individual part of the movement, the main supporting leg is substantial, and the leg that assist in supporting or moving is insubstantial; the arm that reflects the main content of the movement is substantial, and the auxiliary and cooperative arm is insubstantial. As we distinguish the substantial and insubstantial movements, we can make a difference between different situations and exert balanced strength. For substantial movements and body parts, the strength should be calm and substantial; for insubstantial movements and body parts, the strength should be light and reserved. For example, when the movement reaches the fixed form or tends to be completed, sink and stabilize the waist, spine and joints. When the movement changes, relax and flex the joints of the whole body. When the movement of upper limbs changes from insubstantial state to substantial state, stabilize the forearms, gradually extend the fingers, relax the palms and the wrists (also known as settling wrists), and make a tight fist. When the movement of upper limbs changes from substantial state to insubstantial state, the forearm should be light and flexible, the palm should be slightly contained, and the fist should be loose. According to the changes of substantiality and insubstantiality, the practice can be light and calm and the practitioners can distinguish the primary and non-primary movements, avoiding average strength and redundant and dull movements.

After we understand the opposition between insubstantiality and substantiality, rigidness and softness, we should also understand their unification. All movements of Tai-chi are the movement transformation process in which the contradictions coexist in a unity (in most cases, the two hands and legs are in the substantial and insubstantial state alternately). When the movement reaches the end point, all joints and muscles maintain a little room for expansion and transition. As a saying goes, "there is substantiality in the insubstantiality and vice versa". The force should not be rigid. We should distinguish the primary and secondary state of the movement to ensure there is substantiality in the insubstantiality and there is insubstantiality in the substantiality, avoiding rigidity and softening. Every movement and moment of Tai-chi is carried out in mutual restraint and confrontation under several opposite and complementary forces. For example, for the movement of pushing forward with arms, push forward the palm, sink the elbows, contain the shoulders, and relax the upper body as much as possible to ensure solid strength without stiffness. For the movement of retracting the arms, relax and retract the shoulders, turn the elbows outward (inward), relax the writs slightly, rotate the forearm rotate naturally and roundly and do not suddenly stop the strength, and do not deliberately wind and swing the arms, achieving light and flexible movement without flotation or loosening.

The substantiality and insubstantiality of the movement is closely related to the shift of the center of gravity. As one posture is connected with another, the change of position and direction involves the transformation of footwork and the shift of the center of gravity. In exercise, we should also pay attention to the use of body postures and hand movements. In terms of the transition between substantiality and insubstantiality, we should distinguish one from the other to make coherent movement at one go. If there is no clear change between insubstantiality and substantiality, the changes of forward and backward movements will be ineffective, resulting in movement retardation, unstable center of gravity and deflection. In the past, some people said that "people should step forward like a cat and mobilize the *Jin* (strength) like drawing/pulling silk". Therefore, when practicing Tai-chi Chuan, we should ensure light footwork and constant movement.

Regardless of the complexity of the movement, the top rule is to be comfortable when practising Tai-chi Chuan and this is the basic requirement of "upright and comfortable body". As for the rotation, stabilize the body first, then lift the legs and change steps. As for the forward and backward movement, stand on the foot first, and then slowly shift the center of gravity. At the same time, sinking the shoulder, relaxing the waist and the crotch and the mastery of substantiality and insubstantiality in hand movements will also help stabilize the center of gravity. In this way, regardless of the speed of the movement, practitioners will have stable and appropriate center of gravity to avoid instability.

### 2.6　Combination of mind, movement and breath

In Tai-chi Chuan, body coordination and movement coherence are only parts of "coordination and integrity", and the close combination of mind, movement and breath is the key to achieve unity, harmony and integrity of the whole body.

By the combination of mind, movement and breath, it refers to the combination of movement and breath under the guidance of mind. The mind and breath process should meet the requirements of movement, and promote the perfection of the movement. In Tai-chi Chuan, as mind plays a leading role, it requires "mobilizing *qi* with mind and body". In other words, the mind guides the movement and the movement should coordinate with the breath.

As for the movement guided by the mind, it requires the combination of imagination and movement and make the movement driven by the imagination guide. The guidance is not the same for all movement and the mind should lead the main parts in the transformation of solidness and emptiness. For example, for the movement "waving hands like clouds", although the eyes gaze at the right hand which constantly rotates with the waist, the eyes also notice the swing of the left hand and the shift of the center of gravity with its focus on the right hand; when the left hand rotates upward, its attention will turn to the left hand. In this continuous movement, the mind leads and regulates the movements.

As for the movement led by the mind in Tai-chi Chuan practice, the following aspects should be specially focused.

First of all, concentration doesn't mean emotional tension and rigid movement. As a matter of fact, the mind should be consistent with the substantial and insubstantial strength and relaxation to form rhythmic and changing movements. The movement consists of mind activity and strength application, which should be "solid but not stiff, light but not floating".

Second, when practicing Tai-chi, practitioners should be in full spirit and concentrated (including the use of eyes), which is an important embodiment of mind activities. During the practice, it is not allowed to be strained or tired. Instead, the practitioners should be energetic, natural, and full of vitality internally and display calmness and peace.

Third, the mind, strength and movement are united. And they are in a subordinative relationship.

The mind guides strength, and strength produces movement. Therefore, in Tai-chi Chuan, "the mind leads the body movement". The strength connects as practitioners change the postures, and the mind connects as they change the strength. However, this subordinative relationship doesn't involve disconnection and separation. The change of mind should be reflected in strength and movement. As practicing Tai-chi Chuan, it is not right to only pursue "insubstantiality and stillness" and "the movement with the intention of circle rather than the shape of circle". In this way, it is impracticable to guide the movement with the mind, making people confused and puzzled.

How can practitioners coordinate the movement with the breath?

In terms of the combination of movement and breath, in Tai-chi Chuan, it requires deep, long, fine and uniform breath which is smooth and natural. At the very beginning, it only requires natural breath. After practitioners get familiar with the movement, they can consciously guide the breath according to the experience and needs of personal exercise naturally, so as to make it better adapt to the requirements of strength and movement. This breathing is called "breathing following movement". For example, when the movement of Tai-chi is coming to close, in most cases, it requires calm and full strength to stabilize the movement. Meanwhile, practitioners should sink the shoulders, contain the chest, sink *qi* to the abdomen and consciously exhale to promote the movement of abdominal and diaphragm muscles. The movement transformation in Tai-chi is complex. Generally speaking, while using slight strength, extending shoulder blades and relaxing chest, practitioners should consciously inhale; and while using solid and steady strength, and containing the shoulder blades and the chest, practitioners should exhale. Inhale when getting up and exhale when squatting down; inhale when raising hands and exhale when arm falls. The breathing following movement is to turn this spontaneous cooperation into a conscious guiding process. Practitioners can also appropriately use the reverse abdominal breathing method to increase the activity range of abdominal muscles and diaphragm, deepen and lengthen the breathing, and make the movement more calm and flexible.

## Section 3   Breathing Method of Tai-chi Chuan[①]

## 1. Natural Breathing

Natural breathing means that people breathe according to the original breathing rate and breathing method, but it is softer. It is required to be natural, soft and uniform, without any force or intentional control. It can be achieved by nasal inhalation and nasal exhalation, as well as nasal exhalation and mouth exhalation.

## 2. Abdominal Breathing

### 1. Following abdominal breathing

Relax the abdominal muscles when inhale and the diaphragm descends and the abdomen

---

① Wang Changfang et al. *Traditional Health-preserving Sports Course* [M]. Beijing: Beijing Sport University Press. 2014.04.

bulges. The abdomen slightly retract when exhale.

### 2. Reverse abdominal breathing

Contract the abdominal muscles when inhale and the diaphragm descends and the abdomen contains; relax the abdominal muscles when exhale to uplift the abdomen.

Abdominal breathing is completed through the movement of diaphragm, which enhances the movement of diaphragm, increases the volume of thoracic cavity and increases the amount of respiration. It can ensure complete respiration, decrease the functional residual capacity, and improve the ventilation function of the lower part of both lungs. Therefore, it has a good curative effect on respiratory diseases. As it enhances the contraction and relaxation of abdominal muscles, it directly massages the abdominal viscera and helps to improve the function of digestive system.

## 3. Breathing Following Movement

This method requires the full coordination of breath and movement and can be used when the practitioner is skilled. During the practice, special attention should be paid to the adjustment of the depth and frequency of breathing. When practicing Tai-chi, when it comes to opening, raising, lifting, bending and the like, it is necessary to consciously inhale deeply, and uplift the spirit lightly For example, in the movements of "White Crane Spreads Wings" and "Apparent Close Up" where hands lift up and retract, inhaling deeply is needed. On the contrary, when it comes to closing, falling, lowering, stretching and the like, it is necessary to consciously and evenly exhale deeply, and sink the related parts accordingly. For example, in the squatting and pressing forward in the movements of "needle at sea bottom" and "grasp bird's tail", exhaling deeply is needed. In short, generally, for the movement shifting from the solid state to the empty state, inhale and make the movement light and natural; for the movement shifting from the empty state to the solid state, exhale and ensure the make the movement calm and stable.

In some movements, the opening and closing are not obvious, or the arms are one up and one down, or one front and one back with both flexion and extension, it is necessary to distinguish the primary and non-primary movement. The main movement should prevail with the coordination of the breathing and the movement of legs and shift of the center of gravity. For example, for the movements of "needle at sea bottom" after the movement of "fan through the back", raise the right hand, move the body and hands upward and inhale. When the left foot steps forward and the left hand pushes forward, although the right arm continues to lift, the focus should be shifted to the pushing forward with the left hand and the bow stance with the left foot and the movement can be closed in coordinated with deep exhalation. It is not absolute to use the "breathing following the movement". As the structure of Tai-chi routine and the arrangement of movements take in account of the connection and coherence of each movement and the comprehensive exercise, therefore breathing is not the only factor influencing the routine arrangement. Different routines in Tai-chi differ in the number and depth of breathing. Even for the same routine, people with different physiques may differ in speed and breath in the practice. Therefore, the "breathing following movement" is only suitable for active movement and the movement with obvious opening and closing of chest and shoulders. As for some transitional movements, and when individuals find it difficult to coordinate breathing, natural breathing is still recommended, or auxiliary breathing (short breathing) can be used for transitional adjustment. Therefore, regardless the skills of Tai-chi, the combination of "breathing following movement" and "natural breathing" will ensure the smooth and proper combination of breathing and movement to meet one of the principles of Tai-chi, "when cultivated in a straightforward manner, there will be no harm". Do not simply list the "breathing procedure table", or the breathing is rigid and unnatural. In particular, patients or people with weak physique should practice Tai-chi Chuan according to personal conditions and maintain the natural and smooth breathing. They can't use strength to make *qi* in a stiff and reluctant manner. Otherwise, they are contrary to the natural law of breathing, which is harmful to their health.

# 第三章 现代科学健身中的太极拳

太极拳是中华民族的武术瑰宝，不仅蕴藏着深厚的文化内涵和哲理思想，而且兼具健身、防身和养生功能，其"天人合一的哲学思想、性命双修的保健原则、平和柔顺的人文内涵、默识揣摩的心行方式、道德健康的人品要求"[1]，以及"阴阳相济、动静相随、刚柔相间"[2]等技术特色，在调节人的中枢神经系统功能、促进心血管功能、调节呼吸吐纳等养生健身方面具有重要作用。本章从太极拳对中枢神经系统的作用、太极拳对心血管系统的作用、太极拳对呼吸系统的作用、太极拳对消化系统的作用、太极拳对免疫功能的作用、太极拳对心理健康的作用等六个方面加以说明。

## 第一节 太极拳对中枢神经系统的作用

### 一、认识中枢神经系统及其功能

无论从中医还是西医的角度来看，作为中枢神经系统的重要组成部分——脑，都占据极其重要的地位。"以心行气，务令沉着，乃能收敛入骨"。中医认为，脑为元神之府，头为诸阳之首，人体生命是大脑皮层调节功效的结果，意识的形成必不可少人脑这一思维逻辑的内脏。

在现代医学发源地的西方，发达国家也启动全民健脑工程。美国国会通过公共法提出"脑的十年"，日本宣布"强脑科学计划"。正是因为中枢神经系统作为各种反射弧的中枢部分，是学习、记忆的神经基础，使人类能产生各种思维活动。

中枢神经系统是调节某一特定生理功能的神经元群，如呼吸中枢、体温调节中枢、语言中枢等。例如，动物遇到伤害性的东西，会逃避躲开，这是一种反射动作。这个反射动作就经过中枢的加工才引起肌肉的活动。中枢神经系让人产生"感受"。有些感觉信息传入中枢后，经过学习的过程，还可在中枢神经系统内留下痕迹，成为新的记忆。

---

① 王朝琼，何克. 试论太极拳对青少年心理健康的增进作用 [J]. 贵州社会科学，2008/07:130.
② 李慎明. 世界太极拳发展报告（2019）. 北京：社会科学文献出版社，2020.5：426.

## 二、习练太极拳对中枢神经系统的作用

在高强度工作之下，许多现代人处于亚健康状态，随着年龄增长，人们会出现过疲劳、头昏脑涨、记忆减退、注意力分散、反应迟钝的情况，说话不再口出连珠，而是要停下来想一想，而这一瞬间的迟钝则表明中枢神经系统收到抑制。而练习太极拳时，练习者盘拳在松、柔、圆、缓、匀的运行中，似行云流水，有氧运动锻炼周身各个器官，特别是人脑得到氧的充分供应后，对健脑益智有促进作用。

太极拳运动柔和舒缓，讲究心静和意念主导，可以有效调节大脑皮层的兴奋和抑制过程的转换过程。当大脑皮层的运动中枢处于兴奋状态时，其他区域则处于抑制状态，缓解了大脑皮层的局部压力。同时，进行一定强度的太极拳运动，能够有效促进全身的血液循环，加强大脑皮层的新陈代谢，进而提高中枢神经系统的机能。另外，太极拳讲求神气贯串、绝不间断的意气之连。正所谓外形虽微停，而内中之意不可止；节节相贯，一气串成，最为重要的是，太极拳由单纯的运动感受器传递神经冲动，刺激运动中枢兴奋，变为了对大脑及其神经系统的主动与被动刺激相结合的双重积极性诱导，从而更加有效地提高了神经系统的机能。因此，对于大学生来说，在紧张的学习和生活之余，可以通过练习太极拳来缓解疲劳，改善中枢神经系统功能，提高其敏锐度，进而放松大脑，提高学习效率。

太极拳对神经系统，尤其是它的高级部分，有重要的调节与支配作用。人类依靠神经系统的活动，以适应于外界环境并改造外界环境。人依靠神经系统的活动，使身体内各个系统与器官的机能活动按照需要统一起来。太极拳的练习，对中枢神经系统起着良好的影响，因为太极拳一开始，就要求体舒心静，排除杂念，注意力集中，用意不用力，这些都是对大脑活动的良好训练。此外，从动作上来讲，太极拳练习时要如行云流水，连绵不断，如长江大河滔滔不绝，"其根在脚，发于腿，主宰于腰，行于手指，由脚而腿，而腰总须完整一气"。由眼而手部、腰部、足部，上下照顾毫不散乱，前后连贯，同时动作的某些部分比较复杂，必须有良好的平衡能力，因此需要大脑在紧张的活动下完成，也间接地对中枢神经系统起训练作用。这样就提高了中枢神经系统的紧张度，从而活跃了其他系统与器官的机能活动，加强了大脑方面的调节作用。

## 第二节　太极拳对心血管系统的作用

### 一、认识心血管系统及其功能

无论从中医还是西医的角度来看，心脏和血管都是人体健康的中心枢纽。中西医均认为心血管系统与神经系统、内分泌系统、免疫系统间互相影响，这也解释了为什么我们平日常用"担心""心碎"等词语来形容自己的状态。如果我们跳出医学视角，甚至可以把爱情、勇气、智慧、诚信甚至记忆的品质和心脏相关联起来，从中医的角度来说，从心而传导出来的"气"同时控制着人的身体、心理和整个精神世界。

这是因为心脏和血液构成血液运输的网络——心血管系统，血液通过该系统泵入身体的

大血管系统，血液将养分和氧气运送至细胞，并带走细胞代谢产生的废物。在压力的作用下，血液离开心脏，并通过动脉的分支系统运输到全身。接着，最后一级动脉——微动脉将含氧丰富的血液运送至毛细血管。氧气、养分、代谢产生的废物及细胞外液中的其他物质在由毛细血管构成的毛细血管床中进行交换；血液再经毛细血管床进入类似毛细血管的薄壁微静脉；微静脉的血汇入小静脉，小静脉再汇入较大的静脉，最后由大静脉——腔静脉把含氧较低的血液又运回心脏。

## 二、练习太极拳对心血管系统的作用

哈佛医学院一项调查显示，在练习太极拳后，一位 80 多岁心脏病患者病情得到改善。他在采访中说道："太极拳的动作就如微风般轻柔，让我很放松。经过一段时间的练习，我站得更直、睡得也更好了。我发现我自己做家务时能'自由切换'，十分自如。"

医学研究表明，练习太极拳对于提高心血管系统功能有重要作用。太极拳锻炼中一般采用腹式呼吸，通过螺旋和圆弧动作，挤压揉搓了身体各部脏器，达到按摩的功效，从而加速全身的血液循环，有助于扩张毛细血管，增强血管弹性。同时，因为周身松弛放松，静脉血管外周压力下降，使静脉血管的血容量增加，随血液输送的氧气和营养物质等也随之增加，这不仅减轻了心脏压力，并且促进了身体内部的物质交换，提高机体新陈代谢，经常参加太极拳运动可以有效提高心血管系统功能。

太极拳的动作包括了各组肌肉、关节的活动，也包括了有节律的、均匀的呼吸运动，特别是腹式呼吸的横膈肌运动。全身各部骨骼肌肉的周期性的收缩与舒张，可以加强静脉的血液循环，肌肉的活动保证了静脉血液回流，以及向右心室充盈必要的静脉压力。在腹式呼吸中，随横膈肌的一升一降，也使胸腹腔的压力一张一弛，腹部压力随之有规律地升降，这种运动极有利于推动胸腹腔内的动脉和静脉的血液输送和回流，尤其使静脉网流。因为静脉压比动脉压要低得多，腰以下的静脉血回流又受着地心引力的影响，所以静脉血回流不仅要靠血管内压力的推动、静脉瓣的调节，而且也依靠血管外的肌肉的一张一弛和腹部压力的一升一降来促进其回流。腹式呼吸所形成的腹压升降，有利于血液的循环，这样就使躯体和内脏获得更充足的血液营养。练习太极拳时，深长均匀的自然呼吸，并且要气沉丹田，更好地加速了血液与淋巴的循环，加强了心肌的营养，为预防心脏各种疾病及动脉硬化建立了良好的条件。太极拳的动作柔和、协调，也促使全身血管弹性增加、血管神经的稳定性增强。

经常练习太极拳，可以有效地强化人心脏功能，加强微循环功能，有利于毛细血管内外的物质交换，促进组织对氧的利用率，减少肌酸的蓄积，减缓疲劳，益于疾病的恢复，特别是对慢性冠心病、高脂血症、动脉硬化症都有较好的防治作用。心脏作为人体血液运行的动力器官，能够对周身各组织器官的血液起到营养作用，而毛细血管是微循环物质交换的场所。经常习练太极拳，也可以使心神得到静养，并且延缓心脏舒张期，使心肌得以充分休整，收缩力加强，输出增加，提高了心脏的工作能力。太极拳动作圆活自然，可以让全身肌肉有节奏地收缩弛张，使血液流畅，静脉回流增加，从而加速了血液循环，减轻了心脏负担，对心脏起到了保健作用。

## 第三节　太极拳对呼吸系统的作用

### 一、认识呼吸系统及其功能

人在生命中，是离不开呼吸的。一个正常的成年人，每天约呼吸 2 万次，呼吸近 20 公斤空气。如果短暂离开食物和水，生命尚可持续，但一旦失去呼吸，生命将无法延续。太极拳讲究心神合一，对呼吸的要求也很高，只有正确的呼吸才能保证效果。所以正确的呼吸方法也是学习太极拳过程当中的重要一环。如何掌握太极拳中的呼吸方法呢？首先要了解呼吸系统及其功能。

"嘘吸庐外，出入丹田"，太极拳将导引和吐纳结合起来，使练习太极拳时的呼吸轻柔而舒缓。太极拳的呼吸是静与松的结合，两者应是一致的。在练习过程中，习练者将缓慢入静，头脑无杂念，全身放松，达到动静交流和内外统一的自然呼吸。这是中国源远流长的呼吸方法所倡导的一种开合虚实、呼吸自然的方法。在西医临床上常说的呼吸系统，指人体与外界空气进行气体交换的一系列器官的总称，包括鼻、咽、喉、气管、支气管及由大量的肺泡、血管、淋巴管、神经构成的肺，以及胸膜等组织。在呼吸系统中，各器官都有一定的分工，从鼻到各级支气管都是负责传送气体的器官，其中鼻腔有加温、湿润和清洁空气等作用，还能在发音时产生共鸣。

### 二、练习太极拳对人体呼吸系统的作用

近年来，诸多实验研究结果证明，太极拳练习中所采取的呼吸形式特征，以及呼吸与动作的协调配合，对提高人体的心肺机能改善、缓解精神压力等方面均有良好的促进作用。同时，太极拳的腹式呼吸，可以使肺活量得以大大提升，呼吸功能得到改善。

太极拳注重意念的练习，以养气为主，与调息有关，要用动作去引导呼吸，使呼吸也成为一个运动，方能在完整的运动中得到更高的功效。太极拳要求"气沉丹田""以气导力"，采用深长的腹式呼吸，使胸部宽静、肺部充实，提高呼吸机能的持久性，改善肺部的通气功能。具体的作用表现在对肺通气的影响，以及对肺换气的影响。

太极拳对肺通气有积极影响。专家研究发现，长期系统的太极拳训练可使心肺功能发生适应性变化，表现为肺活量增大，这与深细长匀的腹式呼吸，以及动作与呼吸的自然配合所产生的影响分不开。腹式呼吸可使横膈膜上下移动的范围扩大，使胸腔容积增大。胸内负压增加，肺泡壁弹性纤维网被动拉长，其收缩力增大，从而改善肺组织的弹性、提高肺的全部潜在通气能力。临床试验发现，太极拳运动组最大通气量、肺活量在安静运动时都比对照组大，这反映出运动组具有良好的肺通气功能。

太极拳的呼吸方法可养生调息、缓解压力。中国古人常说，调息，小用可以养生，大之可以入道。中国古人有修炼调息，以改善睡眠，强化人体阳气的循环内守。通过一呼一吸，感觉身体内部废气排出，深吸洁净空气，修炼纯净状态。人们在练拳过程中，精神放松、思想集中并调整呼吸，每次练拳下来可以心情舒畅、精神饱满，身体微微出汗，增加体内的新

陈代谢。练习太极拳不仅能灵活四肢，还能舒缓大脑，有利于人们的心态平衡，从而缓解精神压力。

## 第四节　太极拳对消化系统的作用

### 一、认识消化系统及其功能

人体的消化系统由消化道、消化腺两部分组成。其中，消化道是一条很长的肌性管道，包括口腔、咽、食管、胃、小肠、大肠等。消化腺又可分为小消化腺、大消化腺两种。小消化腺散布于各消化管内壁，大消化腺有腮腺、舌下腺、下颌下腺、肝脏、胰脏等。

消化系统的基本功能包括三个，即消化食物、吸收营养、排出残渣。消化食物是指在消化道内将食物分解成结构简单、可以吸收的小分子物质的过程，包括物理消化过程和化学消化过程。物理消化是指消化道对食物进行咀嚼、吞咽、蠕动等机械作用，以磨碎食物、与消化液混合、推动食团下移等过程。化学消化是指食物被消化腺分泌的消化液进行化学分解，以便小肠吸收营养。吸收营养是指上述分解的小分子物质通过消化道黏膜上皮细胞的作用，进入人体的血液和淋巴液的过程。食物中的营养物质，如维生素、无机盐、水可以被直接吸收，蛋白质、脂肪、糖类等物质不能被直接吸收，需分解为结构简单的小分子物质才能被吸收。最后，未被吸收的残渣则通过大肠以粪便形式排出。

### 二、练习太极拳对人体消化功能的作用

太极拳运动的特点是柔和的、缓慢的、舒展的，对提高人体的消化功能具有特殊作用。实践证明，长期练习太极拳可以很好地提高人体的消化功能，主要表现在增强消化腺分泌消化液的功能、保持消化道畅通两个方面。可见太极拳运动有利于提高人体的食物消化、营养吸收和排便功能。

练习太极拳，通过"改善消化系统的血液循环"，达到"有利于营养物质的消化和吸收"的目的。因为练习太极拳可以提高神经系统活动能力，可以预防某些因神经系统机能紊乱导致的消化系统疾病。而且，经常练习太极拳能"改善消化系统的机能，由于肌肉活动的加强，对物质的消化和吸收非常有利……对胃肠发生按摩作用……能够使胃肠肥厚、弹性增加、蠕动加快，从而改善消化系统的血液循环，这对防止和推迟消化系统的老化十分有益"[1]。

练习太极拳时往往要求舌尖轻抵上颚，上下齿轻合，旨在刺激唾液分泌，发挥唾液湿润、抗菌、辅助消化的作用。同时，大幅扭转腰身，让腹腔中各消化器官受到刺激，在呼吸膈肌运动的配合下，增加肝脏的血液循环，增强肝脏消化功能，促进胃肠蠕动，加快消化吸收。因为"腑以通为顺"，"故胃肠通畅，食欲好、大便通，则消化功能良好"。田桂华的实验也证实了这个事实，实验中通过对 28 例消化不良患者安排 4 周 42 式太极拳训练，他发现，28 名患者的消化不良症状均明显好转，有效率为 100%。尽管该实验样本量偏小，但实验效果

---

① 贾震. 关于太极拳的运动特点及生理功效的分析与研究［J］. 吉林省教育学院学报，2012/04:52-53.

还是比较明显的。

陈广德认为，练习"气功"（指传统气功站桩太极五行拳，笔者注，下同）对消化系统疾病治疗有效，"中国科学院等单位用气功治疗 1 385 例胃及十二指肠溃疡病，治愈率为74.7%，好转率为 20.1%，总有效率高达 98.3%"。他还认为，练习太极拳对"加强肠胃、肠等消化系统功能，起到较好作用"，"对人体内物质代谢和消化系统起着良好作用"，"老年人进行体育锻炼大概 30 分钟后，血内胆固醇含量明显下降。有动脉硬化老人进行 6 个月体育锻炼后，化验证明他们血中蛋白含量增加，球蛋白和胆固醇含量明显减少，他们的动脉硬化程度也大大减轻"[1]。陈炎林也认为，练习太极拳能"促进消化功能，使肠胃吸收营养更加有效"，并且可使人身体"从虚胖变成结实"[2]。

## 第五节　太极拳对免疫功能的作用

### 一、认识免疫系统及其功能

人体的免疫系统由免疫器官、免疫细胞、免疫分子三部分组成。免疫器官包括骨髓、胸腺、脾脏、淋巴结、扁桃体等。免疫细胞包括淋巴细胞、吞噬细胞、嗜碱粒细胞、嗜酸粒细胞、中性粒细胞、肥大细胞等。免疫分子包括抗体、补体、溶菌酶、干扰素、免疫球蛋白等。人体的免疫系统能识别、排除抗原性异物，并与其他系统协调，维持机体内环境稳定和生理平衡[3]。

人体的免疫系统是防止病原体入侵人体的最有效的武器，通过发现并清除外来异物、外来微生物入侵，防止引起人体内环境不良变化而导致人体致病。具体来说，人体的免疫系统具有免疫防御、免疫监视、免疫调控的作用。免疫防御是指免疫系统防止外界病原体入侵，同时识别和清除已入侵病原体及其他有害物质的功能，从而使人体免于细菌、病毒、污染物、疾病的攻击。免疫监视是指免疫系统随时发现和清除人体内出现的"非己"成分的功能，如衰老细胞、肿瘤细胞、死亡细胞或其他有害成分，又如人体新陈代谢所产生的废物以及免疫细胞攻击病毒所留下的废物。免疫调控是指人体通过调节自身免疫耐受力，维持人体免疫系统内环境稳定的功能，如通过修补免疫细胞，进而修复受损器官，使其恢复功能[4]。

人体中的免疫系统是无可取代的。健康的免疫系统应该处于一种平衡状态。此时，它就像一支军队，能分清敌友，一致对外，攻无不克，护佑我们机体的"和平"。如果人体的免疫系统不健全，功能低下，就像"侦查员"玩忽职守，造成病原体有机可乘；"战士"战斗力不强，造成病原体大量入侵，我们就会生病。但人体的免疫系统并不是越强越好。如果人体的免疫系统过强，功能亢进，就像"侦查员"分不清敌友，误将友军当敌军；"战士"战斗力超强，摧枯拉朽一顿猛攻。此时我们会误伤自身器官或组织，导致人体处于高度敏感状

① 陈广德，传统气功站桩太极五行拳 [M]．北京：中国人民公安大学出版社，1995：7．

② Yearning K. Chen, *Tai-chi Chuan: Its Effects and Practical Application* [M]. Shanghai: Millington Limited, 1947:10.

③ 陈淑增，等．病原生物学与免疫学（第 2 版）[M]．武汉：华中科技大学出版社，2015.08：9．

④ 金伯泉．医学免疫学 [M]．北京：人民卫生出版社，2008.6：12-74．

态，出现过敏症状。为了使人体的免疫系统处于平衡状态，就要注意几点影响因素，如健康均衡的饮食、生活规律、睡眠充足、适度运动锻炼、良好的卫生习惯、乐观积极的心态等。

## 二、练习太极拳对人体免疫功能的作用

国外研究发现，练习太极拳 15 分钟后，人体免疫细胞数量明显提高。国内实验发现，练习太极拳一次，唾液中的分泌型免疫球蛋白液含量可增加 16mg/100。加州大学洛杉矶分校的麦可欧文通过对 112 人进行分组对比研究，发现练习太极拳 6 个月的一组（打拳组）对抗病毒的免疫能力，要比接受健康教育的一组（上课组）高出将近一倍。

郑传锋通过对陕西师范大学 18 名退休女教师为期 6 个月的太极拳锻炼进行检测与记录。研究发现，其白细胞计数及 IgG、IgA、IgM 水平呈上升的趋势，差异性显著；IL-2、IL-6 呈上升的趋势，FC 呈下降的趋势。说明长期练习太极拳可以增强中老年女性免疫功能，并延缓衰老所产生的免疫抑制[①]。

张勉对 24 名 50 岁以上老年人进行分组对比研究，发现参加太极拳运动 5 周时间的一组（T 组），较之于未参加任何训练的一组（C 组），其 T、B 淋巴细胞的功能均显著提升，说明太极拳运动可以有效地增进老年人机体免疫能力，并对老年人的心理健康起到积极的作用[②]。

齐敦禹对 20 名 II 型糖尿病男性患者练习太极拳 5 周前后自身的对比研究，发现 C3 值显著上升，补体 C4 值也上升，但无统计学意义，IL-2 显著上升，S-IL-2R 的浓度显著下降，$CD^{4+}$ 值明显升高，$CD^{4+}/CD^{8+}$ 比值有上升，但由于时间短，变化并不明显。这说明 II 型糖尿病患者通过练习太极拳能稳定和提高其免疫功能[③]。刘丽萍等的研究也有类似的发现，$CD^{3+}$、$CD^{4+}$、$CD^{4+}/CD^{8+}$ 比值在运动 2 小时后增高，说明身体的免疫应答能力提高。他们还发现，练习太极拳后的中老年女性 bcl-2 基因蛋白值升高，$Ca^{2+}$ 浓度降低，说明习练太极拳使中老年女性机体发生了适应性的变化，细胞凋亡率降低，人体的衰老进程得以延缓[④]。

陈广德指出，"练气功有改善肾虚症状、纠正血浆性激素环境异常之功效"，"对老年人来说，练气功有'赔本补肾，抗衰防老'的效果"[⑤]。Wang Chenchen（拼音名）汇总的 2 个实验表明：一个 98 名老人参加的实验，练习太极拳 10 年后，其内分泌功能，包括脑垂体—甲状腺、脑垂体—性腺系统，广受影响，脑垂体新陈代谢反应得以加强；一个 60 名老人参加的实验，练习太极拳 4 年后，其中 30 名太极组人员，较之于 30 名对照组，其循环 T 细胞总量，含活跃 T 淋巴细胞总量明显高于对照组[⑥]。

练习太极拳还可以增加唾液中的分泌型免疫球蛋白含量，而该物质对于排除入侵的微生物具有很好的抗局部感染作用。练习太极拳时，舌抵上颚，牙齿轻咬，容易产生唾液。这被

① 郑传锋. 太极拳锻炼对中老年人免疫系统的影响 [J]. 辽宁体育科技，2012/05·46-58.

② 张勉.老年人参加太极拳运动对自身免疫功能的影响 [J]. 河南师范大学学报（自然科学版），2002/03:85-88.

③ 齐敦禹. 太极拳运动对 II 型糖尿病患者免疫机能影响的研究 [J]. 北京体育大学学报，2008/07:933-950.

④ 刘丽萍. 太极拳运动对中老年女性身体免疫功能的影响 [J]. 中国临床康复，2005/40:98-99.

⑤ 陈广德，传统气功站桩太极五行拳 [M]. 北京：中国人民公安大学出版社，1995：7.

⑥ WANG C, Collet JP, Lau J. *The Effect of Tai-Chi on Health Outcomes in Patients with Chronic Conditions: a Systematic Review* [J]. Arch Intern Med, 2004, 13(5):12—13.

视为"金津玉液"，只能吞下不能吐掉，叫作"引天河水"，滋润周身，增加黏膜系统的免疫功能。

此外，研究还发现，长期练习太极拳可以使身体保持较高的脱氢表雄酮硫酸盐水平[①]，抗氧化酶活性、血液中的免疫球蛋白的数量与活性和练习时间是正相关性质[②]，抑制促炎细胞因子产生，降低促炎信号[③]。

## 第六节　太极拳对心理健康的作用

### 一、对身心健康的关系以及健康标准的理解

我国自古就对身心健康的关系有过诸多描述，很早就认识到身体健康与心理健康互相影响。关于身体健康影响心理健康的语句如"心者，五脏六腑之大主也，精神之所舍也"，"主明则下安，以此养生则寿，殁世不殆"，反之则"因病而致郁"。可见，身体健康是保持心理健康的重要前提。

关于心理健康影响身体健康的语句，如"怒伤肝，喜伤心，思伤脾，忧伤肺，恐伤肾"，"心定则气顺，气顺则血道畅通，精气内充，正气强盛"。反之则"悲哀愁忧则心动，心动则五脏六腑皆摇"，"因郁而致病"，"愁一愁，白了头"等。陈炎林也指出，"性情与体质紧密相关，意念影响体质"[④]。可见，不良情绪可能会引起五脏气血紊乱、脏腑功能失调，从而导致疾病的产生。只有保持心理健康，才会有助于保持身体健康，"笑一笑，十年少"。而保持心理健康，还要注意有个度的问题，即要做到"喜不过旺，怒不过激，思不过滤，恐不过惧，惊不过神"。

要认识太极拳对心理健康的作用，还要了解健康的标准。过去，人们较多倾向于认为，身体无疾病即是健康。这种生物学上的健康观念虽然无错，却是低层次的。随着社会进步和人类对自身认识的加深，公众的健康观念发生了变化，"无疾病即健康"的生物健康观已不再适应新的健康标准，取而代之的，是集"生物—心理—社会"为一体的、以现代医学知识为基础的健康观。也就是说，健康绝非仅指一个人无疾病、不体弱，而应该包含一个人的身体、心理和社会功能在内的三种功能，均处于良好状态。《现代汉语词典（第6版）》对"健康"的定义也是基于上述健康观，健康是指"（人体）发育良好，机理正常，有健全的心理和社会适应能力"[⑤]。在《世界卫生组织宪章》中，"健康是整个身体、精神和社会的一种良

① LAI H.M.，LIU M.S.Y，LIN T.J，et. al. *Higher DHEAS Levels Associated with Long-term Practicing of Tai-chi*［J］. Chin J. Physiol，2017，60(2):124-130.

② NIU A. *Effect of "Tai-chi" Exercise on Antioxidant Enzymes Activities and Immunity Function in Middle-aged Participants*［J］. Afr.J.Tradit Complement Altern Med，2016，13(5):87-90.

③ BOWER J.E.，IRWIN M.R. *Mind-body Therapies and Control of Inflammatory Biology:A Descriptive Review*［J］. Brain Behav Immun，2016，51:1-11.

④ Yearning K. Chen, *Tai-chi Chuan: Its Effects and Practical Application* [M], Shanghai: Millington Limited, 1947:10.

⑤ 中国社会科学院语言研究所词典编辑室. 现代汉语词典（第6版）［M］. 北京：商务印书馆，2015:639.

好状态"，该提法"核心是强调肉体与精神的统一、人与社会的统一、人与自然的统一"[①]。联合国教科文组织对健康的定义，也是包含了身体健康、心理健康和良好的社会适应能力三个方面。心理学家许金声还提出了包含身体、心理、社会结构和生态环境四个方面的大健康概念[②]。

## 二、太极拳运动对心理健康的作用及其机理

运动对身心健康的作用似乎是不言自明的。《吕氏春秋·尽数》中，"流水不腐，户枢不蠹，动也。形气亦然，形不动则精不流，精不流则气郁。郁处头则为肿为风，处耳则为挶为聋，处目则为眵为盲，处鼻则为鼽为窒，处腹则为张为疛，处足则为痿为蹶"，这一表述清楚地说明，不运动则易致病，而运动则有益于维持身心健康。近代的研究结果更是直接证实了这一点。运动人体学的研究结果表明，当人的心率每分钟介于 120～160 次时，即人体进行中等强度的运动时，对人体健康最有利，因为此时心脏功能调动最充分，脉搏输出量达到最大化。有氧运动的结果也表明，当人的心率每分钟介于 120～130 次时，健康效果最佳。

太极拳为一项中等强度的体育运动，对心理健康的作用十分突出，较多学者均论述过。例如，王朝琼、何克认为，"太极拳'天人合一'的整体观可以帮助青少年克服膨胀的'自我'、孤立的'小我'"，"性命双修的保健原则可以帮助青少年身心同步发展，缓解生理和心理发育不平衡的矛盾"，"太极拳人文内涵可以不断地对练习者产生正面影响，使之强化并定型为青少年文化心理品质"，"太极拳要求意识从平时的向外驰散状态回归到心神内敛的境界，可以有效提升青少年的自知力"，"太极拳崇尚武德的特征，必然对青少年人格培养和道德健康产生积极的作用"等[③]。其余类似的论述也不少，如冯支波、周怡君、陆庆春等学者的研究结果，此处不一一赘述。

然而，在现代社会中，人们的生活节奏快，工作和生活压力大，往往自誉为"上了发条的陀螺"，导致人们身心紧张，容易急躁上火；情感脆弱，容易冲动；身心疲惫，睡眠不好。许多人长期处于亚健康状态，甚至面临精神方面的问题。此时，人们常常利用相关运动进行自我调节，太极拳往往成了很好的解药。那么太极拳对心理健康的作用机理又是如何呢？笔者将从直接机理和间接机理予以说明。

### （一）直接作用机理

众所周知，练习太极拳有助于产生和增加积极、正向的思想情感。同时，这些正向的情感对抑郁、焦虑等消极情绪具有很好的抑制、抵消作用。练习太极拳还可以缓解疼痛，例如 Hall 等人对 160 个人为期 10 周的研究表明，"背痛症状减轻"，"强度降低"[④]。一增一减，对于保持人的心理健康发挥了倍加作用。

太极拳以太极为拳理，主张道义，要求练习者身怀道义之心，多做对国家、社会、集体

① 旷文楠. 道家保健体育的新使命 [J]. 成都体育学院学报，1997(1):21.

② 许金声，活出你的最佳状态 [M]. 北京：经济日报出版社，2002：338.

③ 王朝琼，何克. 试论太极拳对青少年心理健康的增进作用 [J]. 贵州社会科学，2008/07:130-132.

④ A. M. Hall et all, *Tai Chi Exercise for Treatment of Pain and Disability in People with Persistent Low Back Pain: A Randomized Controlled Trial, Arthritis Care and Research*[J], 2011(11)3:1756-1783.

有益的事情，多奉献，少索取，不争名利，不计个人得失，更不能争强好胜、逞凶斗狠。所以说，太极拳是道义之拳、重德之拳，要"致虚极，守静笃"，始终保持恬淡虚无状态，强调从思想深处解放自己。"拳虽武艺，得其正道，中庸之首，不偏不倚，无过无不及，无往不宜"，"学太极拳不可不敬"，"学太极拳不可狂"，"学太极拳不可满"，"学太极拳不可凌厉欺压人"[①]。从这个角度来说，太极拳是正道，练习者可以从中悟出立身之本、做人之礼，因而可以不断促进练习者走向精神健康、道德高尚之境。

练习太极拳，尤其是长时间练习太极拳，有助于保持积极进步的心态和良好的情绪，"使人清理思维，强化大脑"，"使人思维顺畅，思想平和，脾气柔和，增加活力"[②]。因为太极拳理念是隐忍含蓄、后发制人，动作总体上是动静相随、以静制动，是刚柔相间、以柔克刚。太极拳讲究"以意导气"，"以气运身"，"身正体舒"，"心静体舒"，动作松柔圆活，但松而不泄；力道舒缓沉着，但借力打力；运气上放松舒展，但气沉丹田；效果上看似绵软，但内劲节节贯穿。太极拳的身正、心静，对于导引经络、通常血气、维持心理健康是十分有益的。

练习太极拳，有利于发挥性格中的积极一面，抑制其反面。人的性格分类，因分类标准不同而有多种类型，如内向型、外向型；A 型、B 型；理智型、情绪型；多血质、胆汁质、黏液质、抑郁质等。以最后一种分类为例，练习太极拳，一方面可以增强性格中的积极性因素，如多血质性格中的活泼、热情、开朗、豁达、健谈、适应力强，工作效率高；胆汁质性格中的精力充沛、乐观、率直、果敢、坚持；黏液质性格中的沉静、谨慎、稳重，性情平和，有韧性；抑郁质性格中的严肃、不怕困难、善于体察别人不易发现的问题等。同样，上述四种性格之人，通过练习太极拳，也可以较好地改善其不足的一面，如多血质性格中的浮躁、轻率不踏实、缺乏耐力与毅力等；胆汁质性格中的暴躁、冲动、莽撞、易怒、自制力差等；黏液质性格中的不灵活、适应力差、冷淡、被动、迟钝等；抑郁质性格中，畏缩胆小、脆弱顺从、多愁善感、冷漠多疑、犹豫不决等。Wayne 实验中的 67 岁受试者活动表明，练习太极拳可以减轻关节炎、肌肉疲劳所带来的疼痛，练习两周后，受试者可以轻松下楼，"像个 40 岁的健康人"，不再"用两脚才下一级"[③]。

另外，练习者由于要保持性格谦逊随和，考虑周围人群和环境因素，往往能改善人际关系，一定程度上促进社会和谐安定。习练太极拳，能改善人脑的信息加工速度，提高信息处理的稳定性和顺畅度。因为能较好地延缓记忆力、注意力的衰退，从而延缓生理衰老和心理衰老的进程。而且，练习太极拳能较好分散习练者对负面情绪的注意力，不给负面情绪产生、发展的机会和时间，以达到解除紧张度，减轻心理压力，使冷落感、孤独感、抑郁感等消极情绪逐渐减轻和消失。

最后，太极拳文化内涵深奥，动作、套路较为复杂，吐纳配合不易掌握，初学者学习起来困难不少。如果练习者通过自身努力，完成了学习任务，获取了相应的段位，这将极大地提高练习者的自我成就感，从而提高其自信和自主效能。

① 陈鑫. 陈氏太极拳图说［M］. 太原：山西科学技术出版社，2006：74,93-94.

② Yearning K. Chen, *Tai-chi Chuan: Its Effects and Practical Application* [M], Shanghai: Millington Limited, 1947:10.

③ Peter M. Wayne, *The Harvard Medical School Guide to Tai-chi* [M], Boston：Harvard Health Publications，129.

### （二）间接作用机理

太极拳对心理健康的间接作用机理，也就是太极拳运动对心理健康的调节机制。练习太极拳涉及对松—紧、刚—柔、弛—张等辩证关系的认识，以松、柔、弛等为主，在此基础上让意识做螺旋缠绕运动。这种运动方式，对于调节人的心理发挥着良好的作用。以松为例，松实际上蕴含了松、静之意。松，既指形体方面的放松，又指精神方面的放松；静，既指思想方面的安静，又指情绪方面的安静。松静之合，通过"人法地，地法天，天法道，道法自然"，最终以自然为法，以舒适为度，也是最高的遵循。遵循自然而然，则能够减轻人的精神压力和对环境的应激反应，减轻焦虑和紧张的心态，减少躯体化反应，从而使人的中枢神经系统具备最佳的调节功能，护佑人的心理健康。Wang Chenchen（拼音名）汇总的 6 个实验表明：2 个实验的 283 名老年人通过练习太极拳 16 周或 6 个月，与对照组相比，其沮丧感、悲伤感明显减轻，对生命的满意度、健康感知都增加；1 个实验的 90 名学生参加 12 周的太极拳练习，其焦虑感降低，自我能力、视角—运动一体感增加；2 个实验的 186 名病人习练太极拳 1~46 个月，悲伤感、焦虑感降低，心情好转；9 个老年痴呆症病人经过 7 周的练习，其前后测显示，状况好转，结构性回忆能够聚焦，富有洞察力[①]。

练习太极拳必须注意，太极拳是一项整体运动，涉及意、气、形整体协调，要做到既练意，也练气；既练神，又练形，才能做到意气相随、形神兼备。练习太极拳的过程中，要发挥大脑对身体运动过程的调控作用，即意识指导肌肉做精微运动，当意念收紧，刺激人体经络，使内气充实鼓荡，继而意念放松，内气外吐，鼓荡之气平舒。在一紧一松的调控中，内气运行顺畅有节律，肌肉收缩合意有规律，人体运动节律与人体生物节律保持一致，便于下一个循环、往复。练习太极拳还必须注意，太极拳也是一种圆弧运动，涉及脊柱、双腿、双手协调，要做到脊柱为轴心、肢体随心意。练习太极拳过程中，注意发挥脊柱的轴心作用，两腿虚实移动不断变换重心，双手不断抱球变换姿势，利用离心力和向心力带动肢体进行圆弧运动，心意缓发，肢体慢随。由于运动强度低，便于长时间练习，既避免了刚性运动的返挫力致人受伤的危险，又有利于人体功能的有序化维持和发展。人体处于这种有序化状态，便于人本身调控精神、塑造行为，保持精神健康、行为合范。

## 三、太极拳对心理健康的具体作用

作为我国传统文化的重要组成部分，太极拳具有鲜明的民族特色和浓厚的文化底蕴。更重要的是，太极拳秉持的辩证的养生之道、超然的运动心态都足以说明，于外它有利于练习者的身体健康，于内它有利于练习者的心理健康。此外，太极拳低调、内敛、不事张扬的风格，有利于练习者塑造谦和的道德情操。太极拳对心理健康的具体作用，包括如下几点。

#### 1. 改善情绪

情绪影响心态。情绪稳定能使一个人发挥积极的心态，有效地开展工作或完成其他任务。练习太极拳，尤其是长期练习太极拳者，有助于其产生和增加积极的情绪，同时抑制消极情

① WANG C, Collet JP, Lau J. *The Effect of Tai-chi on Health Outcomes in Patients with Chronic Conditions: a Systematic Review* [J]. Arch Intern Med, 2004, 13(5):12—13.

绪的产生，或者转移对消极情绪的注意力，"有助于使人产生较少的紧张、沮丧、疲劳和焦虑状态"①。

### 2. 培养意志

意志决定了一个人的努力程度。心理健康的人一般具有明确的人生目标，并为达到此目标而具有很强的自制力，表现出坚韧果敢意志品质。练习太极拳一般需要克服艰苦、疲劳等身体感觉，还需要克服重复、枯燥、长时间等心理感受，在参加考试定级时候还需要克服强烈的情绪起伏和意志力不佳等心理因素的影响。所以，练习太极拳，尤其是长时间练习太极拳，有助于培养人勇敢顽强、坚持不懈、谦虚谨慎、不怕困难、敢于胜利的意志品质，保持积极健康的心理。

### 3. 和谐人际关系

人际关系影响社会。习练太极拳，既有单独形式的练习，也有小组或群体形式的练习。对于单独形式的练习，存在着练习者个人之间相互沟通、相互学习、相互指点甚至相互切磋等情况。对于小组或群体形式的练习，存在着个人之间、个人与集体之间、集体与集体之间更多的协同，如统一练习时间和地点、统一服饰、统一伴奏音乐、使动作同步、使风格一致、是否安排指点和切磋及竞赛等。所以说，在练习太极拳的过程中，存在着诸多的人际交往，练习者之间相互作用，相互影响、相互学习、相互促进，容易促进感情、融洽关系、增进彼此之间的团结协作，同时有助于弥合分歧、消除隔阂。这对于和谐人际关系，促进社会和谐发展具有较好的作用。

### 4. 正确认知自我

正确认知自我才能恰当地待人处物，对于单独形式的练习者来说，练习太极拳往往能使人修身养性，通过与武术假想敌对练，通过"内圣外王"式的自检，不断提高对自我武术水平和认知能力的认识。对于小组或群体形式的练习者来说，练习太极拳往往是通过群练、表演等形式进行的，通过观察对比和反思，能够认知自我武术水平和修养层次。尤其是对于参加太极拳定级考试或比赛等群体形式的练习者来说，更容易通过展现长处、优势，发现自己的缺点和不足来增加自我认知。

---

① 李慎明，世界太极拳发展报告（2019）［M］. 北京：社会科学文献出版社，2020.5：428.

# Chapter 3  Tai-chi Chuan in Modern Fitness Science

Tai-chi Chuan is a pearl on the crown of Chinese martial art. This form of martial art is culturally profound and deeply philosophical, not only serving as self-defense but also providing fitness and wellness benefits. In Tai-chi Chuan, practitioners aim to be calm and gentle, to cultivate both body and mind, and to attain harmony of heaven and man. Practitioners should "silently memorize and thoroughly ponder the essence of Tai-chi Chuan and to be ethically healthy" [1]. On techniques, Tai-chi Chuan underscores the principles of "combining vigor and suppleness, activity and inactivity, firmness and softness" [2]. It regulates human's central nervous system, cardiovascular functions and breathing. This chapter is focused on illustrating how Tai-chi Chuan strengthens human's central nervous system, cardiovascular system, respiratory system, digestive system, immune system and mental health.

## Section 1   The Effect of Tai-chi Chuan on Central Nervous System

### 1. The Central Nervous System and Its Functions

The brain is an integral and vital part of the central nervous system from either Chinese or western medicine's perspectives. According to Chinese medicine, "use the intent to move the Qi (vital force). Let the Qi sink so that it is able to collect in the bones." The brain is the house of primordial spirit. And all Yang meridians meet in the head. Human life is resulted by the regulation of cerebral cortex. The formation of consciousness lays the foundation of creating mind and logic in human's brain. In the west, the origin of modern medicine, developed countries inaugurates numerous public brain health campaigns. The US congress designated a 10-year initiative of the "Decade of the Brain" project; Japan announced its brain mapping project

---

[1]  WANG Chaoqiong, HE Ke. *Enhancing Adolescent Mental Health through Tai-chi Chuan* [J]. Guizhou Social Sciences, 2008/07:130.

[2]  LI Shenming, *Annual Report on World Tai-chi Development* (2019), Beijing: Social Sciences Academic Press, 2020.5: 426.

Brain/MINDS. As the central part of reflex arcs, the central nervous system acts as the neural basis for learning and memorization, enabling human kind to generate thinking activity, which is a main function of the central nervous system.

The central nervous system is the neuronal group that regulates certain physiological functions, including the respiratory center, the heat regulating center and the language center. Reflex actions such as animalistic escapes from potential attacks are muscular movements triggered and processed through centers. The central nervous system generates sensations. Some sensory information leaves traces within the central nervous system and produces new memory.

## 2. The Impact of Practicing Tai-chi Chuan on Central Nervous System

The intensive work stress and strain take toll of many people's health. With aging, many may start having rising fatigue, dizziness, hypomnesia, and rhembasmus. Some find themselves no more speaking fluently but often making pauses during their speech. Those pauses in fact indicate that the central nervous system is being suppressed. To the contrary, Tai-chi Chuan emphasizes practitioners to make movements loose, soft, slow and balanced. The movement flow is an effective aerobic exercise that activates all organs of the practitioner, and hence it enhances brain functions by transmitting ample oxygen to the brain.

Tai-chi Chuan is a gentle exercise underscoring being calm inside and using the intent to lead all movements. It can effectively regulate the stimulants of the cerebral cortex and the cortex suppression transition. When the motor center of the cortex is excited, other regions of the cortex would be suppressed to relieve the local pressure accumulated in the cortex. And the intensity of Tai-chi Chuan as an exercise can simulate blood circulation of the whole body, boosting metabolism of the cortex and thus strengthening the functional performance of the central nervous system. Furthermore, Tai-chi Chuan emphasizes consistent breathing without random intermission. The intent is always leading the movements despite pauses of movements. More importantly, breathing consistency and the connection between breathing and movements create dual positive mood inductions on the brain and the nervous system with active and passive stimulation. Therefore, practicing Tai-chi Chuan is beneficial for college students to improve their central nervous system function and sensory acuity, to reduce fatigue and relax the brain, so that their learning productivity would be bolstered.

Tai-chi Chuan vitally guide and regulate the nervous system, especially the advanced parts of it. Human beings count on the activities of the nervous system to adapt to and change the physical environment. Through neural activities, people coordinate all systems and organ functions for specific needs. The practice of Tai-chi Chuan is conducive to the central nervous system, because Tai-chi Chuan accentuates being concentrated and relaxed, and using the intent to guide the movement. All such are excellent exercises for the brain. Beyond that, Tai-chi Chuan's movements

shall be like floating clouds and flowing water with no ceasing. "The force exerted in Tai-chi Chuan is rooted in heels, generated from legs, controlled within the waist, reaching fingers, and going through the spine. It transmits from feet to legs to the waist as a whole." When the force is exerted, it requires the force to be a complete one, in the way that the upper and lower body coordinate to generate this force through eyes, hands, the waist and feet. Practitioners are required to have a good sense of balance to master some complex movements. The brain is under an intensive working mode to complete Tai-chi Chuan movements, which also helps train up the central nervous system, enhancing its acuity, activating other systems and organs' functional activities, strengthening the brain's regulatory ability.

## Section 2　The Effect of Tai-chi Chuan on Cardiovascular System

### 1. The Cardiovascular System and Its Functions

Both the heart and blood vessels are central hubs of human health from Chinese medicine and western medicine perspectives. The cardiovascular system interacts with the nervous system, the endocrine system and the immune system. It explains why we often use adjectives like "heart-wrenching" and "heart-broken" to describe their mental state. Apart from medicine, we can even associate "the heart" with many other qualities such as love, bravery, wisdom, integrity and memory. From Chinese medicine perspective, the "Qi" (vital force) derived from the heart commands one's physics, mentality and the whole spiritual world.

It's because the cardiovascular system, the transmission network that consists of the heart and the blood, pumps the blood into the large arteries, and the blood sends nutrients and oxygen to cells and carries metabolic waste away from cells. Under pressure, the blood is pumped away from the heart and being transported to the whole body through arteries. Then, the last level of arteries, arterioles, carry oxygen-rich blood to capillaries. Oxygen, nutrients, metabolic waste and other substances in the extracellular fluid are exchanged in the capillary bed; the blood penetrates the capillary bed and enters capillary-like thin-walled venules. The blood in venules goes to small veins, then to larger veins, and eventually to the largest veins, vena cava, which carry deoxygenated blood back to the heart.

### 2. The Impact of Practicing Tai-chi Chuan on Cardiovascular System

A study from Harvard Medical School shows that the conditions of an eighty-year-old patient with heart disease have been improved after him practicing Tai-chi Chuan. He said in the interview, "the movements of Tai-chi Chuan are like a gentle breeze taking my stress away. After practicing for a period of time, I feel that I can stand more upright and sleep better. And I find myself more multi-tasking when doing housework, and feeling more at ease.

Some medical research shows that practicing Tai-chi Chuan can significantly enhance the cardiovascular system function. Tai-chi Chuan practitioners use abdominal breathing. Its spiral and arc movements squeeze and rub organs within the body with sound massage effect, expediting the blood circulation, facilitating to expand capillaries and to strengthen vascular elasticity. Meanwhile, by relaxing the whole body, the decline of veins peripheral pressure increases blood volume, and the oxygen and nutrients transmitted by the blood also increase. Not only does it reduce cardiac stress but also it stimulates substance exchange within the body and boosts metabolism. And hence the overall cardiovascular function would be markedly strengthened.

Tai-chi Chuan's movements involve movements of muscle groups and joints, rhythmic and even breathing with intended diaphragmatic movements. The cyclical contraction and relaxation of skeletal muscles strengthen venous blood circulation while muscular movements assure venous return and the necessary venous pressure for filling the right ventricle. During abdominal breathing, the diaphragm rises and falls, the pleuroperitoneal cavity is contracted and relaxed, so that the abdominal pressure is up and down alternatively at pace. Such an exercise can strengthen arterial and venous blood transmission and return, and the venous network blood flow would be particularly reinforced. Because venous pressure is much lower than arterial pressure, the venous blood return below the waist is impacted by gravity, so venous blood return not only needs the push of the pressure inside vessels, the regulation of venous valves, but also the contraction and relaxation of the muscles outside vessels, and the ups and downs of the abdominal pressure to stimulate its blood return. The up-and-down intra-abdominal pressure generated by abdominal breathing benefits the blood circulation, supplying nutrients better to the body and organs through blood. The deep and even natural breathing used in Tai-chi Chuan requires the practitioner to sink the breath to the navel psychic-center, which speeds up the blood and lymphatic circulation, bolsters cardiac nutrients, prevents various heart-related diseases and arteriosclerosis. The smooth and coordinated movements of Tai-chi Chuan fortify both vessel elasticity and vascular stability.

Regular practice of Tai-chi Chuan can effectively strengthen human cardiovascular functions and microcirculation, facilitating substance exchange inside and outside the capillaries, increasing the utilization of oxygen in tissues, decreasing the accumulation of creatine, reducing fatigue, and facilitating the recovery of diseases. It's a great exercise to take to prevent chronic coronary heart diseases, hyperlipidemia and arteriosclerosis. The heart is a main power organ of blood circulation for human, nourishing the blood of all organs and tissues of the body. Capillaries are where substances are exchanged through microcirculation. Regular practice of Tai-chi Chuan can calm the mind, extending cardiac dilation, giving cardiac muscles an adequate rest, enhancing cardiac output and cardiac contractility, improving the overall cardiac performance. The circular and agile movements of Tai-chi Chuan make muscles contract and relax at pace, strengthening the blood flow and venous blood return, so that the blood circulation would be fastened and the heart's work

load would be reduced to better protect the heart.

# Section 3   The Effect of Tai–chi Chuan on Respiratory System

## 1. The Respiratory System and Its Functions

One cannot live without breathing. A normal adult breathes 20,000 times per day, inhaling and exhaling around 20kg of air. Life can still sustain during temporary fasting of food and water, but life would end once breathing is lost. In Tai-chi Chuan, it emphasizes heart and mind being one, so breathing is an essential part with strict requirements for practice. Only when one masters the correct breathing methods of Tai-chi Chuan can one attain the practice benefits. Therefore, correct breathing methods are a critical part in learning Tai-chi Chuan. So how shall one master Tai-chi Chuan's breathing methods? First of all, they should understand human's respiratory system and its functions.

"Breathing in and out of 'Dantian' (the navel psychic-center)" is the doctrine of Tai-chi Chuan on combining "Daoyin"(guided breathing exercise) and "Tuna" (the art of inhalation and exhalation). By following this principle, practitioners' breathing would be light, gentle and slow. The Tai-chi Chuan breathing shall be concentrated as well as relaxed. During the practice, practitioners should dwell into silence with a clear mind. The whole body should be relaxed to achieve natural coherent breathing uniting the static and the dynamic, the inside and the outside. This historical breathing method originated in China advocates combining substantiality and insubstantiality in natural breathing. According to western medicine, the respiratory system is referred to the sum of organs responsible for air exchange within the human body, including the nose, the pharynx, the larynx, the trachea, the bronchus, with plenty of alveoli, blood vessels, lymph vessels, the lung that consists of neurons, the pulmonary pleurae and other tissues. In the respiratory system, each organ has a certain division of labor, the nose and the bronchi of all levels are responsible for air transmission, in which the nasal cavity has the functions of heating, moistening and air cleaning, also it resonates when a person makes sounds.

## 2. The Impact of Practicing Tai–chi Chuan on Respiratory System

Recent laboratory research shows that the breathing techniques, the coordination between breathing and movements play a positive role on cardiopulmonary performance and in relieving mental stress. The abdominal breathing of Tai-chi Chuan greatly increases human's vital capacity and improves the respiratory performance.

Tai-chi Chuan focuses on the practice of intent, cultivating "Qi" (vital force) and regulating breathing. Bodily movements are used to guide breathing, transforming breathing to an exercise, so that a greater efficacy of practicing Tai-chi Chuan would be attained. Practitioners are required to sink the "Qi" to the navel psychic-center, and using the intent to guide the force. The long deep abdominal breathing makes the chest wide and quiet, strengthening the lungs to improve breathing durability and the overall pulmonary ventilation performance, particularly on pulmonary ventilation and gas exchange.

The practice of Tai-chi Chuan significantly strengthens pulmonary ventilation. Research shows that the regular practice of Tai-chi Chuan produces considerable adaptive cardiopulmonary changes including the increase of vital capacity through the training of long deep even abdominal breathing and the natural coordination of movements and breathing. The abdominal breathing can enlarge the up-and-down movement area, increasing the chest volume. The negative intrathoracic pressure increases the elongation of the elastic fiber network of the alveolar wall. The increase of contraction force enhances the elasticity of the lung tissue and uplifts the full potential pulmonary ventilation capacity. Clinical studies show that the vital capacity of the maximum ventilation volume of the Tai-chi Chuan exercise group when at rest is even higher than that of the control group, which demonstrates the robust pulmonary ventilation performance of the Tai-chi Chuan group.

The breathing methods of Tai-chi Chuan nourish health and relieve stress. As an ancient Chinese saying goes, regulating breathing can nourish health at least and attain the "Tao" (to become an immortal) at best. Ancient Chinese people are habitual to regulate breathing so as to improve sleep and to strengthen and secure the circulation of Yang energy within the body. Through inhaling and exhaling, the waste gas would be discharged and the clean air would be taken in to purify the practitioner. During the practice, one feels relaxed and concentrated while regulating the breathing. Every session of practice helps refresh one's mind and mood with mild perspiration and accelerated metabolism. The limbs would be trained to be more agile, the brain would be calmer, the mood would be more balanced, so that the stress would be channeled out.

# Section 4   The Effect of Tai-chi Chuan on Digestive System

## 1. The Digestive System and Its Functions

The human digestive system consists of the digestive tract and the digestive glands. Among them, the digestive tract is a long muscular duct, including the mouth, the pharynx, the esophagus, the stomach, the small intestine and the large intestine. The digestive glands can be divided into two kinds: small digestive glands and large digestive glands. Small digestive glands are scattered in the lining of all digestive tubes. Large digestive glands include the parotid glands, the sublingual glands, the submandibular glands, the liver and the pancreas.

The digestive system has three basic functions: digesting food, absorbing nutrients and excreting residues. Digesting food is the process of breaking down food into absorbable small molecules in a simple structure, which includes physical digestion and chemical digestion. The physical digestion is the process of the digestive tract grinding food, mixing food with digestive juices, pushing down the food mass through mechanical actions of chewing, swallowing and peristalsis. The chemical digestion means the food being chemically decomposed by digestive juices secreted by the digestive glands to facilitate the small intestine to absorb nutrients. Absorption of nutrients is referred to the process of the aforementioned decomposed small-molecule substances passing through epithelial cells of the digestive tract mucosa and entering the blood and lymphatic fluid of the body. The nutrients in food such as vitamins, inorganic salts and water can be absorbed directly, while proteins, fats and sugars cannot be and need to be broken down into simple-structured small molecules for absorption. Lastly, the unabsorbed residues are excreted in the form of feces through the large intestine.

## 2. The Impact of Tai–chi Chuan on Human Digestive Functions

As an exercise, Tai-chi Chuan is known as gentle, slow and smooth, and hence it provides considerable benefits to human digestive functions. It's proven that regular practice of Tai-chi Chuan can markedly improve human digestive functions, especially on enhancing the function of secreting digestive juices by the digestive glands and keeping the digestive tract clear of buildup and waste. Strengthening human digestion, nutrients absorption and bowel movements are proven benefits of playing Tai-chi Chuan.

Practicing Tai-chi Chuan can enhance nutrients digestion and absorption by quickening the blood circulation of the digestive system. It also helps prevent some digestive diseases caused by neural functional disorders, thanks to the improvements of neural system performance. Moreover, regular practice of Tai-chi Chuan can "strengthen digestive functions profited from the increase of muscular exercise which is truly beneficial for digestion and nutrient absorption. It massages the stomach and intestines, which can thicken the gastrointestinal walls, increase their elasticity, fasten their movements and thus fasten the digestive system's blood circulation. It's essentially helpful to prevent and slow down the aging of the digestive system"[1].

The practice of Tai-chi Chuan also requires the practitioners to place the tip of the tongue lightly against the palate with the upper and lower teeth lightly combined, aiming to stimulate saliva secretion and strengthening its effects of moistening, being anti-bacterial and aiding digestion. Meanwhile, the wide range of waist twisting can stimulate the digestive organs in the

---

[1] JIA Zhen. *Analysis and Research on the Exercise Characteristics and Physiological Efficacy of Tai-chi Chuan* [J], *Journal of Educational Institute of Jilin Province*, 2012/04:52-53.

abdominal cavity. With the assistance of abdominal breathing movements, it accelerates the blood circulation of the liver, reinforcing the digestive function of the liver, facilitating gastrointestinal movements, expediting digestion and absorption. As organs should be clear of buildup and waste, so that one can have smooth and sufficient gastrointestinal movements, a good appetite, regular bowel movements and robust digestion. An experiment conducted by TIAN Guihua proves that. In this experiment, 28 patients with dyspepsia practiced the 42-Stance Tai-chi Chuan for four weeks. After the practice, all 28 patients' dyspepsia has been well lessened with 100% efficacy. Despite of the small sample size of the experiment, the findings are still significant.

CHEN Guangde thinks practicing "Qigong" (referred to Standing-Stance Five-Element Chuan), is effective in treating digestive diseases. In the Chinese Academy of Science, 1,385 patients with gastric and duodenal ulcers were treated with "Qigong". The recovery rate is 20.1% and the total efficacy rate is up to 98.3%. He also thinks that practicing Tai-chi Chuan can fortify gastrointestinal digestive functions and boost human metabolism. When elderly people practice 30 minutes of Tai-chi Chuan, their cholesterol level in the blood drops significantly. For elderly people with arteriosclerosis, after six months of practice of Tai-chi Chuan, their blood protein content increases while the content of globulin and cholesterol falls a lot, and their arteriosclerosis has been greatly reduced[1]. CHEN Yanlin also thinks the practice of Tai-chi Chuan can make digestion and nutrient absorption more effectively. It also can help one transform their figure from "a weak fat one to a solid healthy one" [2].

# Section 5   The Effect of Tai-chi Chuan on Immune System

## 1. The Immune System and Its Functions

Human's immune system comprises immune organs, immune cells and immune molecules. Immune organs include bone marrow, the thymus, the spleen, lymph nodes and tonsils; immune cells include lymphocytes, phagocytes, basophils, eosinophils, neutrophils and mast cells; immune molecules include antibodies, complement, lysozyme, interferon and immunoglobulins. Human's immune system can recognize and eliminate antigenic foreign substances, and coordinate with other systems to maintain the stability and physiological balance of the internal environment of the body[3].

---

① CHEN Guangde, *Traditional Qigong Standing-Stance Tai-chi Five-Element Chuan* [M], Beijing: Chinese People's Public Security University Press, 1995: 7.

② Yearning K. Chen, *Tai-chi Chuan: Its Effects and Practical Application*[M], Shanghai: Millington Limited, 1947:10.

③ CHEN Shuzeng, *Pathogen Biology and Immunology (2nd ed.)* [M]. Wuhan: Huazhong University of Science and Technology Press,2015.08: 9.

The human immune system is the most powerful weapon to prevent pathogen invasion into the human body, by detecting and removing foreign substances and foreign microorganisms that cause adverse changes in the body's internal environment. Specifically, the human immune system takes on the roles of immunodefense, immunosurveillance and immunoregulation. Immunodefense is referred to the function of the immune system that prevents the invasion of external pathogens, identifies and removes the invading pathogens and other harmful substances, so that the human body is protected from the attack of bacteria, viruses, pollutants and diseases; immunosurveillance is referred to the function of the immune system to detect and remove "non-self" components in the body, such as senescent cells, tumor cells, dead cells and other harmful components, as well as the waste generated by metabolism and the waste left by the immune cells after attacking viruses; immunoregulation is the function of the body to maintain the stability of the internal environment of the immune system by regulating the immune tolerance. For instance, by repairing immune cells, it makes damaged organs recover and the function of damaged organs restored[1].

The immune system in the human body is irreplaceable. A healthy immune system should be in a state of balance. It is like an army who are able to distinguish between friends and foes, and to assert solidarity to conquer enemies and to protect the "peace" of our body. If the body's immune system is not sound with low functional performance, it's like the investigators in the troop are negligent and pathogens take the chance to invade; the "soldiers" are not competitive enough for the combat, causing a large amount of pathogens succeeding invading the body. So, we fall ill. But the human immune system is not the stronger the better. If the system is too strong and hyperfunctional, the "investigators" would not be able to tell apart friends from foes, and might mistakenly see friends as foes; meanwhile the "soldiers" are overly aggressive in combating so our own organs or tissues might be hurt, and the person would be under a hypersensitive state inflicted with allergies. To achieve a robust immune balance, healthy and balanced diet, regular life routines, sufficient sleep, moderate exercise, good hygiene and a positive attitude are all key influencing factors.

## 2. The Impact of Practicing Tai–chi Chuan on Human Immune Functions

Foreign studies found that the number of immune cells in the body increased significantly after 15 minutes of Tai-chi Chuan practice. And an experiment done in China found that the amount of secreted immunoglobulin in saliva was increased by 16 mg/100 after practicing Tai-chi Chuan once. Michael Owen from UCLA conducted a comparative study of 112 people, and he found that the group that practiced Tai-chi Chuan for 6 months (the pugilism group) had the level of the immunity to viruses twice as much as that of the group who received health education only

---

① JIN Boquan *Medical immunology* [M]. Beijing: People's Medical Publishing House, 2008.6: 12-74.

(the class group).

ZHENG Chuanfeng recorded and studied the 6-month Tai-chi Chuan practice of18 retired female teachers from Shaanxi Normal University. It was found that their white blood cell counts, IgG, IgA, and IgM levels showed a rising trend with significant differences; IL-2 and IL-6 showed a rising trend and FC showed a descending trend. It indicates that a long-term practice of Tai-chi Chuan can enhance immune functions and delay the immunosuppression caused by aging among middle-aged and elderly women[1].

ZHANG Mian conducted a comparative study on 24 elderly people of more than 50 years old in groups. He found that the group that participated in Tai-chi Chuan exercise for 5 weeks (group T) had significantly higher T and B lymphocyte functions than the group that did not participate in any training (group C), indicating that Tai-chi Chuan exercise can effectively strengthen the immune capacity of the elderly organisms and their mental health[2].

QI Dunyu conducted a comparative study of 20 male type II diabetic patients before and after practicing Tai-chi Chuan for 5 weeks. He found that their C3 values increased significantly, complement C4 values also increased but were not statistically significant, IL-2 rose significantly, the concentration of S-IL-2R fell significantly, CD4+ values increased significantly, and the CD4+/CD8+ ratio increased but the change was not significant due to the short period of time. This suggests that type II diabetic patients can stabilize and improve their immune functions by practicing Tai-chi Chuan [3]. A similar finding was found in a study done by LIU Liping, where the CD3+, CD4+, and CD4+/CD8+ ratio of participants significantly increased after 2 hours of Tai-chi Chuan exercise, indicating a rise in immune response. They also found that bcl-2 gene protein values increased and Ca2+ concentrations declined in middle-aged and elderly women after practicing Tai-chi Chuan, suggesting that the practice of Tai-chi Chuan induced adaptive changes in the body of middle-aged and elderly women, and the apoptosis rate was lowered, slowing down human's aging process[4].

CHEN Guangde pointed out that "practicing Qigong (referred to traditional Qigong Standing-Stance Five-Element Chuan) can lessen kidney deficiency symptoms and correct abnormalities in the plasma sex hormone environment" and "for the elderly, practicing Qigong can reinforce kidneys, strengthen resistance and prevent aging" [5]. The two studies summarized by WANG Chenchen (pinyin spelling) show the findings as follows. In one study of 98 elderly

① ZHENG Chuanfeng. *The Effect of Tai-chi Chuan on the Immune System of Middle-aged and Elderly people* [J]. Liaoning Sport Science and Technology,2012/05:46-58

② ZHANG Mian. *Effects of Elderly People's Participation in Tai-chi Chuan on the Immune Function* [J]. Journal of Henan Normal University (Natural Science Edition), 2002/03:85-88.

③ QI Dunyu. *Study on the Effects of Tai-chi Chuan on the Immune Function in Type II Diabetic Patients* [J]. Journal of Beijing Sport University, 2008/07:933-950.

④ LIU Liping. *Effects of Tai-chi Chuan on the Immune Function in Middle-aged and Elderly Women* [J]. Chinese Journal of Clinical Rehabilitation, 2005/40:98-99.

⑤ CHEN Guangde, *Traditional Qigong Standing-Stance Tai-chi Five-Element Chuan* [M], Beijing: Chinese People's Public Security University Press, 1995: 7.

people, after practicing 10 years of Tai-chi Chuan, their endocrine functions including pituitary-thyroid and pituitary-gonadal systems have been well improved, and their metabolic response of the pituitary gland has been strengthened; in a study of 60 elderly people participated, 30 participants from the Tai-chi Chuan group had much higher total circulating T cells containing active T lymphocytes than that of the control group, after practicing more than four years of Tai-chi Chuan. [1]

Practicing Tai-chi Chuan can also increase the amount of secretory immunoglobulins in the saliva, which can prevent local infection by eliminating invading microorganisms. During the practice, the tongue is placed against the upper palate and the teeth are gently clenched, which easily produces saliva. This is deemed to be "golden fluid", which can only be swallowed but not spit out, and is called "attracting water from the river of heaven", which nourishes the body and fortifies the immune functions of the mucous membrane system.

Furthermore, it was found that a long-term practice of Tai-chi Chuan can help one maintain relatively high level of dehydroepiandrosterone sulfate within the body [2]. And the antioxidant enzyme activity, the amount and activity of immunoglobulins in the blood are positively correlated with the duration of practice[3]. Such elements inhibit pro-inflammatory cytokine production and reduce pro-inflammatory signals. [4]

# Section 6   The Effect of Tai-chi Chuan on Mental Health

## 1. Tai-chi Chuan's Impact on Well-being and the Criteria of Health

The relationship between physical and mental health has been described in China since ancient times. From very early on, it was recognized that physical health and mental health influence each other. For instance, "the heart is the master of the five viscera and six bowels, as well as the house of one's spiritual world." "When the master is sound and wise, the subordinates will be well and at ease. Adopting this as a principle to safeguard health is going to be sustainable. Or else one would be diseased and depressed." As illustrated, physical health is the prerequisite to

---

[1] WANG C, Collet JP, Lau J. *The Effect of Tai-chi on Health Outcomes in Patients with Chronic Conditions: a Systematic Review* [J]. Arch Intern Med, 2004, 13(5):12—13.

[2] LAI H.M., LIU M.S.Y, LIN T.J, et. al. *Higher DHEAS Levels Associated with Long-term Practicing of Tai-chi* [J]. Chin J. Physiol, 2017, 60(2):124-130.

[3] NIU A. *Effect of "Tai-chi" Exercise on Antioxidant Enzymes Activities and Immunity Function in Middle-aged Participants* [J]. Afr.J.Tradit Complement Altern Med, 2016, 13(5):87-90.

[4] BOWER J.E., IRWIN M.R. *Mind-body Therapies and Control of Inflammatory Biology:A Descriptive Review* [J]. Brain Behav Immun, 2016, 51:1-11.

mental health.

Mental health can affect physical health tremendously. "Anger hurts the liver, exhilaration hurts the heart, reminiscing hurts the spleen, worry hurts the lungs and fear hurts the kidneys." "If the mind is calm, the Qi would be smooth so that blood vessels would be clear, with robust intrinsic energy and vital force." Otherwise, "sadness and sorrow hurt the heart, and all organs will be shaken." "One would fall ill because of depression." "A dose of sadness would make your hair grey overnight." CHEN Yanlin also points out that "temperament and physique are closely linked, and the intent affect the physic." [1] Therefore, bad moods may cause organ disorders, problems of the blood circulation, so that one might be diseased. Only when mental health is kept can physical health would be well maintained. "A good laughter can make you ten years younger." However, one should be moderate in keeping his/her mental health by "neither overthinking nor feeling "overjoyed, outrageous, overly frightened or scared."

To understand the role of Tai-chi Chuan on mental health, it is essential to understand the criteria of health. In the past, people assumed that health means that the body is without diseases. This biological concept of health cannot be calledwrong, but it is superficial. With social progress and the deepening of people's thoughts on health, the concept of public health has evolved. The former definition of health no longer fits. In other words, health is not only about an individual's health with no diseases, but it is about one having balanced performance of three key functions, physical, psychological and social functions. [2] According to the WHO Charter, "health is a good state of conditions of the whole body, the mind and the social life." The core of its concept is the unity of body and soul, the individual and the society, people and nature. [3] UNESCO's definition of health also includes three aspects: physical health, mental health and good social adaptabilities. Psychologist XU Jinsheng also proposed the concept of greater health that shall include four aspects of health: physical health, mental health, social structure and ecological environment.[4]

## 2. Tai-chi Chuan's Impact on Mental Health and Its Mechanism

It's self-evident to say that exercise benefits greatly to one's physical and mental health. According to Chinese ancient classic *Master Lv's Spring and Autumn Annals*, "when the energy is dynamic, the water keeps flowing without being rotten, nor the house beams would be worm-eaten. Likewise, if the form is not moving, the energy would not flow, and the stagnation would cause energy suppression. The accumulated suppression in the head would make the head swollen, the ears deaf, the eyes blind, the nose congested or suffocated, the abdomen bloating and the feet frail." This clearly illustrates that a sedentary life style is prone to

① Yearning K. Chen, *Tai-chi Chuan*: *Its Effects and Practical Application* [M], Shanghai: Millington Limited, 1947:10.

② The Dictionary Editorial Office, Institute of Linguistics, Chinese Academy of Social Sciences. *Modern Chinese Dictionary (6th ed.)* [M]. Beijing: The Commercial Press, 2015:639.

③ KUANG Wennan. *The New Mission of Taoist Health Sports* [J]. Journal of Chengdu Sport University , 1997(1):21.

④ XU Jinsheng, *Live Out Your Best* [M]. Beijing: The Economic Daily Press, 2002:338.

diseases, while exercise is pivotal for maintaining physical and mental health. Recent studies prove that. Findings from human kinesiology research also show that when one's heart rate is between 120-160 times per minute doing moderate exercise, it offers biggest benefits to human health, for the cardiac function is fully mobilized and the pulse output reaches the maximum. Aerobic exercise research findings also indicate that health is at its best when one's heart rate is between 120-130 times per minute.

As a moderate physical exercise, Tai-chi Chuan generates remarkable effects on improving mental health, as discussed by many scholars. For instance, WANG Chaoqiong and HE Ke argue that "Tai-chi Chuan's holistic view of harmony of heaven and man can help adolescents overcome their inflated egos and isolated egos. The principle of training both body and mind can help adolescents develop their physical and mental capabilities in a balanced way, while the physiological and psychological development gaps would be bridged". The essence of Tai-chi Chuan in humanity can continuously produce positive influence on the practitioners, so as to strengthen their will and character." "Tai-chi Chuan requires the practitioner's intent to be collected and concentrated regardless of the chaos of the outside world, that would help train up young people's cognitive abilities." "That Tai-chi Chuan accentuates the value of ethics inevitably will shape and cultivate young people's qualities and ethics." [1] Similar comments have been reiterated by many others, too. e.g., FENG Zhibo 2018; ZHOU Yijun 2017 and LU Qingchun 2013, which are not going to be elaborated here.

However, the fast pace of modern society overwhelms people with soaring stress from life and work. People call themselves as "wound-up gyroscopes" often. That leads to excessive physical and mental tensions, emotional vulnerability, fast impulsiveness, physical and mental fatigue and poor sleep. Many people have been in a state of chronic subhealth for long, and even with psychological issues. To tackle them, Tai-chi Chuan can be a substantial solution where people can self-regulate themselves through exercise. So how does Tai-chi Chuan act on improving mental health? It's going to be illustrated here from its direct and indirect mechanisms.

### (1) The mechanism of direct impact

It is well known that practicing Tai-chi Chuan helps to generate and increase positive, upbeat thoughts and emotions. At the same time, these positive emotions have a good inhibiting and counteracting effect on negative emotions such as depression and anxiety. Practicing Tai-chi Chuan can also relieve pain. For example, in a study of 160 participants for 10 weeks by Hall, it shows that "the practice of Tai-chi Chuan can lessen participants' back pain or the pain intensity has been lowered." [2] The rise of joy and the fall of pain brought by Tai-chi Chuan can immensely strengthen one's mental health.

---

[1] WANG Chaoqiong, HE Ke. *Experimental Discussion on the Enhancing Effect of Tai-chi Chuan on Adolescent Mental Health* [J]. Guizhou Social Sciences, 2008/07:130-132.

[2] A. M. Hall et all, *Tai-chi Exercise for Treatment of Pain and Disability in People with Persistent Low Back Pain: A Randomized Controlled Trial*, Arthritis Care and Research [J], 2011 (11) 3:1756-1783.

Tai-chi Chuan is based on the principle of morality and righteousness, requiring practitioners to be moral and righteous, to do more things that are beneficial to the country, the society and the community; to give more, to take less, not to compete for fame and fortune, not to care about personal gains and losses, and not to be aggressive or vicious. Therefore, Tai-chi Chuan is the pugilism of morality and virtue, and should "be in the void, keep quiet and relieve". One should always maintain a state of tranquility and emptiness, focusing on emancipation from the depth of thoughts. "Tai-chi Chuan is a martial art in its own right neutral way. Neither biased, nor excessive, little or vicious." "Learning Tai-chi Chuan cannot be disrespectful." "Learning Tai-chi Chuan cannot be complacent." "Learning Tai-chi Chuan cannot be arrogant." "Learning Tai-chi Chuan cannot be harsh or oppressive." [1] From this point of view, Tai-chi Chuan is the righteous path, from which the practitioners can learn the essence of being a person and the rituals of being a human being, and thus it can continuously help the practitioners attain their spiritual health and moral nobility.

Practicing Tai-chi Chuan, especially for long, helps one maintain positive and progressive mindset and good emotions, "clear the mind and strengthen the brain." "It makes people think smoothly and calmly, with a soft temper and rising vitality" [2]. All such are resulted from the concept of Tai-chi Chuan, where the practitioner should be patient and subtle, and the actions in general are to move and brake with stillness, and to overcome rigidity with softness. Tai-chi Chuan is about "guiding Qi with the intent", "using Qi to move the body", "the postures should be upright and the body should be relaxed", "the mind is quiet and the body is comfortable". The movements are loose and round, but the energy is well-kept with no leaking; the force is soothing and calm, but the it is borrowed; the breathing is relaxed and deep, but the Qi sinks to the navel psychic-center; the effect looks soft, but the internal force is running through. Hence, the upright postures and calm mind Tai-chi Chuan underscores are truly helpful for guiding the meridians, clearing the blood and energy, and preserving one's mental health.

The practice of Tai-chi Chuan helps bring out one's positive side of personality and contain his/her negative side. There are various types of human personality classification, depending on the classification criteria, such as introvert and extrovert; type A and type B; rational and emotional; polycystic, bilious, mucous, depressive, etc. Take the last classification as an example, practicing Tai-chi Chuan can enhance the bright side of the personality, such as lively, enthusiastic, cheerful, open-minded, talkative, adaptable and efficient qualities in a polycystic personality; energetic, optimistic, straightforward, bold and persistent qualities in a bilious personality; quiet, cautious, steady, calm and resilient qualities in a mucous personality; the qualities of being serious, being not afraid of difficulties, being good at finding issues others take for granted in a depressive personality. On the other hand, the shortcomings of a personality can be corrected by practicing

① CHEN Xin, *Chen's Tai-chi Chuan Illustrated* [M], Taiyuan: Shanxi Science and Technology Publishing House, 2006: 74, 93-94

② Yearning K. Chen, *Tai-chi Chuan: Its Effects and Practical Application* [M], Shanghai: Millington Limited, 1947:10.

Tai-chi Chuan. For instance, impetuousness, rashness, lack of stamina and perseverance in a polycystic personality; irritability, impulsiveness, recklessness, irritability and poor self-control in a bilious personality; inflexibility, poor adaptability, apathy, passivity and sluggishness in a mucus personality; and fearfulness, fragility, submissiveness, and indifference in a depressive personality. All such can be well contained with the help of Tai-chi Chuan. A study done by Wayne shows that Tai-chi Chuan practice can help 67-year-old participants significantly reduce the pain caused by arthritis and muscular fatigue. After two weeks of practice, participants could easily go down the stairs "like a healthy 40-year-old person" and no longer "use two feet to move down only one step."[1]。

In addition, practitioners tend to improve interpersonal relationships and promote social harmony and stability to a certain extent because they have to maintain a humble and easy-going personality, and to be considerate about people and the environment around. Practicing Tai-chi Chuan can improve the speed, the stability and smoothness of information processing in the human brain, because it can better delay the decline of memory and attention, thus slowing down the process of physical and psychological aging. Moreover, practicing Tai-chi Chuan can better distract the practitioner from negative emotions, depriving the opportunity and time for negative emotions, in order to release their tension sand reduce psychological stress, making negative emotions such as coldness, loneliness and depression gradually reduce and disappear.

Lastly, the culture of Tai-chi Chuan is profound, the movements and routines are complex, and it is not easy to master the breathing and the coordination, so it is difficult for beginners to learn. If the practitioner completes the learning task through his/her own efforts and gets certified with a certain grade, this will boost the practitioner's sense of self-achievement, thus fortifying his/her self-confidence and autonomous effectiveness.

### (2) The mechanism of indirect impact

The mechanism of indirect impact of Tai-chi Chuan on mental health is the mechanism of regulation of mental health by Tai-chi Chuan exercise. The practice of Tai-chi Chuan involves the awareness of the dialectical relationship of loose and tight, rigid and flexible, relax and contract. Based on that, the consciousness is allowed to do spiral winding movements. This kind of movements plays a vital role in regulating human psychology. Take "set loose" as an example, "loose" actually implies relaxation and stillness. The relaxation is physical as well as mental; The "stillness" refers to both the quietness of the mind and the quietness of the emotions. The combination of relaxation and stillness is the evidence of obeying the principle of "people learning from the earth, the earth learning from the heaven, the heaven learning from the truth and the truth learning from nature." Learning from nature is the ultimate goal to achieve the ultimate comfort. Naturally over time, one can emancipate from emotional and environmental stress, anxiety and tensions, so that somatoform response would be reduced and their central nervous system would

---

① Peter M. Wayne, *The Harvard Medical School Guide to Tai-chi* [M], Boston: Harvard Health Publications，129.

attain the optimal regulation function to assure one's mental health.　The six studies summarized by WANG Chenchen (pinyin spelling) show the findings as follows. The 283 elderly people in two studies practiced Tai-chi Chuan for 16 weeks or 6 months. Compared to the control group, their degree of frustration and sadness is much decreased, and their degree of happiness towards life, their sense of feeling healthy is increased; in another study of 90 students, after 12-week practice of Tai-chi Chuan, their anxiety level is down, and their sense of self-competence and perspective-motor integration is increased. In two studies of 186 patients, after practicing Tai-chi Chuan for 1 to 46 months, their sadness and anxiety level are down and their mood is improved; in a study of nine Alzheimer patients, their conditions are improved with rising ability to focus on the structural memory, and with the enhancement of insightfulness. [1]

When practicing Tai-chi Chuan, one must keep in mind that Tai-chi Chuan is a holistic exercise, involving the coordination of the intent, the Qi and the form as a whole, so as to realize the intent along with the Qi while rendering the correct form and essence of Tai-chi Chuan. During the practice, one should pay attention to the regulation by the brain, that is, using the intent to guide the muscles to accomplish fine movements. When the intent is on, the meridians are stimulated, the intrinsic Qi is solid; and when the intent is set loose, the Qi is exhaled, the whole body is finally relaxed and soothed. Under the tight-loose regulation, the intrinsic Qi is flowing within the body rhythmically, so are the muscle contraction, human kinetic movements and biological movements. The synchronized pace of such all makes the practitioner get ready for the next cycle and repetition of Tai-chi Chuan. It should also be noted that Tai-chi Chuan is a circular movement, involving the spine, the legs and the hands. It's required that the spine should act as the axis, and the limbs should move guided by the intent. The practitioner should pay attention to keeping the spine as the axis while changing the center by switching between substantiality and insubstantiality, with both hands changing gestures while keeping the ball-holding posture, using centrifugal and centripetal forces to lead the limbs for circular movements. The intent-guiding movement process is slow and calm. The low intensity of the exercise supports practitioners for long practice sessions, while avoiding the risks of injury caused by the reaction force of strenuous exercises. It also stabilizes and enhances human organs functional performance. When one is at such a balanced, well-controlled state, it's beneficial for one to optimize their mental wellness, improve behavioral compliance, and maintain mental health.

## 3. Tai-chi Chuan's Specific Impact on Mental Health

As an essential part of our traditional culture, Tai-chi Chuan has distinctive national characteristics and a strong cultural heritage. More importantly, the dialectical approach to health

---

① WANG C, Collet JP, Lau J. *The Effect of Tai-chi on Health Outcomes in Patients with Chronic Conditions: a Systematic Review* [J]. Arch Intern Med, 2004, 13(5):12—13.

and the transcendent attitude of movements suffice to show that Tai-chi Chuan benefits practitioner's physical health as well as mental health. In addition, the understated, restrained and unassuming style of Tai-chi Chuan is conducive to cultivate practitioner's humility and ethics. The specific effects of Tai-chi Chuan on mental health are as follows.

1. Improve the mood. Emotions affect the mind. Emotional stability enables a person to exert a positive state of mind and work effectively or to accomplish tasks. Practicing Tai-chi Chuan, especially for those who have been practicing it for long, helps them generate and enhance positive emotions while suppressing the generation of negative emotions or diverting their attention from negative emotions, which "helps to produce less tensions, frustration, fatigue and anxiety" [1]

2. Cultivate the will. Will determines a person's degree of efforts. Mentally healthy people generally have a clear goal in life, and have strong self-control to achieve this goal, revealing their tenacity and will. Practicing Tai-chi Chuan requires practitioners to overcome physical hindrances such as setbacks and fatigue, as well as psychological feelings such as boredom, tedium, and long-awaiting. One also needs to well control their emotional swings and the lack of will power when attending Tai-chi Chuan grading exams. Thus, a long regular practice of Tai-chi Chuan can forge people's will, reinforcing their tenacity, humility and mental health.

3. Harmonious interpersonal relationships. Interpersonal relationships influence one's social wellbeing. On practicing Tai-chi Chuan, there are individual forms of practice, but there are also group sessions or group practice. For individual practice, there are situations where individual practitioners communicate with each other, learn from each other, point out practice issues for each other, and even spar with each other. For group sessions or group practice, there is more synergy among individuals, between individuals and the group, and among groups. For group practice, plenty of coordination needs to be done to confirm the practice time and place, the outfits, the background music, the step synchronization, the collective style, the coaching session arrangement, the peer-to-peer review, contests etc. Therefore, there are a lot of interpersonal communication and collaboration opportunities during the group practice, where practitioners can enhance their teamwork, collaborating to reach the common goal, which is beneficial for them to develop interpersonal skills and enhance their social well-being.

4. Correct self-perceptions. Only when one has a correct self-perception can he/she interact with people and deal with matters appropriately. For individual practitioners, the practice of Tai-chi Chuan can often nourish their body and mind, promote their deepened understanding of martial art, by them practicing against imaginary opponents and implementing the stringent ethical doctrine of "being a sage inside and being a king outside". For group practitioners, their Tai-chi Chuan level and skills would make remarkable progress by periodic group practice sessions, performance, comparative review and self-reflection. For practitioners bracing for Tai chi Chuan grading exams or group competitions, they might be able to have more opportunities to identify their own strengths and weaknesses, so as to deepen their self-perceptions.

---

[1] LI Shenming, *Annual Report on World Tai-chi Development* (2019) [M], Beijing: Social Sciences Academic Press, 2020.5: 428.

# 第四章 太极拳的基本形态和功法

## 第一节 基本形态[①]

### 一、静态

#### （一）身型

头：虚领；肩：松沉；肘：下垂；腕：塌活；腰：松塌；髋：松缩；膝：裹住；踝：灵活；腿：微屈；胸：内含（图 4-1-1）。

#### （二）手型

##### 1. 拳

四指自然卷屈，拇指扣于食指和中指的第二指节上（图 4-1-2）。

要求：拳面齐平，不可僵硬。

图 4-1-1

图 4-1-2

---

① 冯志强. 太极拳全书［M］. 北京：学苑出版社，2000.1.

### 2. 掌

五指自然伸直，手指微分，虎口撑圆，掌心内凹（图 4-1-3）。

要求：掌要自然伸直，掌心微含空，形如荷叶状。

### 3. 勾

五指第一指节自然捏拢，屈腕（图 4-1-4）。

要求：掌心含空，五指不可用力。

图 4-1-3           图 4-1-4

拳、掌、勾示意图（图 4-1-5）。

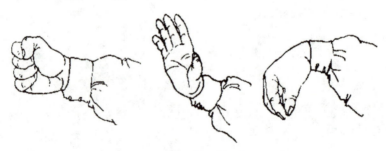

图 4-1-5   拳、掌、勾

## （三）步型

### 1. 弓步

前腿全脚着地，屈膝前弓，另一腿自然伸直，脚尖内扣朝斜前方约 45 度（图 4-1-6）。分顺、拗两种，顺弓步指出手和出脚同侧，如左手左脚在前的单鞭式；拗弓步是异侧手脚在前，如右手在前，左腿在前的搂膝拗步。

要求：顺弓步一般要求两脚之间横向 10 厘米；拗弓步为 20 厘米，后胯微屈。

### 2. 马步

两腿屈膝半蹲，两脚尖微微内扣，两脚约 3 个脚长（图 4-1-7）。

要求：屈膝松胯，开胯圆裆。

图 4-1-6　　　　　　　　　　　图 4-1-7

### 3. 仆步

一腿屈膝全蹲，另一腿自然伸直（图 4-1-8）。

要求：两脚跟不可离地。

### 4. 虚步

一腿屈膝支持，另一脚脚跟着地，或脚尖虚点地，前后脚之间距离根据身体条件架势而定（图 4-1-9）。

要求：虚实分明。

图 4-1-8　　　　　　　　　　　图 4-1-9

### 5. 丁步

一腿屈膝半蹲，重心在屈膝腿上，另一腿以脚前掌着地，点于支撑腿脚内侧（图4-1-10）。

要求：虚实分清，点地腿小腿肌肉不可紧张。

### 6. 独立步

一腿微屈支撑，另一腿屈膝提起，大腿水平（图4-1-11）。

要求：支撑稳定，提膝脚尖自然松垂。

图4-1-10        图4-1-11

## 二、动态

### （一）手法

### 1. 掤法

屈臂呈弧形，横于体前，掌心向内，高于肩平，力达前臂外侧（图4-1-12）。

要求：肘尖下垂，既不可软缩也不可僵硬，劲力上做到掤在两臂。

### 2. 捋法

两臂稍屈，两掌心斜相对，由体前向后划弧摆至腹前（图4-1-13、图4-1-14）。

要求：两肘微屈，用腰带手回捋，动作走弧形，不可硬拉强拽，劲力上做到捋在掌中。

### 3. 挤法

一臂屈于胸前，另一手抚于屈臂手的腕内侧，两臂同时向前用力推出（图4-1-15）。

要求：两臂撑圆，低不过胸口，高不过肩，劲力上做到挤在手背。

### 4. 按法

单手或双手自上向下为下按，自后经下向前弧形推出为前按（图4-1-16、图4-1-17）。

要求：两臂不可伸直，劲力上做到按在腰攻。

### 5. 单推掌

一掌由肩上或胸前沿弧形向前推出，指尖向上（图4-1-18）。

要求：推时沉肩垂肘。

图 4-1-12　　　　　图 4-1-13　　　　　图 4-1-14

图 4-1-15　　　　　图 4-1-16

图 4-1-17　　　　　图 4-1-18

### 6. 搂手

一掌经腹前弧行由异侧髋前向同侧髋前划弧，掌心向下（图4-1-19、图4-1-20）。

要求：以腰带手划平圆。

图 4-1-19                     图 4-1-20

### 7. 云手

两掌弧行经体前上下交叉划圆（图4-1-21）。

要求：两臂松沉不可僵硬，以腰带臂。两腕内外旋翻，高不过眼低不过裆。

### 8. 双分掌

两掌十字交叉合抱于胸口前，向左右弧形旋臂分开，掌心朝外，腕与肩同高（图4-1-22）。

要求：两臂成弧形，不可直臂高举腕过头顶。

图 4-1-21                     图 4-1-22

### 9. 插掌

手臂由屈到伸，直腕向斜前下方伸出，力达指尖，另一手常按于同侧胯旁（图 4-1-23）。

要求：臂自然伸直，力达掌尖。

### 10. 架掌

手臂内旋自下向前上，架在头侧上方，掌心向外（图 4-1-24）。

要求：手臂保持弧形，高过头。

图 4-1-23　　　　　　　　图 4-1-24

### 11. 冲拳

手握拳由腰间平拳或立拳向前冲出（图 4-1-25）。

要求：利用周身合力，力达拳面，臂微屈，沉肩坠肘。

### 12. 双贯拳

双拳经两侧臂内旋向前弧行，两拳眼相对合击，基本上两拳之间与头宽（图 4-1-26）。

要求：两肩下沉，臂呈弧形，拳眼与耳同高，松腰送臂。

图 4-1-25　　　　　　　　图 4-1-26

### （二）步法

步法是指脚步移动的方法。太极拳对步法要求"迈步如猫行，行步如临渊，所谓有不得机得势处，身便散乱，其病必腰腿求之"。"腿"主要指步法的变化，动作的灵活与迟重全在步法。

步法总要求：轻灵稳健，步点准确，轻起轻落，点起点落。

#### 1. 上步

后脚越过支撑腿脚内侧向前迈步（图4-1-27～图4-1-29）。

要求：弧形上步。

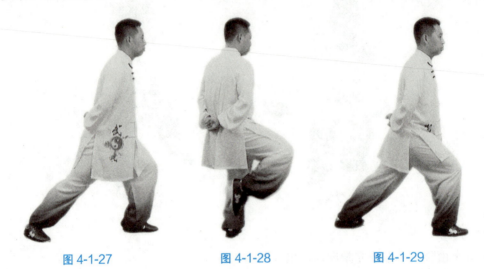

| 图 4-1-27 | 图 4-1-28 | 图 4-1-29 |

#### 2. 退步

前脚越过后脚支撑腿内侧退一步（图4-1-30、图4-1-31）。

要求：弧形退步。

| 图 4-1-30 | 图 4-1-31 |

### 3. 碾步

以脚掌或脚跟为轴转动（图 4-1-32、图 4-1-33）。

要求：转动灵活。

图 4-1-32                            图 4-1-33

### 4. 进步

两脚连续交替向前上步（图 4-1-34～图 4-1-37）。

要求：身体移动平稳。

图 4-1-34                            图 4-1-35

图 4-1-36                    图 4-1-37

## 5. 侧行步

两脚交替向体侧行进（图 4-1-38～图 4-1-41）。

要求：提脚时脚跟先起，落脚时脚尖先落，保持身体平稳移动。

图 4-1-38                    图 4-1-39

图 4-1-40                    图 4-1-41

### 6. 跟步

前脚不动，后脚上半步不越过前脚（图 4-1-42～图 4-1-43）。

要求：前脚落地后脚起如跷跷板。

图 4-1-42　　　　　　　　　　　　图 4-1-43

## （三）眼法

在武术中，眼神与各种动作配合的方法叫眼法。眼法是体现精神的重要环节，拳谚中有"手眼相随""手到眼到"说法。太极拳要求"神似捕鼠之猫"，一般要威而不猛，眼随手动，不仅使动眼神经、视神经得以锻炼，更体现形神兼备的气势。切不可半开半闭，毫无神气。通过眼神能反映内里变化，反之眼神也能诱导精神放松，不能忽视。眼法主要包括注视和随视两类。

### 1. 注视

以主动手为目标，向主动手的方向投目远视。

### 2. 随视

随主动手动转，眼随手转。

# 第二节　常见功法[①]

桩功，亦叫站桩，是我国传统武术特有的练功手段，各流派都非常重视站桩的功法练习，而且各有其独特的练法。太极拳讲究以意行拳，要将意念与拳势动作完善地结合起来，通过站桩达到调身、调息、调心的功效，并增强下肢功力，使膝关节得到锻炼。要想在太极拳的功力和健身祛病方面有所收获，应重视站桩的练习，在站桩上下功夫。这里就太极拳通常采用的几种站桩功法进行介绍。

## 一、无极桩

### 1. 动作过程

（1）两脚并步站立，舌抵上颚，呼吸均匀，松静自然（图4-2-1）。

（2）重心歇在右腿，右髋关节上提，左腿顺势向左划开半步，与肩同宽；随即重心落于两腿中间，使百会穴、会阴穴和两脚涌泉穴连线中点在一条垂直线上。

（3）两手自然伸直，贴于大腿两侧；眼帘自然下垂，目视前下方（图4-2-2）。

图 4-2-1　　　　　　　　图 4-2-2

### 2. 动作要领

（1）虚灵顶劲，含胸拔背，呼吸自然；整个开步过程思想意识从右边到左边然后过渡到身体中心位置。

（2）左脚先从大拇指依次向外划弧过渡到脚跟踩实。

## 二、太极桩

### 1. 动作过程

（1）两脚平行分开，与肩同宽，自然站立，两膝微屈，重心落于两腿中间，使百会穴、会阴穴和两脚间距中点在一条垂直线上。松肩，松腰，松胯，全身松静，意念集中，无杂念，呼吸自然。

（2）两臂慢慢前平举，微屈，相抱于胸前，手指自然舒展，掌心向内，指尖相对，指尖相距10～20厘米。

（3）两腿半屈蹲，上体保持正直，眼平视前方（图4-2-3）。

### 2. 动作要领

（1）虚领顶劲，含胸拔背，松腰竖脊，沉肩坠肘，圆臂舒指，收腹敛臀，气沉丹田，全身松而不懈，实而不僵。

图 4-2-3

（2）时间长短因人而异，随功力的增长，逐渐延长时间，初练时每次站 3～5 分钟即可。

## 三、开合桩

### 1. 动作过程

（1）与无极桩动作（1）相同。

（2）两臂前按，随后慢慢向外撑开。同时，两腿左右移动重心，并做深度吸气。

（3）稍停，两臂再慢慢收合。同时，重心回到中间，并呼气（图 4-2-4、图 4-2-5）。

图 4-2-4 图 4-2-5

### 2. 动作要领

（1）两臂外掤时，如抱着个大气球在充气，两臂意在随气球增大四面胀出，外掤与吸气同步。

（2）两臂收合时，如两臂要把气球中的气挤出，随气球缩小，两臂收合，并同步呼气。

（3）此开合桩宜用顺式呼吸，力求通畅顺遂，不可憋气，随练习时间的增加，逐步延长开合时间，加深呼吸深度。

## 四、升降桩

### 1. 动作过程

（1）与无极桩动作（1）相同。

（2）两臂徐徐前平举，与肩同高、同宽，手心向下，肘微屈，肩要放松。

（3）稍停，两腿屈膝下蹲。两掌随之向下轻轻按至腹前，停顿片刻，两腿慢慢站立，两臂随之升起。如此循环，次数因人而异，随功力的增长增加练习次数。

（4）收功时，两臂徐徐下落收至大腿两侧，两脚并拢（图 4-2-6、图 4-2-7）。

### 2. 动作要领

（1）升降时上体保持正直，不可前俯后仰。两掌下按时，两肩放松前送，两肘坠沉，两手如将水中木板下按。上升时，不可耸肩，以肩催肘，肘催腕，腕推掌，向前送劲，与腰背形成对撑。

（2）身体下降后，可随功力的增强逐渐延长停顿时间。

图 4-2-6　　　　　　　　　　　图 4-2-7

## 五、虚步桩

### 1. 动作过程

（1）两脚并步站立，两臂自然下垂，右脚尖向右打开，重心徐徐移至右脚并屈膝半蹲，左脚向前迈出半步，脚跟着地，脚尖跷起，膝微屈。

（2）同时，两手向前上方举起，在体前合抱，左掌心向右偏下，指与鼻同高，指尖斜向前上。右掌在左肘内侧下方，掌心向左偏下，指尖斜向前上，目视左掌（图 4-2-8）。

（3）左右式交替练习，动作相反。

### 2. 动作要领

（1）两腿虚实分明，收腹敛臀，实腿要屈膝，稳固支撑身体；虚腿膝部微屈，不可挺直，脚跟轻轻支撑。

（2）上体保持中正安舒；两臂要沉肩坠肘，舒指坐腕，劲贯指尖；头部要虚领顶劲，心念集中。

## 六、定势桩

定势桩是指在太极拳的演练中，为了更好地掌握某一动作而刻意固定或重复该动作，然后通过太极拳的八个维度对该动作进行逐一自查，以提高太极拳基本技术的方法。

图 4-2-8

以上各种桩功练习完毕均要走动遛腿，不宜大声说话，以增加养功。

## 七、行功

### 1. 前进步

身体自然直立，两手背贴附后腰两侧，两腿屈膝，重心移至右腿，左脚跟提起（图4-2-9），左腿抬起向前上步，脚跟着地成虚步（图 4-2-10）。重心移至右腿，全脚着地，成左弓步（图4-2-11），眼视前方。上体后坐，重心后移，右腿屈膝，左腿自然伸直，成左虚步（图4-2-12），再上体稍左转，左脚外展踏实，重心移至左腿并屈膝（图4-2-13），右腿上步屈膝收于左腿旁（图4-2-14）。上体稍右转，出右脚。重复上述动作，左右相换。最后，后脚向前跟步，两脚靠拢，两腿慢慢伸直立正。

图 4-2-9　　　　　　　　　　图 4-2-10

图 4-2-11　　　　　　　　　　图 4-2-12

图 4-2-13　　　　　　　　图 4-2-14

　　动作要点：上体始终保持正直，重心保持平稳，不要忽高忽低，步法的转变要虚实分明，连贯稳定。眼平视，呼吸要自然。虚步时为吸气，弓步和碾步时为呼气。

### 2. 后退步

　　身体自然站立，两脚并拢，两手背贴附后腰两侧，眼平视（图 4-2-15）。身体重心移至右腿，两腿屈膝，左腿向左后方撤一步，前脚掌先着地（图 4-2-16）。左腿屈膝后坐，右腿自然伸直，脚尖抬起，成右虚步；右腿提起经左腿内侧向后方撤一步，前脚掌先着地；重心后移右腿屈膝后坐，左腿自然伸直，翘脚尖，成左虚步，眼平视（图 4-2-17）。重复上述动作，左右相换。最后前脚向后撤步，与后脚并拢，两脚伸直，两臂自然下垂于体两侧。

　　动作要点：上体始终保持正直平稳，行进过程中不可忽高忽低。动作要连贯，虚实要分明。呼吸要自然，身体后坐时为呼气，抬腿撤步时为吸气。

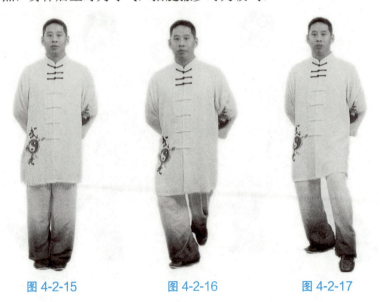

图 4-2-15　　　　　　图 4-2-16　　　　　　图 4-2-17

### 3. 侧移步

身体松静站立,两脚并拢,两手置于腰部。精神集中,呼吸自然,眼向前平视(图 4-2-18)。屈膝蹲坐,身体重心移至右腿,左脚提起;随即上体右转,左脚向左侧移动一步,脚尖点地(图 4-2-19)。上体左转,身体重心左移,左脚踏实,右脚收至左脚内侧约 20 厘米,脚尖点地(图 4-2-20)。身体重心移至右腿,右脚踏实,左脚提起;上体右转,左脚再向左侧移动一步,脚尖点地(图 4-2-21)。上体左转,动作同前。如此连续练习,左行数次后,可反向右行练习。

图 4-2-18　　　　　　　　　图 4-2-19

图 4-2-20　　　　　　　　　图 4-2-21

动作要点:顶头竖颈,沉肩含胸,上体中正,松腰活胯,重心平衡,动作连贯均匀。脚步移动要轻提轻落,点起点落。初学时自然呼吸,逐步过渡到一步一呼吸。如动作较慢也可一步两呼吸,即左右转腰提脚时吸气,开步、并步时呼气。

# Chapter 4   Basic Forms and Practicing Methods of Tai-chi Chuan

## Section 1   Basic Forms[1]

### 1. Static State

#### (1) Body Shape

The head is upright and straight without using strength; the shoulders hang downward in a relaxed way; the elbows are relaxed downward; the wrist softens; the waist relaxes; knees bend; ankles keep flexible; legs bend slightly; chest is slightly reserved inward. (Figure 4-1-1)

#### (2) Hand Shape

1. Fist: The four fingers are naturally flexed, with the thumb clasped on the second knuckle of the index and middle fingers. (Figure 4-1-2)

Figure 4-1-1                    Figure 4-1-2

① FENG *Zhiqiang. Pandect of Tai-chi Chuan*[M]. Beijing: Xueyuan Publishing House. 2000.1.

Requirements: The face of the fist should be flat and free from stiffness.

2. Palm: Stretch all fingers naturally and keep fingers slightly apart. The web between the thumb and the index fingers should be extended to round and the center of the palm is inward. (Figure 4-1-3)

Requirements: The hand should be naturally straight, and the palm is slightly hollow, which is like a lotus leaf.

3. Hook: Pinch the first knuckles of all fingers together naturally and bend the wrist. (Figure 4-1-4)

Requirements: The palm is hollow and all fingers should not use any strength.

Figure 4-1-3          Figure 4-1-4

Fist, Palm, and Hook (Figure 4-1-5)

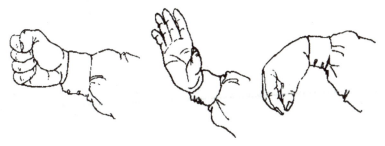

Figures 4-1-5   Fist, Palm, and Hook

## (3) Foot Shape

### 1. Bow Stance

Step the whole front foot on the ground and bend the knee; straighten the other leg naturally with the toes inwards about 45°diagonally. (Figure 4-1-6) Bow stance can be classified into homolateral lunge and heterolateral lunge. By homolateral lunge, it refers to the moving hand and foot are on the same side, such as single whip which is formed by pushing left hand and stepping forward the left foot. By heterolateral lunge, it refers to the moving hand and foot on different sides, such as brush knee and twist step which are formed by pushing right hand and stepping forward the left foot.

Requirements: For homolateral lunge, the distance between two feet horizontally should be 10cm; for heterolateral lunge, it should be 20cm. And hip should flex slightly.

### 2. Horse Stance

Bend the knees and squat with the feet slight inward. The distance between the feet is about 2 to 3 times of the length of foot. (Figure 4-1-7)

Figure 4-1-6                 Figure 4-1-7

Requirements: Buttocks should be tucked in and knees should be bent with open legs and round crotch.

### 3. Drop Stance

Squat on one leg until the thigh is parallel to the ground and extend the other leg out to the side naturally. (Figure 4-1-8)

Requirements: The two feet should not get off the ground.

### 4. Empty Stance

Bend one leg as the supporting leg and touch the ground with the heel or tip of the other foot. The distance between the front and rear feet is determined according to the individual physical conditions. (Figure 4-1-9)

Requirements: The weight should be totally given to the supporting leg and the frontal leg has no weight placed on it.

### 5. T-shaped Stance

Squat on one leg and place the center of weight on the bending leg. Place the other foot beside the supporting leg with half sole touching the ground. (Figure 4-1-10)

Figure 4-1-8                    Figure 4-1-9

Requirements: The weight should be totally given to the supporting leg. The other leg has no weight placed on it and the calf muscle of it should not be stressed.

### 6. Crane Stance

Stand on one leg which bends slightly and raise the other leg and bend the knee to make the thigh parallel to the ground. (Figure 4-1-11)

Requirements: The base leg should be stable and the toes of the raised leg drop naturally.

Figure 4-1-10                    Figure 4-1-11

# 2. Dynamic State

## (1) Hand Movement

### 1. P'eng (Wardoff)

Bend the arms in an arc across the chest with the palm facing the chest. Strength comes from

the lateral forearms. (Figure 4-1-12)

Requirements: Bend down the elbow tip without retraction or stiffness. The strength comes from two arms.

### 2. Lu (Rollback)

The two palms are obliquely opposite, yielding from the front of the body to the front of the abdomen. (Figure 4-1-13, Figure 4-1-14)

Figure 4-1-12          Figure 4-1-13          Figure 4-1-14

Requirements: Bend the elbows slightly and roll back hands with the movement of waist. The movement should form an arc without pulling or dragging. The force should come from the palm.

### 3. Chi (Press)

Bend one arm in front of the chest and put the other hand on the medial wrist of the bending arm. Both arms should put forth strength at the same time. (Figure 4-1-15)

Requirements: Two arms should form a round and the position of the arms should not lower than chest or higher than the shoulder. The force should be pressed upward to the back of the hands.

### 4. An (Push)

Practitioners can push down with single hand or both hands or push down from back to forward direction in an arc. (Figure 4-1-16, Figure 4-1-17)

Figure 4-1-15

Requirements: Don't straighten arms. And the movement should be finished in a systematic way.

### 5. Singling palm push

Extend one upright palm from the shoulder to the front by the corner of mouth. Contain chest and relax shoulders. (Figure 4-1-18)

Figure 4-1-16          Figure 4-1-17          Figure 4-1-18

Requirements: While pushing, relax shoulders and bend down elbows.

## 6. Brush

Extend one palm from the abdomen on the opposite side to the hip on the same side. (Figure 4-1-19, Figure 4-1-20)

Requirements: The palm should circle from one side to the other side driven by the movement of waist.

Figure 4-1-19                    Figure 4-1-20

## 7. Wave Hands like Clouds

Two hands rotate up, down, to the left and to the right respectively. (Figure 4-1-21)

Requirements: The two arms should be relaxed without stiffness and driven by the movement of waist. Turn the wrists inside and outside, and the position of two wrists shouldn't be higher than the eyes or lower than the abdomen.

### 8. Two Palms Extending

Cross two palms in front of the chest and extend the palms to the right and left respectively with palms facing outward. The wrists are at the shoulder level. (Figure 4-1-22)

Figure 4-1-21                    Figure 4-1-22

Requirements: Two arms should be in an arc form. Don't raise arms above head.

### 9. Thrust Palm

Extend the curved arm and make the straight wrist extending forward and downward. The strength passes to the tip of fingers. Keep the other hand on the same side of the hip. (Figure 4-1-23)

Requirements: Extend the arm naturally and the strength should reach the tip of fingers.

### 10. Blocking Palm

Move the palm from below to above to parry overhead, with the palm facing upward. (Figure 4-1-24)

Figure 4-1-23                    Figure 4-1-24

Requirements: Keep arms arched over head.

### 11. Punch

Make a horizontal or vertical fist and punch out from the waist level. (Figure 4-1-25)

Requirements: Use the force of the whole body and pass the strength to the fist face. Bend the arms slightly, and lower the shoulders and elbows.

### 12. Double roundhouse punch

Rotate both arms inward and arc forward two fists, two thumbs striking together. The distance between two fists is basically the width of the head. (Figure 4-1-26)

| Figure 4-1-25 | Figure 4-1-26 |

Requirements: Drop shoulders and keep arms in an arc. The thumbs are at ear level. Relax waist and extend arms.

## (2) Footwork

Footwork refers to the method of footstep movement. In Tai-chi Chuan, it requires that "people should step forward like a cat and walk like standing by an abyss. If the body easily falls into disorder, the problem must be in waist and legs". "Leg" mainly refers to the change of footwork, and the flexibility and steadiness of action are all in footwork.

General requirements for footwork: The steps should be light, flexible and accurate. Practitioner should raise up and put down the foot gently on the toes or on the heel.

### 1. Step Up

Step Up with the rear foot over the inside of the supporting leg. (Figure 4-1-27~Figure 4-1-29)

Requirements: Step up in an arc.

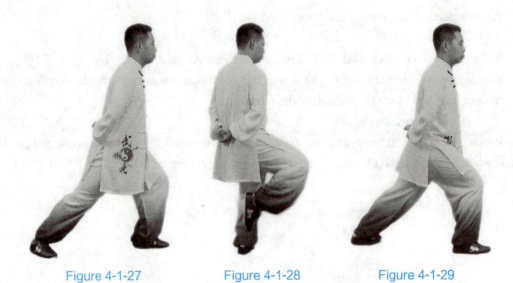

Figure 4-1-27      Figure 4-1-28      Figure 4-1-29

## 2. Step Back

Step Back with the front foot over the inside of the supporting leg. (Figure 4-1-30，Figure 4-1-31)

Requirements: Step backward in an arc.

Figure 4-1-30      Figure 4-1-31

## 3. Grinding Step

Rotate on the sole or heel of the foot. (Figure 4-1-32，Figure 4-1-33)

Requirements: The rotation shall be flexible.

Figure 4-1-32                    Figure 4-1-33

## 4. Step Forward

Step forward with two feet alternately. (Figure 4-1-34～Figure 4-1-37)

Requirements: The body should move steadily.

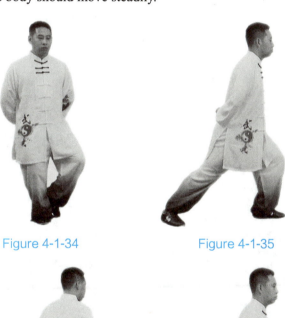

Figure 4-1-34                    Figure 4-1-35

Figure 4-1-36                    Figure 4-1-37

### 5. Side Step

Move feet to body's side alternately. (Figure 4-1-38～Figure 4-1-41)

Figure 4-1-38                    Figure 4-1-39

Figure 4-1-40                    Figure 4-1-41

Requirements: When raising up foot, practitioners should raise up the heel first. When putting down the foot, practitioners should put down on the toes first. The body should move steadily.

### 6. Following Step

Don't move the front foot and take half a step forward with the rear foot which shouldn't cross the front foot. (Figure 4-1-42, Figure 4-1-43)

Requirements: As putting down the front foot, practitioners should raise up the rear foot, which is like a seesaw.

Figure 4-1-42          Figure 4-1-43

### (3) Eye Movement

In martial arts, eyes movement is required for various movements to reflect the spirit of the practitioner. As a saying goes in fist practicing, "hand and eye should follow each other" and "eyes and hands movement shall be coordinated". In Tai-chi Chuan, it requires that "the body status is like a cat catching mice". Generally, people should be powerful but not fierce, and the eyes should follow the hand. Thus, it not only enables the oculomotor nerve and optic nerve exercise, but also reflects the unity of form and spirit. Do not half open and half close the eyes, or it will show no spirit at all. The eyes can reflect the internal changes, and they can also induce mental relaxation. Therefore, the eye movement is of great significance.

#### 1. Fixed eyes

Taking the hand as the target, stare at the direction of the main hand.

#### 2. Followed eyes

The eyes follow the movement of the main hand.

## Section 2  Common Practicing Methods[1]

Standing practice is also known as standing stance. As a unique practice method of traditional Chinese martial art, it is highly valued by all schools and each school has distinctive practicing methods. In Tai-chi Chuan, it requires the combination of movement and mind. And standing stance enables people to regulate their body, breath and mind, strengthen the force and skills of

---

[1] LI Shoutang . *24-Stance Tai-chi Chuan Learning and Practice*[M]. Taiyuan: Shanxi Science and Technology Publishing House, 2009.1.

their lower limbs and exercise their knees. If practitioners want to benefit from Tai-chi Chuan in terms of force and skills and fitness, they should attach great importance to stance practice. The common practicing methods of standing stance are as follows.

## 1. Infinite Stance

### 1.1 Action Process:

(1) Stand with feet parallel, with the tongue placed against the upper palate, breathe evenly, and be relaxed and natural (Figure 4-2-1).

(2) The center of gravity is shifted to the right leg, the right hip joint is lifted, and the left leg slide to the left with a half step, shoulder-width apart; Then the center of gravity falls between the legs, so that Baihui Point, Huiyin point and the midpoint of Yongquan point between feet are on a vertical line.

(3) The arms and hands should be naturally straight, and put on both sides of the thigh; Eyes naturally droop, and gaze at the lower front. (Figure 4-2-2)

### 2. Movement Essentials

(1) Straighten the head and body, hollow the chest and raise the back, and breathe naturally; Throughout the process of stepping forward, the mind moves from the right to the left and then to the center of the body.

(2) The left foot circles outward from the big toe in turn making the heel reach the ground gradually.

Figure 4-2-1                Figure 4-2-2

## 2. Tai-chi Stance

### 2.1　Movement Instruction

(1) Stand with feet parallel and shoulder-width apart. Bend knees slightly and the center of gravity falls between the legs, enabling *Baihui Point*, *Huiyin point* and the midpoint between feet are on a vertical line. Relax shoulders, waist and hip. Stay relaxed and quiet. Concentrate mind without distractions and breath naturally.

(2) Slowly lift arms forward, slightly bend arms and hold them in front of the chest. Stretch fingers naturally with palm facing inward. Fingertips are opposite and 10-20 cm apart.

(3) Squat with both legs. Keep the upper body straight and gaze forward evenly. (Figure 4-2-3)

Figure 4-2-3

### 2.2　Movement Essentials

(1) Straighten the head and body, hollow the chest, raise the back, relax the waist, erect the spine, and lower the shoulders and the elbows. Arc the arms and relax the fingers, keep abdomen in and buttocks not protruding. Sink the *qi to* the *Dantian* or the navel psychic-center. The whole body should be relaxed but not loosened, solid but not stiff.

(2) The duration of practice depends on individuals. With the improvement of skills, the duration can be lengthened gradually. At the beginning, each practice can last 3-5 minutes.

## 3. Opening and Closing of Tai-chi

### 3.1　Movement Instruction

(1) The movement is the same as that of the movement 1 in Infinite Stance.

(2) Ward off arms gradually on ball holding stance. At the same time, bend the knees to squat and breathe in deeply.

(3) Make a slight pause, and slowly bring the arms back. At the same time, stand naturally on legs and exhale. (Figure 4-2-4, Figure 4-2-5)

### 3.2　Movement Essentials

(1) When warding off arms, it feels like that practitioners are holding a large balloon being inflated and the arms are expanding as the balloon is gradually inflated. Breathe in while warding off arms.

(2) When bringing arms back, it feels like the balloon is released with the arms and the arms are back together as the balloon shrinks. Exhale in the process.

(3) When practicing this opening and closing of Tai-chi, practitioners should use the following breath method. Don't hold breath and ensure the breath is smooth. With the increase of practice, the

duration of opening and closing can be lengthened and the depth of respiration can be deepened.

Figure 4-2-4　　　　　　　　　　　　Figure 4-2-5

# 4. Yin Yang Stance

## 4.1　Movement Instruction

(1) The movement is the same as that of the Movement 1 in Infinite Stance.

(2) Slowly lift arms forward to the shoulder level and ensure that the arms are shoulder-width apart with palm facing downward. Bend elbows slightly and relax shoulders.

(3) Make a slight pause, and slightly bend knees to squat. Descend arms to the front of the abdomen. Make a slight pause and stand up gradually with legs and raise up arms at the same time. Repeat in this way and the number of repetition depends on individuals. With the improvement of skills, the number of practice can increase.

(4) In terms of the ending, drop the arms slowly to the sides of the thighs, and the feet are placed together. (Figure 4-2-6, Figure 4-2-7)

Figure 4-2-6　　　　　　　　　　　　Figure 4-2-7

### 4.2   Movement Essentials

(1) Keep the upper body upright during lifting and descending. Do not bow forward or lean backward. When two palms are descending, relax the shoulders and make them forward. Bend down the elbows and it feels like pressing the wooden board in the water with both hands. When lifting, do not shrug shoulders. Push elbows with shoulders, the wrists with elbows, and palms with wrists. Push the strength forward, and form an opposite support with waist and back.

(2) After descending, the duration of the pause can be lengthened with the improvement of skills.

## 5. Empty Step Stance

### 5.1   Movement Instruction

Stand with two feet in parallel, and drop arms naturally. Turn the right foot to the right, and move the center of gravity slowly to the right foot and squat with the bending right leg. Make a half step forward with the left foot and step on the ground with the heel. Lift the tip of the foot and bend the knee slightly. At the same time, raise hands forward and upward, and hold arms in front of the body, with the left palm facing to the right downward. The fingers are at the nose level, pointing obliquely forward. The right palm is under the inner side of the left elbow and facing left downward. The fingers of right hand are pointing obliquely forward. Eyes gaze at the left hand. (Figure 4-2-8)

Practice the left style and right style alternatively. The movement direction of them are opposite.

### 5.2   Movement Essentials

(1) The center of gravity should be on the supporting leg. Keep abdomen in and buttocks not protruding. Bend the supporting leg to

Figure 4-2-8

make the body stable. Slightly bend the other leg and support the body with the heel slightly.

(2) Keep the upper body upfront. Lower the shoulders and elbows. Relax fingers and settle wrists. The strength should reach the tip of fingers. Hold the head erect with hidden energy and concentrate mind.

## 6. Fixed Posture Stance

In Tai-chi Chuan practicing, in order to master a certain movement, people can fix or repeat that movement deliberately, which is called fixed posture stance. And then people can make self-check on that movement through the eight dimensions of Tai-chi Chuan, so as to improve the basic skills of this.

For all of the above standing practice, after completing the practice, practitioners should walk around. Don't talk loudly. In this way, practitioners can improve the skills.

# 7. Walk Practicing

### 7.1 Forward Walking

Keep the body upright naturally, and put the back of both hands closely on the waist. Bend the knees of both legs and shift the center of gravity to the right leg. Lift the left heel (Figure 4-2-9) and step forward with the heel touching the ground to make an empty step (Figure 4-2-10). The center of gravity is on the right leg. Step on the whole right foot to form a bow stance with the left foot forward (Figure 4-2-11), and gaze forward evenly. Lower back the upper body slowly to a sitting stance, shifting the center of gravity back. Bend the right leg and straighten the left leg naturally into a left empty step. (Figure 4-2-12). Then, turn the upper body slightly to the left, stretch out and step on the whole left foot to shift the center of gravity to the left leg and bend the knee (Figure 4-2-13). Step forward with the right leg and bend the knee next to the left leg (Figure 4-2-14). Turn the upper body slightly to the right and step forward the right foot. (Figure 4-2-15) Repeat the above left-style and right-style movements alternatively. In closing, the rear foot steps forward to get close to the other foot and stand upright slowly.

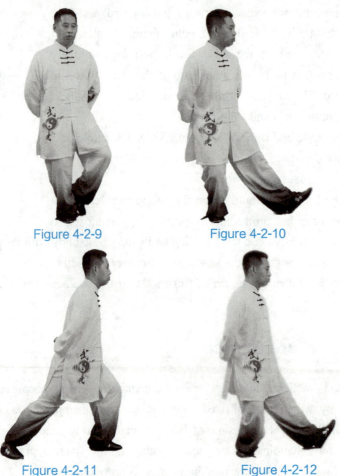

Figure 4-2-9          Figure 4-2-10

Figure 4-2-11          Figure 4-2-12

Figure 4-2-13                Figure 4-2-14

Movement essentials: Keep the upper body upright and the center of gravity steady. The shift of footwork should be coherent and stable with the right transition of the center of gravity. The eyes should gaze forward evenly and the respiration should be natural. Breathe in when making an empty step and breath out when making a bow stance and grinding step.

### 7.2   Backward Walking

Stand naturally with feet together. Pile hands on the abdomen and gaze forward evenly. (Figure 4-2-15). Shift the center of gravity to the right leg, bend knees and step back to the left with the left leg and make the sole of foot touch the ground first (Figure 4-2-16). Bend the left leg and sit back, straighten the right leg naturally, and lift toes into a right empty step. Lift the right leg and step backward and make the sole of foot touch the ground first. Shift the center of gravity backward, bend the right knee and sit back. Strengthen the left leg naturally and tilt up toes into a left empty step, and gaze forward evenly (Figure 4-2-17). Repeat the above left-style and right-style movements alternatively. Finally, the front foot steps backward to get close to the other foot. Stand upright, and put two arms on both sides of the body naturally.

Figure 4-2-15           Figure 4-2-16           Figure 4-2-17

Movement essentials: Keep the upper body upright and stable during walking. The movement should be coherent with the right transition of the center of gravity. The respiration should be natural. Breath out when sitting back and breathe in when stepping backward.

### 7.3　Side Walking

Relax the body and stand upright with feet together. Put hands at the waist. Concentrate mind, breathe naturally and gaze forward evenly (Figure 4-2-18). Bend knees to sit back, shift the center of gravity to the right leg and lift the right foot. Turn the upper body to the right, move the left foot to the left, and touch the ground with the toes. (Figure 4-2-19) Turn the upper body to the left, shift the center of gravity to the left, step on the whole left foot, bring back the right foot to about 20 cm inside the left foot, and touch the ground with the toes (Figure 4-2-20). Shift the center of gravity to the right leg, step on the whole right foot and lift the left foot. Turn the upper body to the right, step left with the left foot again, and touch the ground with the toes (Figure 4-2-21). Turn the upper body to the left, and repeat the above movement. Practitioners can practice the left style first and then the right style.

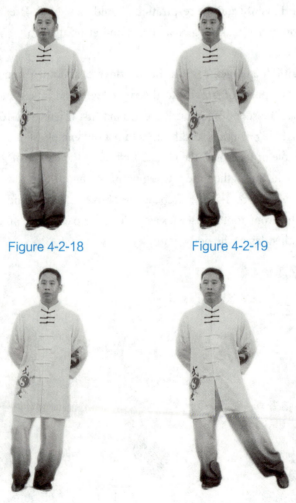

Figure 4-2-18　　　　　　　　　Figure 4-2-19

Figure 4-2-20　　　　　　　　　Figure 4-2-21

Movement essentials: keep the head and neck upright. Relax shoulders and contain chest. Keep the upper body upright, relax the waist and hip and keep balance of the center of gravity. The movement should be smooth and coherent. Practitioners should raise up and put down the foot gently on the toes or on the heel. At the beginning, practitioners can breathe naturally. Gradually, they can take a breath for each step. If the movement is relative slow, practitioners can breathe two times for each step, i.e. breathe in when turning the waist to left or right and lift the foot and breathe out when stepping forward or bringing feet together.

# 第五章  教学与训练

与他人交流的过程中，人们通常使用语言来沟通。正如你想用语言表达自己的想法一样，武术运动是演练者通过自身的肢体语言来讲述和表达其思想、观点和看法的。教学与训练就是在这一表达过程中的两个互为联系且彼此依赖的行为和过程，是先后关系，更是学会、掌握与提高的关系。

## 一、教学与教学法

在教学过程中，安排科学、合理的教学内容，划分完整有序的教学阶段，采用针对性的教学方法非常重要。接受过武术教育的人都知道，同样的拳套内容，由不同的教师来教，其结果是完全不一样的。有的教学班级的学生，在老师的带领下，精神饱满，信心满满，动力强劲，自觉练习的积极性高涨；有的教学班级的学生，其结果则完全相反，学习中既感觉内容空洞，言之无物，无知识所学，无技能可练，练之乏味，反而还觉得可以自由任性，没有什么规矩、规范，甚至认为练武随便动一动都行，也无所谓技法、技能可言，更别说可以"未曾习武先有德"和防身自卫了。毫不夸张地说，这是目前我们许多学校和社会武术教学组织，在学生上过武术课之后，对其课堂教学认知的一个现实写照。

### （一）教学概说

#### 1. 概念
教学是由教师的"教"和学生的"学"所组成的一种人类特有的人才培养活动。

#### 2. 任务
（1）向学生传授系统的科学知识，训练学生形成基本技能、技巧，发展学生的智力和能力。

（2）培养学生具有坚定正确的政治方向、辩证唯物主义的世界观和共产主义的道德品质。

（3）使学生身体正常发育，健康成长。

（4）培养学生具有正确的审美观，获得感受美、鉴赏美和创造美的知识和能力。

（5）使学生掌握现代工农业生产的基本知识，学会使用基本生产工具的技能。

#### 3. 教学阶段的划分
第一阶段：基本功和基本动作教学。

第二阶段：动作的打"点"与连"线"。

第三阶段：组合动作的学与练。

第四阶段：全套动作的学与练。

第五阶段：攻防转换的拆招及其讲解与示范。

第六阶段：推手学习阶段。

第七阶段：散手学习阶段。

### 4. 备课及其应用

运用科学的教学法，是上好一堂课的保证，而备课是教师课前的必要准备，是上好课的基础和前提，必须充分、完整且具有明确的针对性，可见备课环节至关重要。那么，如何才能备好课呢？

（1）严格遵循"教学大纲"的要求制订教学计划，备课工作必须清楚"教学链条"上的多种关系。

众所周知，写教案是每个教师课前必须完成的一项任务，但这只是一个完整的教学链条上一个很小的环节，教案要根据教学计划来撰写，教学计划又是根据教学大纲来安排的。一个完整的教学链条包括：人才培养方案（课程设置）—教学大纲—教学计划—教案。只有提前写好教案，教师才可依据教案实施课堂教学。

（2）充分了解教学对象的基本情况。撰写教案之前，还要针对性地充分了解、分析教学对象。例如，他们求学的目的、动机，现有基础，甚至包括性格、爱好、氛围等。

（3）熟知并掌握教学内容。除了掌握课堂教学的内容之外，教师还要拓展自己的知识面和技术运动的能力与类别。主要涉及体育基本知识与技能，专项运动的技理、技法与文化等。针对内容和课时情况，进一步分析其内容在教学环节中的比重、重点难点、易犯错误、攻防含义、相关知识或纠正技术错误法等。对于学生提出的难以辨析和解答的问题，即使教师自己不知道，也不能问而不答，要引导思考，开源开窍。分清楚故事、传说、小说、历史的关系，便于学生课后科学地认识和理解。

（4）领会和理解教案模板的写作要求。尽管教案所写的内容和要求是相通的，但不同的教学单位对于教案的规定是不一样的。因此教案格式及其要求是有所差别的。不过万变不离其宗，课程的结构均包括准备部分、基本部分和结束部分。教案的内容基本涵盖了教学内容、教法与要求、组织与计划、时间、强度、密度等。

（5）科学分配不同教学内容在本次课堂教学中的比重，实施针对性的组织与教法。教师要依据常规内容进行思考、组织和撰写教案。例如，包括课堂练（礼节礼仪、课堂常规、专项素质等），复习内容（基本功和基本动作、上次课及其已学内容等），新授内容等。

（6）掌握武术教学法，并要区别其一般教学法与太极拳课堂教学法。掌握一般教学法是前提，在此基础上，根据太极拳运动的内容、特点和规律，有针对性地开展教学活动（教师主体及其主动作用）。

## （二）常用的教学法及其运用

教学方法是完成教学任务的途径、手段和方式，是提高教学质量的关键。太极拳教学中常用的教学方法主要有讲解法、示范法、领做与口令、练习法等。

### 1. 讲解法

讲解的主要内容包括：动作规格、攻防含义、基本技法、关键环节和易犯错误。

讲解的主要方法如下。

（1）顺序化讲解。动作的讲解，一般先讲下肢步型、步法；接着讲上肢手型、手法；再讲上下肢配合方法；最后讲动作技法含义和攻防用法。

（2）术语化讲解。武术动作名称是按照动作结构、形象和运动方法而取名的，一般能表达动作的全貌，如"野马分鬃""左蹬脚"等。讲解时，要把动作规格和动作术语结合起来，便于学生记忆动作和正确理解动作要领。太极拳的术语，特别是传统太极拳的术语，许多在表达时有形、有意、有法，需与动作方法和用法联系起来，认真领会。

此外，还有形象化讲解、单字化讲解和口诀化讲解。

### 2. 示范法

示范在武术教学中占主导地位，太极拳教学的示范所占比重更大。太极拳示范要求动作规范、熟练，力点准确，并突出太极拳的技术风格特点。它可以使学生了解所学动作的形象、结构、要领和方法，是学生通过直观的感性认识获得对太极拳动作方法及其特点、风格的了解的整体表现。通常有完整示范法和分解示范法。

在下列情况下，可运用完整示范法。

（1）对新授教学内容的武术动作，可采用完整示范，能帮助学生建立第一印象。

（2）对结构简单和难度不大的动作可采用完整示范法。

（3）对有一定基础的学生可采用完整示范法。

在下列情况下，可运用分解示范法。

（1）动作结构和方法路线较复杂繁难，可分为上、下肢两部分或几个小节来进行示范教学。

（2）攻防因素较多的动作，可按攻防含义的顺序进行示范教学。

（3）富于顿挫的动作，可按动作结构的顺序进行示范教学。武术套路中顿挫性动作掌握的好坏，直接影响着节奏的鲜明。这类动作必须具备以下基本特征（需要分析）：① 在一个动作里含有轻重之分的特征，可按轻重对比因素划分细节进行教学；② 在一个动作里含有突然改变方向的特征，可按突然变向的部分划分出细节进行教学；③ 在一个动作里含有擒纵或拿打的特征，可按一擒一纵或一拿一打之分进行教学。

分解示范是为了使学生更好地掌握动作，因此不宜将动作分解过细，应尽快地向完整动作过渡。分解示范与完整示范应有机地结合起来运用，一般应遵循"完整—分解—再完整"的原则。

采用示范法进行教学，是为了解决学生学习中的问题，因此，也要注意示范面、示范位置和示范速度的选择与运用，便于学生能全貌、完整地看清并领会动作。

### 3. 领做与口令

在教学中，领做与口令指挥是教师示范和讲解的一种特殊形式，也是武术教学的主要手段和方法，太极拳教学中此法的运用非常普遍，它能有效地引导学生掌握动作，也便于学生统一行动。

领做是教师做动作来带领学生进行模仿练习。通过领做，使学生初步掌握套路动作的方向和路线。口令是学生已基本学会动作后，教师用来指挥学生统一练习的语言行为。正确地运用口令，能统一学生的行动，达到整齐划一的教学效果。需注意以下两点。

（1）领做位置要恰当。教师领做的位置一般应站在套路运动方向的斜前方，要与学生的运动方向一致。当动作方向发生改变时，教师的领做位置也要随着学生运动的方向而转换，同时应利用学生重做或口令提示要领的方法，使教师有时间走向所变换的位置继续领做。这样，不仅能避免学生的记忆发生混乱，而且有利于掌握套路动作。

（2）领做与口令指挥相结合。教师的领做应稍慢一点，便于学生观察与模仿，同时要用简明的语言提示与口令指挥有机结合起来。一般来说，在传授新内容时应以身领为主，口令配合，使学生模仿动作更准确；复习教材时应以口令为主，身领为辅，有利于帮助学生熟记动作。

### 4. 练习法

练习是学生在教师的指导下，通过反复实践掌握和提高武术技术技能的主要方法。教学中经常采用的有模仿练习法、重复练习法、默想练习法等。

太极拳课堂教学组织练习的形式一般有集体练习、分组练习和单人练习等，此外，还有教学比赛、预防与纠正错误法等。它们均具有各自不同的功能，需针对不同的对象，灵活运用，具体实施。

## 二、训练与训练法

### （一）训练概说

#### 1. 概念
训练是指有计划、有步骤、分阶段地通过学习和辅导，反复强化，掌握某种技能。

#### 2. 任务
（1）使受训者获得一项行为方式或技能。

（2）有计划、有步骤地通过学习和辅导掌握某种技能。

（3）有意识地使受训者发生生理反应（如建立条件反射、强健肌肉等），从而改变受训者的身体素质、专项素质和能力的活动。

#### 3. 训练时应遵循的训练原则
在太极拳运动训练的过程中，除遵循训练学的一般训练原则来实施训练外，根据太极拳的运动特点及其训练规律，以及它本身所蕴含的浓郁太极文化，特别是太极拳的呼吸、攻防转换的方法和意识，适度、规范、针对性地加以训练。训练原则如下。

（1）功贯始终、寓含技击的原则。"功贯始终"是指将太极拳基本功的训练贯穿于训练的全过程。通过基本功的练习，获取必须具备的基本技术与技能。太极拳基本手型、手法、步型、步法等是太极拳套路基础阶段的必修内容，而且也是提高受训者技术水平的一种重要手段。"寓含技击"是指在演练过程中，将技击意识寓含于太极拳的技法练习之中，用意识引导动作，并将动作攻防含义的理解贯注于动作的过程之中，以表现太极拳特有的韵味，使动作显得充实饱满。

（2）动静结合、内外互导的原则。太极拳刚柔相济，要有一定的掤劲。在苦练套路的同时，还要练习实战，即对打，强化受训者的反应速度，使反应更加灵活。通过实战训练环节，不断积累实战经验。也通过亲自体验，加深对动与静、内与外的直接感受，为提高训练水平打下坚实的基础。

（3）用心领悟、突出风格的原则。"用心领悟"是指开动思维，用心揣摩动作的精微，细心体验动作的感受，追求动作诀窍的豁然悟通，从而展示出太极拳套路动作的刚柔相济、内外合一、形神兼备的整体性。我们经常看到，练习者演练的是同一个太极拳套路，但其风格却有明显区别。不同的风格则表现不同练习者对太极拳的理解与认识的差异，因此，在训练过程中要着重强调用心领悟，突出拳种特点和风格。

（4）持之以恒、重复渐进的原则。太极拳运动技术水平的长进，是一种技术与功力的缓慢渗透过程，需要日积月累，不断修正，长期练习。所以，它不仅需要练习者一定身体素质的支持，还需要用一定的思维来领悟。它需要时间的磨炼，并通过汗水来积累，方法只是其提高的催化剂，但方法是不能代替的积累，在时间没有积累到一定量时，单一鼓噪的训练方法所起的作用是有限的。

"重复渐进"是指对太极拳教学内容要不断地重复训练，在不断地重复训练中体验内化技艺，循序渐进地提高技术水平，熟能生巧。只有在不断地重复练习中，渐进地领悟太极拳的内在神韵，才能巩固提高技艺，形成正确的动力定型，从而使技术精益求精。

## （二）综合训练法及其运用

在太极拳的传承与发展过程中，有其传统的训练方法，且根据对象的不同，所实施的针对性训练方法也有很大差别，但这些零散的具有个体差异的特殊方法，只有上升到一定的理论层面，归纳总结出其富有共性和规律性的原则、方法，才具有推广和应用价值。

太极拳完全遵循一般武术运动训练过程中常采用的运动训练方法，具体操作方法包括重复训练法、变换训练法、间歇训练法、循环训练法等。除此之外，依据太极拳的结构和运动特点，又有适合于自身运动特点的训练方法，如打点训练法、连线训练法等。它们是对太极拳一般训练方法的具体补充，也是在太极拳的教学和训练过程中，可以互换、互通的切实可行的方法。

### 1. 打"点"

为使动作过程进一步清晰、规范地展示，常将一个完整的太极拳动作分割成几个线段，用短时停顿来加以练习。例如，"野马分鬃"由三个点组成，即收脚抱球、迈步合手、弓步分手。

### 2. 连"线"

经过打"点"环节后，将每一个线段按照动作过程的先后连接起来，连贯完成动作，完整呈现动作过程。

### 3. 默念

默念主要就是想象动作要领、动作形态、动作意识、动作攻防含义、动作方向和路线等。在运用中，我们可以经常想象优秀太极拳运动员的动作意识、形态、节奏、用力，把这种好的感觉，经过自己本体感觉的转换来加强，这样有利于练习者水平的提高。练好太极拳不是单凭肢体的运动多流汗、多花时间、只凭力气就能学有所成的，必须用思想、意识来引导和支配动作，头脑清晰、思维敏捷地反复训练，才能有所成就。为了提升思维训练的有效性，教师或师傅们都曾反复告诫，不是只在训练场上才叫训练，"拳不离手，曲不离口"，平时自己没在训练场上的时候，只要有机会就要想动作，理解具体动作的含义，将身体运动的过程，通过有意识的引导回放，在大脑中再现，反复强化大脑刺激，加强其记忆的痕迹。这种方法用于比赛前可控制赛前情绪，放松紧张状态，充满自信地走向赛场。例如，比赛前，默念一遍套路，想象动作要领和注意事项，这样更有利于运动员水平的发挥；睡觉前，也可以想象当天练习的套路，整体回忆一遍。

总的来说，太极拳训练应遵循太极拳技艺、技理、技能的形成、巩固与提高的规律；注重基础素质、基本内容和核心技法训练；处理好训练量与训练强度之间的关系。

# Chapter 5  Teaching and Training

Language is the medium for interpersonal communication. To be understood, we need to express the thoughts through language. Likewise, martial art is the body language practitioners use to express their thoughts, points of views and perspectives with intended body movements. In martial art, teaching and training are behaviors and processes which are sequential, mutually beneficial and enhancing. They are interconnected and interdependent when the intended body expression is unfolded in martial art.

## I. Teaching and Pedagogy

Teaching should cover all essential subjects, whose content should be curated by the phase based on the learning curve and be delivered scientifically and orderly. It's pivotal that targeted and appropriate pedagogy should be employed. Those who have received martial art education know, that learning outcomes truly vary when the same pugilism routine is taught by different teachers. In some classes, students are energetic, confident and assertive. Being fully motivated, they practice the taught techniques strenuously with strong self-discipline; while in some others, students study it without purpose, finding classes superficial and boring filled with aimless exercise. They are hence misled to assume that they can perform martial art at whim, not needing to follow rules. They even think that there are neither skills nor techniques to acquire, let alone "learning ethics before martial art" and self-defense tactics. The harsh fact is, many martial art schools or private institutes nowadays are inflicted with such downfalls.

### (I) Teaching overview

#### 1. Definition
Teaching is a human-specific activity of cultivating talents, where teachers instruct and students learn.

#### 2. Tasks
(1) Knowledge is imparted systematically to students, to train students to acquire intended skills, techniques, and to develop their intelligence and abilities.

(2) To cultivate students to form correct and firm political stances, view of world with dialectical materialism, and ethics embracing communism.

(3) To empower students to grow up healthily.

(4) To cultivate students' correct values of aesthetics, knowledge and ability of perceiving, appreciating and creating beauty.

(5) To enable students to harness fundamental knowledge of agriculture and production, learning to use basic production tools.

### 3. Teaching planning by the phase

Phase one: fundamental skills and basic movements

Phase two: "points" and "lines" of movements

Phase three: study and practice of combo movements

Phase four: study and practice of the whole routine

Phase five: break-down analysis and demonstration of transition offence and defense

Phase six: pushing hands learning

Phase seven: free fighting learning

### 4. Teaching planning and application

Employing pedagogy scientifically lays the foundation for class success. Teaching planning is an imperative step of preparation. The planning is vital and it should be complete, substantial with clear objectives. So, how shall we do a good teaching planning?

(1) Strictly follow the requirements of the syllabus, set up teaching plan, clearly identify the relations contained in "the chain of teaching".

It's a must for teachers to write up teaching plans before class. People often take for granted though, that actually teaching planning is only a small spart of a complete chain of teaching of a course. The teaching plan needs to be created based on the teaching schedule which is decided based on the syllabus. A complete chain of teaching should include the teaching protocol (course design), the syllabus, the teaching schedule, and the teaching plan. Preparing teaching plans in advance provide guidelines and reference to teachers to conduct teaching accordingly in class.

(2) Thoroughly understand students' conditions

Before writing up teaching plans, teachers should strive to understand students learning conditions including their learning motives, goals, current levels, and even their personalities, hobbies and learning styles.

(3) A good grasp of teaching content

Aside of the teaching content to be delivered in class, teachers should expand their knowledge domain, strengthening their overall ability in martial art and other related disciplines. They should incessantly broaden their knowledge in fundamentals and skills of sports, techniques, expertise and the culture of specialized exercise. Teachers shall further analyze the proportion of teaching content in class, key points, difficulties, common mistakes, meaning of offence and defense, related knowledge, and methods of correcting technical errors. On questions that teachers find difficult or challenging to answer, teachers should help students explore and seek solutions. Teachers shall present the related stories, legends, novels and history logically, so that students can deepen their understanding of the subject after school.

(4) Understand the writing requirements of teaching plan templates (formality requirements)

Though teachers may share similar or even the same teaching content under a same topic, different institutes have different requirements on teaching plans and the formality. The principles however, are similar. And the class structure is almost identical, including the introductory, the fundamental and the ending. The teaching plan should cover the teaching content, the adopted pedagogy, learning goals, organization and planning, time length, class intensity and knowledge density.

(5) Optimize the proportion of teaching points at the class, organizing the class and using appropriate pedagogies accordingly.

Design, organize and write teaching plans based on standard teaching points. That includes exercises in class (etiquette, courtesy, standard exercise in class, conditioning and strength etc.), content review (basic skills and basic movements, the learned content from the previous class), and the newly taught.

(6) Master martial art pedagogies, differentiating general pedagogies and specific pedagogies for Tai-chi Chuan.

Harnessing general pedagogies is the prerequisite, based on which Tai-chi Chuan classes should be developed and led by teachers by taking into account of Tai-chi Chuan's substance, characteristics and patterns.

### (II) Common pedagogies and application

Pedagogy is the means to achieve teaching tasks, a key to improving teaching quality. Common Tai-chi Chuan pedagogies include verbal instruction, demonstration, leading and commands, and practice.

#### 1. Verbal instruction

Key points: movement forms, purpose of offence and defense, basic techniques, key steps and common mistakes.

Mainly two kinds of verbal instruction.

(1) Sequential instruction

The instruction of movements usually starts from foot forms and footwork, then hand forms and hand movements, then combination of the upper and lower body; lastly meaning of movements and techniques, application of offence and defense tactics.

(2) Terminology explanation

Martial art terminology is named after the movement structures, images and movement methods. Generally, the martial art movement terms describe overall movement features, such as Partition of Wild Horse's Mane, and Kick With Left Heel. When explaining, teachers shall combine movement forms and terminology together to help students memorize movements and understand the keys. Tai-chi Chuan's terminology, especially traditional ones, contain the connotation of ideogram, ideology and corresponding methods. They shall be perceived by linking movement methods and practicing principles together.

Furthermore, visualized explanation of terms, detailed explanation of key words, and songs that underscore principles would strengthen the teaching effect.

## 2. Demonstration

Demonstration is a pivotal way to martial art teaching. In Tai-chi Chuan teaching, demonstration takes even a bigger part than others. Tai-chi Chuan demonstration demands correct movements, precise points of force, and the emphasis on Tai-chi Chuan's unique style. Through demonstration, it helps students understand ideograms, structures, key points and methods of the taught movements in a straight-forward manner. Complete demonstrations are often presented in class.

Complete demonstration is employed in the following situations

(1) For the teaching of new martial art movements, complete demonstrations can be employed to help students establish their general understanding of the movements.

(2) For the teaching of simple-structure and non-challenging movements, a complete demonstration can be employed.

(3) Complete demonstrations can be used to teach students with a certain foundation.

In the following scenarios, break-down demonstrations can be employed.

(1) For movements with complex structures and methods, the demonstration can be divided into the upper body and lower body parts, or into several small sessions.

(2) For movements with intensive offence and defense elements, the demonstration can be conducted following the sequence of offence and defense.

(3) For movements with pauses, teachers can conduct demonstrations following the sequence of movement structure. Whether the pause in Tai-chi Chuan is handled well affects the overall rhythm of the whole routine. Such movements possess the following common features (that need to be analyzed):

① For a movement that contains heaviness and lightness, it can be taught by dividing it into heavy parts and light parts.

② For a movement that requires sudden direction-changing, the direction-changing part can be singled out as a focused session for teaching.

③ For a movement that has "catch and release" or "catch and hit" features, each set of "catch and release" and "catch and hit" should be distinguished and be taught.

Break-down demonstration is used to help students better master movements. Movements should be broken down into chunks instead of tiny fragments, so that students can proceed to learn the complete movement soonest possible. Break-down demonstration and complete demonstration should both be used in class, following the principle of "complete, break-down, complete".

Using demonstration to teach is about solving problems students encounter during their study.

### 3. Leading and commands

In teaching, leading and making commands are a special form of demonstration and explanation. It's also a major means in martial art teaching, commonly used in Tai-chi Chuan teaching, which can effectively guide students to master movements.

Leading is a method of teachers doing movements while students follow. By leading, students can master the directions and trajectories of routines. Commands are the language teachers use to guide students to practice after students have basically learned the movements. Using commands correctly can synchronize students' actions in class. Two points to be paid attention to as follows.

(1) Picking the right location for leading

The leading location of the teacher should be in diagonally front of the routine movement trajectory, aligned with students' movement trajectory. When the movement direction is changed, teacher's leading location should be changed accordingly along with the students. Meanwhile the teacher should adjust his/her location of movement during the break when students are repeating the practice or the teacher is making commands and reminders of practice. In this way, it avoids students from messing up their movement memorization and helps students harness routines.

(2) Combining leading and commands.

Teachers should slow down the pace when leading, allowing students to observe and emulate sufficiently. Concise reminders and commands should be used in class. Generally, when teaching new, teachers should lead students with movements complimented with verbal commands, to sharpen students' movement emulation. When reviewing, teachers should mainly make commands complimented with movement leading, serving to help students memorize movements.

### 4. Practice methods

Practice is a method of students repeatedly exercising the taught martial art techniques under teacher's guidance, so as to hone the skills. Common practice methods include emulation practice, repetition practice and ruminating practice.

In Tai-chi Chuan classes, practice form mainly includes group practice, team practice and individual practice. Additionally, contests, error prevention and correction observation are also adopted. They play a different role in class teaching for different groups of students. In implementation, they should be used flexibly to suit students' needs.

## II. Training and Training Methods

### (I) Training overview

#### 1. Definition

Training is the process of studying and practicing repeatedly to master a certain skill.

## 2. Tasks

(1) To enable trainees to acquire a specific behavior or skill.

(2) To study and practice to master a certain skill in a planned and organized manner.

(3) To intend to trigger trainees' physiological reactions (such as flex reactions and muscle strengthening), so as to change trainees' physiques, conditioning and strength.

## 3. Training principles

During Tai-chi Chuan training, aside of general training principles, additional Tai-chi Chuan-specific principles should be set up given the characteristics, training patterns and its cultural background of Tai-chi Chuan. In particular, targeted training should be rendered to breathing of Tai-chi Chuan, methods and awareness of transition offence and defense, moderation of force and code of conduct. Training principles are as follow:

(1) Be solid with fundamental skills, using intent of offence and defense in the routine.

"Being solid with fundamental skills" is about conducting Tai-chi Chuan fundamental skills training throughout the whole process. With practice on fundamental skills, trainees get to acquire basic skills and capabilities. The basic hand movements and hand forms, footwork and foot forms are the basic in Tai-chi Chuan routines learning. They are also foundation to strengthening trainees' techniques. "Using intent of offence and defense in the routine" refers to the intent that should be put in practicing Tai-chi Chuan to guide movements. Practitioners should reveal their understanding on offence and defense in their movements, to bring out the unique essence of Tai-chi Chuan, making their movements solid and rich.

(2) Combine activity and inactivity, connecting the inside and the outside

In Tai-chi Chuan, firmness and softness supplement to each other, supported by sufficient amount of ward-off force. While strenuously practicing Tai-chi Chua routines, practitioners should also practice combat to strengthen practitioners' responsiveness and agility. By practicing combat in training, practitioners can not only accumulate combat experience but also deepen their understanding on activity vs. inactivity, the inside vs. the outside, so as to be well-prepared to move up to the next level.

(3) Think deep and establish style

It's often noted that practitioners show marked difference in styles when playing the same Tai-chi Chuan routine. Different styles express divergent understanding and perception of Tai-chi Chuan. Therefore, practitioners should be encouraged to think deep and establish their own style of Tai-chi Chuan playing during their training.

(4) Repeat, be consistent to progress

Tai-chi Chuan practitioners progress in a slow and consistent way with advances in their technique and expertise thanks to their dedicated efforts day in and day out. Therefore, it not only requires practitioners to have the required physique, but also a clear mindset to perceive Tai-chi Chuan. It takes time to learn and takes sweat to accumulate experience. Methods are just a catalyst for improvement and they cannot replace practitioners' consistent practice. Without consistent practice of a certain scale, the training method only plays a limited role in Tai-chi

Chuan learning.

"Repeat, be consistent to progress" means practitioners should repetitively practice and internalize the taught knowledge of Tai-chi Chuan, so as to advance their techniques by constantly honing skills. Only through repetitive practice can one progressively capture the essence of Tai-chi Chuan, fortify their skills, establish proper dynamic stereotypes, so that their techniques and expertise will see continuous progress.

## (II) Comprehensive training methods and application

In the inheritance and development of Tai-chi Chuan, traditional training methods are preserved and adopted to teach different groups of students. They're sporadic and different in their own way. Hence they need to be elevated to a theoretical level to seek commonality and principles for widespread application.

Tai-chi Chuan completely follows athletic training methods commonly used in martial art training, including repetition, switch training, interval training and cyclical training. Beyond that, pointing and line connecting are also employed as supplementary training to Tai-chi Chuan, given its pugilism structure and movement characteristics. In Tai-chi Chuan teaching, all such above training methods are practical ones that can be switched, connected and complemented to each other.

### 1. Pointing

To make the movement process clearly and precisely presented and explained. A complete Tai-chi Chuan movement can be broken down into several segments for practice with pauses. For instance, Partition of Wild Horse's Mane comprises three points, which are "stretch arms like carrying a ball", "step forward and hold hands" and "take a bow stance and split hands".

### 2. Line connecting

After the step of pointing, every line segment of the movement should be linked up to present the whole movement.

### 3. Ruminating

Ruminating is mainly about picturing the key points of movement, the form of movement, the intent of movement, the connotation of offence and defense, and the movement's direction and trajectory. In application, we can also imagine how top Tai-chi Chuan player think and act on movement intent, form, pace and force exertion. It's a great beneficial training to help practitioners improve significantly by benchmarking the good standard against themselves. To practice Tai-chi Chuan well, physical practice with sweat, time and luck would not be enough to make one succeed. It's the thinking and intent that guide and govern movements that would make one a successful Tai-chi Chuan player, who should possess a clear and agile mind with repetitive and consistent practice. To elevate one's thinking, teachers or coaches often reiterate the importance of consistent practice on and off the field, like "breathing in and breathing out pugilism". While off the field, one should keep practicing movements whenever there's a chance, striving to perceive meaning of movements, replaying movements in mind to strengthen the impression and memory of such. This method can help practitioners control their emotion before contests, calming their nerves and feeling confident to compete. For instance, one can ruminate the whole routine before his competition, picturing the key points and details of movements. It would much help contestants bring up their game. Before sleep, contestants can also picture the whole routine, establishing a thorough review of the routine he/she plays.

Generally speaking, Tai-chi Chuan training should follow the nature of Tai-chi Chuan technique evolution involving formation, consolidation and improvement. Much attention should be paid to elementary ability training, fundamental training and core techniques training. And the training volume and intensity should be well balanced.

# 第六章　简化太极拳

## 第一节　简化太极拳简介

### 一、简化太极拳创编简介

"简化太极拳"是按照由简到繁、由易到难的原则，是对已在群众中流行的太极拳进行改编、整理而成的。它改变了过去先难后易的锻炼顺序，去掉了原有套路中过多的重复姿势动作，集中了原套路的主要结构和技术内容，便于群众掌握，易学易懂。这套拳共分八个组，包括"起势""收势"共二十四个姿势动作。练习者可连贯演练，也可以选择单式或分组练习。

### 二、简化太极拳动作名称及顺序

第一组：起势、左右野马分鬃、白鹤亮翅；
第二组：左右搂膝拗步、手挥琵琶、左右倒卷肱；
第三组：左揽雀尾、右揽雀尾；
第四组：单鞭、云手、单鞭；
第五组：高探马、右蹬脚、双峰贯耳、转身左蹬脚；
第六组：左下势独立、右下势独立；
第七组：左右穿梭、海底针、闪通臂；
第八组：转身搬拦锤、如封似闭、十字手、收势。

### 三、图解说明

在文字说明中，凡有"同时"两字的，不论先写或后写身体的某一部分动作，都要求一齐活动，不要分先后去做。动作的方向是以人体的前、后、左、右为依据的，不论怎样转变，总是以面对的方向为前，背向的方向为后，身体左侧为左，身体右侧为右。假设面向南方起势，对一些完成式面向方向斜度较大的姿势，特别说明了方向。

# 第二节 简化太极拳动作图解

### 1. 起势

（1）动作名称释意。起势是指在整个套路运动中说明套路的开始。

（2）动作过程。

预备势：身体自然直立，两脚并拢；两臂自然下垂，两手放在大腿外侧；眼向前平看（图6-2-1）。

起势：① 身体自然直立，两脚开立，与肩同宽，脚尖向前；两臂自然下垂，两手放在大腿外侧；眼向前平看（图6-2-2）。② 两臂慢慢向前平举，两手高与肩平，与肩同宽，手心向下（图6-2-3）。③ 上体保持正直，两腿屈膝下蹲；同时两掌轻轻下按，两肘下垂与膝相对；眼平看前方（图6-2-4）。

图 6-2-1 　　　　 图 6-2-2 　　　　 图 6-2-3 　　　　 图 6-2-4

（3）动作要点。

① 头颈正直，下颌微向后收，不要故意挺胸或收腹。精神要集中（起势由立正姿势开始，然后左脚向左分开，成开立步）。② 两肩下沉，两肘松垂，手指自然微屈。屈膝松腰，臀部不可凸出，身体重心落于两腿中间。两臂下落和身体下蹲的动作要协调一致。

（4）功法与健身机理。

升降桩功法。动作多采用两掌升降，以利于调息沉气。通过起手吸气和落手呼气，调整呼吸，做到气沉丹田，平心静气，从而进一步为练习套路做准备。实际练习中，往往在起势和收势时采用两手升降调整呼吸（图6-2-5）。

### 2. 左右野马分鬃

（1）动作名称释意。左右野马分鬃是指运动中身体舒展，两手左右，一上一下，交替划弧，似骏马奔腾而头鬃分张，披落两旁，故名野马分鬃。

（2）动作过程。

① 上体微向右转，身体重心移至右腿上；同时右臂收在胸前平屈，手心向下，左手经

体前向右下划弧放在右手下，手心向上，两手心相对成抱球状，左脚随即收到右脚内侧，脚尖点地；眼看右手（图6-2-6）。② 上体微向左转，左脚向左前方迈出，右脚跟后蹬，右腿自然伸直，成左弓步；同时上体继续向左转，左右手随转体慢慢分别向左上右下分开，左手高与眼平（手心斜向上），肘微屈，右手落在右胯旁，肘也微屈，手心向下，指尖向前；眼看左手（图6-2-7、图6-2-8）。③ 上体慢慢后坐，身体重心移至右腿，左脚尖翘起，微向外撇（大约45°），随后脚掌慢慢踏实，左腿慢慢前弓，身体左转，身体重心再移至左腿；同时左手翻转向下，左臂收在胸前平屈，右手向左上划弧放在左手下，两手心相对成抱球状；右脚随即收到左脚内侧，脚尖点地，眼看左手（图6-2-9～图6-2-11）。④ 右腿向右前方迈出，左腿自然伸直，成右弓步；同时上体右转，左右手随转体分别慢慢向左下右上分开，右手高与眼平（手心斜向上），肘微屈；左手落在左胯旁，肘也微屈，手心向下，指尖向前；眼看右手（图6-2-12、图6-2-13）。⑤与③相同，只是左右相反（图6-2-14～图6-2-16）。⑥与④相同，只是左右相反（图6-2-17、图6-2-18）。

图 6-2-5　　　　　图 6-2-6

图 6-2-7　　　　　图 6-2-8

图 6-2-9 图 6-2-10 图 6-2-11

图 6-2-12 图 6-2-13

图 6-2-14 图 6-2-15 图 6-2-16

图 6-2-17                      图 6-2-18

（3）动作要点。上体不可前俯后仰，胸部必须宽松舒展。两臂分开时要保持弧形。身体转动时要以腰为轴。弓步动作与分手的速度要均匀一致。做弓步时，迈出的脚先是脚跟着地，然后脚掌慢慢踏实，脚尖向前，膝盖不要超过脚尖，后腿自然伸直；前后脚夹角成 45°～60°（需要时后脚脚跟可以后蹬调整）。野马分鬃的弓步，前后脚的脚跟要分在中轴线两侧，它们之间的横向距离（即以动作行进的中线为纵轴，其两侧的垂直距离为横向）应该保持在 10～30 厘米。

（4）功法与健身机理。主要锻炼功法：行步—前进步功法。

此动主练颈、臂、胸、腰、胯、腿部位，可治肾病等。

### 3. 白鹤亮翅

（1）动作名称释意。运动过程中两臂左右、上下对称分展，身脊中直形如鸟翼，状如白鹤亮翅而得名，又因两臂升降旋转之势，还有说取单展双亮之意。

（2）动作过程。

① 身体重心前移，右脚跟进半步，上体微向左转；左手翻掌向下，左臂平屈胸前，右手向左上划弧，手心转向上，与左手成抱球状；眼看左手（图 6-2-19）。② 上体后坐，身体重心移至右腿，上体先向右转，面向右前方，眼看右手，然后左脚稍向前移，脚尖点地，成左虚步；同时上体再微向左转，面向前方，两手随转体慢慢向右上左下分开，右手上提停于右额前，手心向左后方，左手落于左胯前，手心向下，指尖向前；眼平看前方（图 6-2-20）。

（3）动作要点。完成姿势胸部不要挺出，两臂上下都要保持半圆形，左膝要微屈。身体重心后移和右平上提、左手下按要协调一致。

（4）功法与健身机理。主要锻炼功法为虚步桩。此势运动胸、背、肩、臂、腰、各部而练习周身纵向伸缩之力。

### 4. 左右搂膝拗步

（1）动作名称释意。做动作时将一手搂膝，另一手前推（异侧手脚在前为拗步），根据攻防含义，称为搂膝拗步。其中武术基本功包括：顺弓步和拗弓步。

图 6-2-19　　　　　　　图 6-2-20

（2）动作过程。

① 右手从体前下落，由下向后上方划弧至右肩外侧，肘微屈，手与耳同高，手心斜向上；左手由左下向上，向右下方划弧至右胸前，手心斜向下；同时上体先微向左再向右转，左脚收至右脚内侧，脚尖点地；眼看右手（图 6-2-21～图 6-2-23）。② 上体左转，左脚向前（偏左）迈出成左弓步：同时右手屈回由耳侧向前推出，高与鼻尖平，左手向下由左膝前搂过落于左胯旁，指尖向前；眼看右手手指（图 6-2-24、图 6-2-25）。③ 右腿慢慢屈膝，上体后坐，身体重心移至右腿，左脚尖翘起微向外撇，随后脚掌慢慢踏实，左腿前弓，身体左转，身体重心移至左腿，右脚收到左脚内侧，脚尖点地：同时左手向外翻掌由左后向上划弧至左肩外侧，肘微屈，手与耳同高，手心斜向上；右手随转体向上、向左下划弧落于左胸前，手心斜向下；眼看左手（图 6-2-26～图 6-2-28）。④与②相同，只是左右相反（图 6-2-29、图 6-2-30）。⑤与③相同，只是左右相反（图 6-2-31～图 6-2-33）。⑥与②相同（图 6-2-34、图 6-2-35）。

图 6-2-21　　　　　　　图 6-2-22　　　　　　　图 6-2-23

图 6-2-24

图 6-2-25

图 6-2-26

图 6-2-27

图 6-2-28

图 6-2-29

图 6-2-30

图 6-2-31              图 6-2-32              图 6-2-33

图 6-2-34              图 6-2-35

动作要点：前手推出时，身体不可前俯后仰，要松腰松胯。推掌时要沉肩垂肘、坐腕舒掌，同时须与松腰、弓腿上下协调一致。搂膝拗步成弓步时，两脚跟的横向距离保持 30 厘米左右。

（3）功法与健身机理。主要锻炼功法：行功-前进步。此势能运动腰、脊、肩、臂、膝、腿各部，特别突出转腰、迈步，对肾足健康有功效。

### 5. 手挥琵琶

（1）动作名称释意。运动中两手一前一后，前后摆动滚转，犹如怀抱琵琶，后面护"中节"的一手（保护肘关节的手），好似弹拨琴弦，故取此为名。

（2）动作过程。右脚跟进半步，上体后坐，身体重心转至右腿上；上体微向右转，左脚略提起稍向前移，成左虚步，脚跟着地，脚尖翘起，膝部微屈；同时左手由左下向上挑举，高与鼻尖平，掌心向右，臂微屈，右手收回放在左臂肘部里侧，掌心向左；眼看左手食指（图 6-2-36、图 6-2-37）。

图 6-2-36                                    图 6-2-37

（3）动作要点。身体要平稳自然，沉肩垂肘，胸部放松。左手上起时不要直向上挑，要由左向上、向前，微带弧形。右脚跟进时，脚掌先着地，再全脚踏实。身体重心后移和左手上起、右手回收要协调一致。

（4）功法与健身机理。主要锻炼功法为虚步桩。本势主练两臂及腰部。

### 6. 左右倒卷肱

（1）动作名称释意。"倒卷肱"，因肱骨回卷屈臂而名。又名倒撵猴：撵，有赶走，驱逐含义，猴子轻灵活跃，性喜扑人，以手引之，待猴前扑时，退步抽手，用另一手推按其头。根据此意，拳中将敌比喻为猴，加之退步挥手如驱赶追击之猴而名为倒撵猴。

（2）动作过程。

① 上体右转，右手翻掌（手心向上）经腹前由下向后上方划弧平举，臂微屈，左手随即翻掌向上；眼的视线随着向右转体先向右看、再转向前方看左手（图 6-2-38、图 6-2-39）。

图 6-2-38                                    图 6-2-39

② 右臂屈肘折向前，右手由耳向侧前推出，手心向前，左臂屈肘后撤，手心向上，撤至左肋外侧；同时左腿轻轻提起向后（偏左）退一步，脚掌先着地，然后全脚慢慢踏实，身体重心移到左腿上，成右虚步，右脚随转体以脚掌为轴扭正；眼看右手（图 6-2-40、图 6-2-41）。
③ 上体微向左转，同时左手随转体向后上方划弧平举，手心向上，右手随即翻掌，掌心向上；眼随转体先向左看，再转向前方看右手（图 6-2-42）。④与②相同，只是左右相反（图 6-2-43、图 6-2-44）。⑤与③相同，只是左右相反（图 6-2-45）。⑥与②相同（图 6-2-46、图 6-2-47）。⑦与③相同（图 6-2-48）。⑧与②相同，只是左右相反（图 6-2-49、图 6-2-50）。

图 6-2-40　　　　　　　　　　　　图 6-2-41

图 6-2-42　　　　　　　图 6-2-43　　　　　　　图 6-2-44

图 6-2-45          图 6-2-46          图 6-2-47

图 6-2-48          图 6-2-49          图 6-2-50

（3）动作要点。前推的手不要伸直，后撤手也不可直向回抽，随转体仍走弧线。前推时，要转腰松胯，两手的速度要一致，避免僵硬。退步时，脚掌先着地，再慢慢全脚踏实，同时，前脚随转体以脚掌为轴扭正。退左脚略向左后斜，退右脚略向右后斜，避免使两脚落在一条直线上。后退时，眼神随转体动作先向左右看，然后再转看前手。最后退右脚时，脚尖外撇的角度略大些，便于接做"左揽雀尾"的动作。

（4）功法与健身机理。

主要锻炼功法：行功—后退步。此动主要锻炼腰、脊、肩、背、膝、足各部位，有助于肾脏和足部的健康。

### 7. 左揽雀尾

（1）动作名称释意

太极拳中将敌人手臂比做雀的头尾，用双手持取雀头雀尾，并随其旋转上下，有如持玩雀尾而称此名。另一说，模拟古代人在与人交战前，首先把长袍的下摆扎入衣带以便利做战，故又称懒扎。

（2）动作过程。

① 上体微向右转，同时右手随转体向后上方划弧平举，手心向上，左手放松，手心向下，眼看左手（图6-2-51）。② 身体继续向右转，左手自然下落逐渐翻掌经腹前划弧至右肋前，手心向上，右臂屈肘，手心转向下，收至右胸前，两手相对成抱球状；同时身体重心落在右腿上，左脚收到右脚内侧，脚尖点地，眼看右手（图6-2-52、图6-2-53）。③ 上体微向左转，左脚向左前方迈出，上体继续向左转，右腿自然蹬直，左腿屈膝，成左弓步；同时左臂向左前方掤出（即左臂平屈成弓形，用前臂外侧和手背向前方推出），高与肩平，手心向后，右手向右下落放于右胯旁，手心向下，指尖向前；眼看左前臂（图6-2-54、图6-2-55）。

图 6-2-51　　　　　　　　　图 6-2-52　　　　　　　　　图 6-2-53

图 6-2-54　　　　　　　　　图 6-2-55

④ 身体微向左转，左手随即前伸翻掌向下，右手翻掌向上，经腹前向上、向前伸至左前

臂下方；然后两手下捋，即上体向右转，两手经腹前向右后上方划弧，直至右手手心向上，高与肩齐，左臂平屈于胸前，手心向后，同时身体重心移至右腿；眼看右手（图 6-2-56、图 6-2-57）。

图 6-2-56　　　　　　　　　　　　图 6-2-57

⑤　上体微向左转，右臂屈肘折回，右手附于左手腕里侧（相距约 5 厘米），上体继续向左转，双手同时向前慢慢挤出，左手心向后，右手心向前，左前臂要保持半圆；同时身体重心逐渐前移变成左弓步，眼看左手腕部（图 6-2-58、图 6-2-59）。

图 6-2-58　　　　　　　　　　　　图 6-2-59

⑥　左手翻掌，手心向下，右手经左腕上方向前、向右伸出，高与左手齐，手心向下，两手左右分开，宽与肩同，然后右腿屈膝，上体慢慢后坐，身体重心移至右腿上，左脚尖翘起，同时两手屈肘回收至腹前，手心均向前下方；眼向前平看（图 6-2-60～图 6-2-62）。
⑦　上式不停，身体重心慢慢前移，同时两手向前，向上按出，掌心向前，左腿前弓成左弓

步，眼平看前方（图 6-2-63）。

图 6-2-60　　　　　　　图 6-2-61　　　　　　　图 6-2-62

（3）动作要点。掤出时，两臂前后均保持弧形。分手、松腰、弓腿三者必须协调一致。揽雀尾弓步时，两脚跟横向距离不超过 10 厘米。

下捋时，上体不可前倾，臀部不要凸出。两臂下捋须随腰旋转，仍走弧线。左脚全掌着地。

向前挤时，上体要正直。挤的动作要与松腰、弓腿相一致。

向前按时，两手须走曲线，手腕部高与肩平，两肘微屈。

（4）功法与健身机理。主要锻炼功法：开合桩。

包含了与人接手、掤架、捋化、挤进、按发的劲法变化过程，这一点说明了太极拳重视四种基本劲法的思想，突出本动重要性。

图 6-2-63

### 8. 右揽雀尾

（1）动作名称释意。

与"左揽雀尾"相同。

（2）动作过程。

① 上体后坐并向右转，身体重心移至右腿，左脚尖里扣，右手向右平行划弧至右侧，然后由右下经腹前向左上划弧至左肋前，手心向上，左臂平屈胸前，左手掌向下与右手成抱球状；同时身体重心再移至左腿上，右脚收至左脚内侧，脚尖点地；眼看左手（图 6-2-64～图 6-2-67）。② 同"左揽雀尾"③ 解，只是左右相反（图 6-2-68、图 6-2-69）。③ 同"左揽雀尾"④ 解，只是左右相反（图 6-2-70、图 6-2-71）。④ 同"左揽雀尾"⑤ 解，只是左右相反（图 6-2-72、图 6-2-73）。⑤ 同"左揽雀尾"⑥ 解，只是左右相反（图 6-2-74～图 6-2-76）。⑥ 同"左揽雀尾"⑦ 解，只是左右相反（图 6-2-77）。

图 6-2-64

图 6-2-65

图 6-2-66

图 6-2-67

图 6-2-68

图 6-2-69

图 6-2-70

图 6-2-71

图 6-2-72

图 6-2-73

图 6-2-74

图 6-2-75

图 6-2-76　　　　　　　　　　图 6-2-77

（3）动作要点。均与"左揽雀尾"相同，只是左右相反。

（4）功法与健身机理。均与"左揽雀尾"相同。

### 9. 单鞭

（1）动作名称释意。太极拳中将人的手臂击人称为鞭，一手吊勾，一手拂面或由胸前挥出，外形上颇似跨马扬鞭而得名。

（2）动作过程。

① 上体后坐，身体重心逐渐移至左腿上，右脚尖里扣；同时上体左转，两手（左高右低）向左弧形运转，直至左臂平举，伸于身体左侧，手心向左，右手经腹前运至左肋前，手心向后上方；眼看左手（图6-2-78、图6-2-79）。② 身体重心再渐渐移至右腿上，上体右转，左脚向右脚靠拢，脚尖点地，同时右手向右上方划弧（手心由里转向外），至右侧方时变勾手，臂与肩平，左手向下经腹前向右上划弧停于右肩前，手心向里；眼看左手（图6-2-80、图 6-2-81）。③ 上体微向左转，左脚向左前侧方迈出，右脚跟后蹬，成左弓步；在身体重心移向左腿的同时，左掌随上体的继续左转慢慢翻转向前推出，手心向前，手指与眼齐平，臂微屈；眼看左手（图6-2-82、图6-2-83）。

图 6-2-78　　　　　　　　　　图 6-2-79

图 6-2-80                                   图 6-2-81

图 6-2-82                                   图 6-2-83

（3）动作要点。上体保持正直，松腰。完成式时，右臂肘部稍下垂，左肘与左膝上下相对，两肩下沉。左手向外翻掌前推时，要随转体边翻边推出，不要翻掌太快或最后突然翻掌。全部过渡动作，上下要协调一致。如面向南起势，单鞭的方向（左脚尖）应向东偏北（大约为 15°）。

（4）功法与健身机理。主要锻炼功法：开合桩。

根据动作结构特点，单鞭主练肩部及四肢，对肩背酸痛，手足麻木等疾病，有疗治功效。

**10. 云手**

（1）动作名称释意。两手在腰脊转动的带动下，分别做上下左右的回旋盘绕，如云气旋绕，似行云飞空，而称云手。

（2）动作过程。

① 身体重心移至右腿上，身体渐向右转，左脚尖里扣；左手经腹前向右上划弧至右肩前，手心斜向后，同时右手变掌，手心向右前；眼看左手（图6-2-84～图6-2-86）。② 上体慢慢左转，身体重心随之逐渐左移；左手由脸前向左侧运转，手心渐渐转向左方，右手由右下经腹前向左上划弧，至左肩前，手心斜向后，同时右脚靠近左脚，成小开立步（两脚距离为10～20厘米）；眼看右手（图6-2-87、图6-2-88）。③ 上体再向右转，同时左手经腹前向右上划弧至右肩前，手心斜向后，右手向右侧运转，手心翻转向右，随之左腿向左横跨一步；眼看左手（图6-2-89～图6-2-91）。④同②解（图6-2-92、图6-2-93）。⑤同③解，（图6-2-94～图6-2-96）。⑥同②解（图6-2-97、图6-2-98）。

图 6-2-84　　　　　　　　　图 6-2-85　　　　　　　　　图 6-2-86

图 6-2-87　　　　　　　　　图 6-2-88

图 6-2-89　　　　　　　图 6-2-90　　　　　　　　图 6-2-91

图 6-2-92　　　　　　　　　　图 6-2-93

图 6-2-94　　　　　　　图 6-2-95　　　　　　　　图 6-2-96

图 6-2-97                    图 6-2-98

（3）动作要点。身体转动要以腰脊为轴，松腰、松胯，不可忽高忽低。两臂随腰的转动而运转，要自然圆活，速度要缓慢均匀。下肢移动时，身体重心要稳定，两脚掌先着地再踏实，脚尖向前。眼的视线随左右手而移动。第三个"云手"，右脚最后跟步时，脚尖微向里扣，便于接"单鞭"动作。

（4）功法与健身机理。主要锻炼功法：行功一侧移步。

此动主练腰、背、臂、腿各部位，对手足腰背疾病有防治作用。

### 11. 单鞭

（1）动作名称释意。太极拳中将人的手臂击人称为鞭，一手吊勾，一手拂面或由胸前挥出，外形上颇似跨马扬鞭而得名。

（2）动作过程。

① 上体向右转，右手随之向右运转，至右侧方时变成勾手，左手经腹前向右上划弧至右肩前，手心向内；身体重心落在右腿上，左脚尖点地；眼看左手（图 6-2-99、图 6-2-100）。

② 上体微向左转，左脚向左前侧方迈出，右脚跟后蹬，成左弓步；在身体重心移向左腿的同时，上体继续左转，左掌慢慢翻转向前推出，成"单鞭"式（图 6-2-101、图 6-2-102）。

图 6-2-99                    图 6-2-100

图 6-2-101　　　　　　　　　图 6-2-102

（3）动作要点。与前"单鞭"式相同。

（4）功法与健身机理。与前"单鞭"式相同。

## 12. 高探马

（1）动作名称释意。此势动作具有象形之意，其动作外型像高高站立在马镫上探路，或像探身跨马之势而得名。

（2）动作过程。

① 右脚跟进半步，身体重心逐渐后移至右腿上；右勾手变成掌，两手心翻转向上，两肘微屈，同时身体微向右转，左脚跟渐渐离地；眼看左前方（图 6-2-103）。② 上体微向左转，面向前方，右掌经右耳旁向前推出，手心向前，手指与眼同高，左手收至左侧腰前，手心向上，同时左脚微向前移，脚尖点地，成左虚步；眼看右手（图 6-2-104）。

图 6-2-103　　　　　　　　　图 6-2-104

（3）动作要点。上体自然正直，双肩要下沉，右肘微下垂。跟步移换重心时，身体不要有起伏。

（4）功法与健身机理。主要锻炼功法：虚步桩。此动主练腰、胯、膝、腿各部，能治肾脏之病。

### 13. 右蹬脚

（1）动作名称释意。此势名称来源于动作特征，以左脚支撑体重，把右脚蹬出，故取此名。

（2）动作过程。

① 左手手心向上，前伸至右手腕背面，两手相互交叉，随即向两侧分开并向下划弧，手心斜向下，同时左脚提起向左前侧方进步（脚尖略外撇）；身体重心前移，右腿自然蹬直，成左弓步；眼看前方（图6-2-105～图6-2-107）。② 两手由外圈向里圈划弧，两手交叉合抱于胸前，右手在外，手心均向后，同时右脚向左脚靠拢，脚尖点地；眼平看右前方（图6-2-108）。③ 两臂左右划弧分开平举，肘部微屈，手心均向外，同时右腿屈膝提起，右脚向右前方慢慢蹬出，眼看右手（图6-2-109、图6-2-110）。

图 6-2-105　　　　　　图 6-2-106　　　　　　图 6-2-107

图 6-2-108　　　　　　图 6-2-109　　　　　　图 6-2-110

（3）动作要点。身体要稳定，不可前俯后仰。两手分开时，腕部与肩齐平。蹬脚时，左腿微屈，右脚尖回勾，劲使在脚跟。分手和蹬脚须协调一致。右臂和右腿上下相对。如面向南起势，蹬脚方向应为正东偏南（约30°）。

（4）功法与健身机理。主要锻炼功法：升降桩和开合桩。此动主练腿部，锻炼腿部柔韧性和肌肉力量。

### 14. 双峰贯耳

（1）动作名称释意。此势动作具有象形之意，以左右两拳由身后到身前，贯击对方两耳，犹如落下两座山峰，劲大无比，故取此名。

（2）动作过程。

① 右腿收回，屈膝平举，左手由后向上、向前下落至体前，两手心均翻转向上，两手同时向下划弧分落于右膝盖两侧，眼看前方（图6-2-111、图6-2-112）。② 右脚向右前方落下，身体重心渐渐前移，成右弓步，面向右前方；同时两手下落，慢慢变拳，分别从两侧向上、向前划弧至面部前方，成钳形状，两拳相对，高与耳齐，拳眼都斜向内下（两拳中间距离为10～20厘米）；眼看右拳（图6-2-113、图6-2-114）。

图 6-2-111　　　　　　　图 6-2-112

图 6-2-113　　　　　　　图 6-2-114

（3）动作要点。完成式时，头颈正直，松腰松胯，两拳松握，沉肩垂肘，两臂均保持弧形。双峰贯耳式的弓步和身体方向与右蹬脚方向相同。弓步的两脚跟横向距离同"揽雀尾"式。

（4）功法与健身机理。主要锻炼功法：开合桩。此动主练肩、臂、肘、腕部。

### 15. 转身左蹬脚

（1）动作名称释意。此势名称来源于动作特征，其动作从前方往左转90°，然后把左脚蹬出，故取此名。

（2）动作过程。

① 左腿屈膝后坐，身体重心移至左腿，上体左转，右脚尖里扣，同时两拳变掌，由上向左右划弧分开平举，手心向前；眼看左手（图6-2-115、图6-2-116）。② 身体重心再移至右腿，左脚收到右脚内侧，脚尖点地，同时两手由外圈向里圈划弧合抱于胸前，左手在外，手心均向后；眼平看左方（图6-2-117、图6-2-118）。③ 两臂左右划弧分开平举，肘部微屈，手心均向外，同时左腿屈膝提起，左脚向左前方慢慢蹬出；眼看左手（图6-2-119、图6-2-120）。

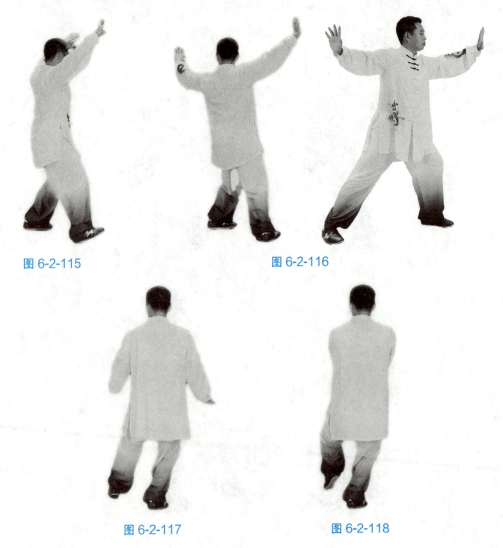

图 6-2-115

图 6-2-116

图 6-2-117

图 6-2-118

图 6-2-119

图 6-2-120

（3）动作要点。与右蹬脚式相同，只是左右相反。左蹬脚方向与右蹬脚成 180°（即正西偏北，约 30°）。

（4）功法与健身机理。主要锻炼功法：升降桩和开合桩。此动主练腿部，锻炼腿部柔韧性和肌肉力量。

### 16. 左下势独立

（1）动作名称释意

在运动中以腿下蹲，身体下降，称下势。

金鸡独立，因外形动作"一脚提起、一脚独立支撑"一手上扬，一手下垂而状如雄鸡独立，故取此名。

（2）动作过程。

①　左腿收回平屈，上体右转，右掌变成勾手，左掌向上、向右划弧下落，立于右肩前，掌心斜向后，眼看右手（图 6-2-121、图 6-2-122）。②　右腿慢慢屈膝下蹲，左腿由内向及侧（偏后）伸出，成左仆步；左手下落（掌心向外）向左下顺左腿内侧向前穿出，眼看左手（图 6-2-123、图 6-2-124）。

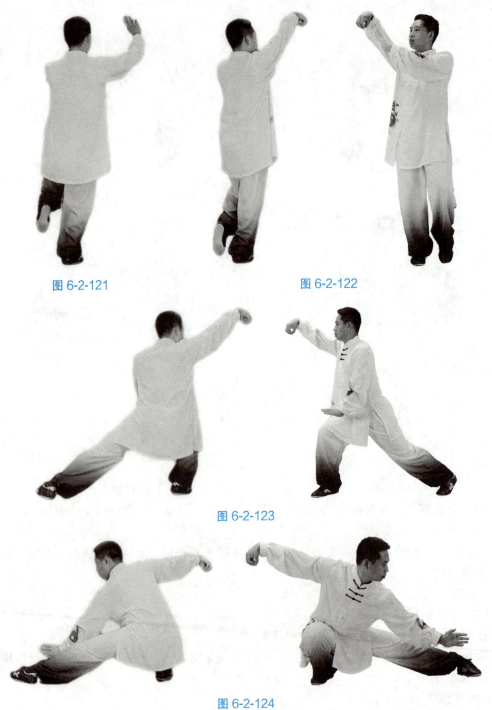

图 6-2-121　　　　　　　　　　　　　图 6-2-122

图 6-2-123

图 6-2-124

③ 身体重心前移，左脚跟为轴，脚尖尽量向外撇，左腿前弓，右腿后蹬，右脚尖里扣，上体微向左转并向前起身，同时左臂继续向前伸出（立掌），掌心向右，右勾手下落，勾尖向后；眼看左手（图 6-2-125）。④ 右腿慢慢提起平屈，成左独立式，同时右勾手变掌，并由后下方顺右腿外侧向前弧形摆出，屈臂立于右腿上方，肘与膝相对，手心向左，左手落于左胯旁，手心向下，指尖向前；眼看右手（图 6-2-126、图 6-2-127）。

图 6-2-125　　　　　　　　图 6-2-126　　　　　　　　图 6-2-127

（3）动作要点。右腿全蹲时，上体不可过于前倾。左腿伸直，左脚尖须向里扣，两脚脚掌全部着地。左脚尖与右脚跟踏在中轴线上。

上体要正直，独立的腿要微屈，右腿提起时脚尖自然下垂。

（4）功法与健身机理。主要锻炼功法：升降桩。下势：此动主练背、膝、腿、足踝各部，锻炼脊椎及腿部力量。

金鸡独立：此动主练腰脊两腿，锻炼平衡能力。

### 17. 右下势独立

（1）动作名称释意。

同"左下势独立"。

（2）动作过程。

① 右脚下落于左脚前，脚掌着地，然后左脚前掌为轴脚跟转动，身体随之左转，同时左手向后平举变成勾手，右掌随着转体向左侧划弧，立于左肩前，掌心斜向后；眼看左手（图 6-2-128、图 6-2-129）。② 同"左下势独立"② 解，只是左右相反（图 6-2-130、图 6-2-131）。③ 同"左下势独立"③ 解，只是左右相反（图 6-2-132）。④ 同"左下势独立"④ 解，只是左右相反（图 6-2-133、图 6-2-134）。

（3）动作要点。右脚尖触地后必须稍微提起，然后再向下仆腿。其他均与"左下势独立"相同，只是左右相反。

（4）功法与健身机理。同"左下势独立"。

### 18. 左右穿梭

（1）动作名称释意。此势动作具有象形之意，传统称"玉女穿梭"，此势动作柔缓，左右运转，交织纤巧灵活，犹如织女在织锦运梭一般，故取此名。简化太极拳，删除"玉女"，改为"左右穿梭"。

图 6-2-128

图 6-2-129

图 6-2-130

图 6-2-131

图 6-2-132

图 6-2-133

图 6-2-134

（2）动作过程

① 身体微向左转，左脚向前落地，脚尖外撇，右脚跟离地，两腿屈膝成半坐盘式，同时两手在左胸前成抱球状（左上右下），然后右脚收到左脚的内侧，脚尖点地，眼看左前臂（图 6-2-135～图 6-2-137）。② 身体右转，右脚向右前方迈出，屈膝弓腿，成右弓步；同时右手由脸前向上举并翻掌停在右额前，手心斜向上，左手先向左下再经体前向前推出，高与鼻尖平，手心向前；眼看左手（图 6-2-138～图 6-2-140）。③ 身体重心略向后移，右脚尖稍向外撇，随即身体重心再移至右腿，左脚跟进，停于右脚内侧，脚尖点地，同时两手在右胸前成抱球状（右上左下），眼看右前臂（图 6-2-141、图 6-2-142）。④同②解，只是左右相反（图 6-2-143～图 6-2-145）。

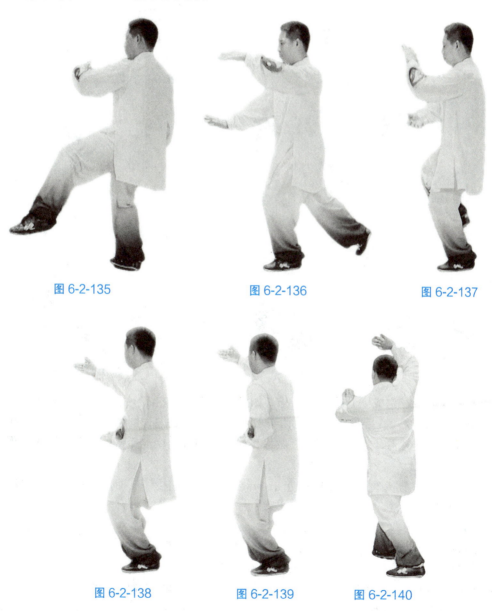

图 6-2-135　　　　　　图 6-2-136　　　　　　图 6-2-137

图 6-2-138　　　　　　图 6-2-139　　　　　　图 6-2-140

图 6-2-141　　　　　　　　　　　图 6-2-142

图 6-2-143　　　　　　图 6-2-144　　　　　　图 6-2-145

（3）动作要点。完成姿势面向斜前方（如面向南起势，左右穿梭方向分别为正西偏北和正西偏南，均约 30°）。手推出后，上体不可前俯。手向上举时，防止引肩上耸。一手上举一手前推要与弓腿松腰上下协调一致。做弓步时，两脚跟的横向距离同搂膝拗步式，保持在 30 cm 左右。

（4）功法与健身机理。主要锻炼功法：开合桩。此动主练肩、肘、腕、腰、腿各部位，锻炼灵轻伸缩之力。

### 19. 海底针

（1）动作名称释意。海底是指"会阴"穴，四指比喻钢针，暗含攻击方法而名为海底针。另一说认为以手喻为金针而点、刺对方之裆部神经（海底穴），故取此名。

（2）动作过程。右脚向前跟进半步，身体重心移至右腿，左脚稍向前移，脚尖点地，成左虚步；同时身体稍向右转，右手下落经体前向后、向上提抽至肩上耳旁，再随身体左转，由右耳旁斜向前下方插出，掌心向左，指尖斜向下，与此同时，左手向前、向下划弧落于左胯旁，手心向下，指尖向前；眼看前下方（图6-2-146、图6-2-147）。

图 6-2-146　　　　　　　　　　图 6-2-147

（3）动作要点。身体要先向右转，再向左转。完成姿势，面向正西。上体不可太前倾。避免低头和臀部外凸。左腿要微屈。

（4）功法与健身机理。主要锻炼功法：升降桩。此动主练腰脊之力。

### 20. 闪通臂

（1）动作名称释意。此势动作具有象形之意，将自己脊背比喻为扇轴，两臂比喻为扇幅，腰转动时两臂向横侧展开，犹如折扇突然放开（与突然收合）一般，其力发于背，故取此名。

（2）动作过程。上体稍向右转，左脚向前迈出，屈膝弓腿成左弓步，同时右手由体前上提，屈臂上举，停于右额前上方，掌心翻转斜向上，拇指朝下，左手上起经胸前向前推出，高与鼻尖平，手心向前；眼看左手（图6-2-148～图6-2-150）。

图 6-2-148　　　　　　　　　　图 6-2-149

177

图 6-2-150

（3）动作要点。完成姿势上体自然正直，松腰、松胯；左臂不要完全伸直，背部肌肉要伸展开。推掌、举掌和弓腿动作要协调一致。弓步时，两脚跟横向距离同"揽雀尾"式（不超过10厘米）。

（4）功法与健身机理。主要锻炼功法：开合桩。此动主练背脊，使力由脊发，贯通于两臂及腿部。

### 21. 转身搬拦捶

（1）动作名称释意。此势直接表达技击动作，指在转身同时，以两手向左右搬移对方之来力，然后用左立掌拦阻来手，随之，以右拳进击其肋、胸部之意，故以此为名。

（2）动作过程。① 上体后坐，身体重心移至右腿上，左脚尖里扣，身体向右后转，然后身体重心再移至左腿上，与此同时，右手随着转体向右、向下（变拳）经腹前划弧至左肋旁拳心向下，左掌上举于头前，掌心斜向下，眼看前方（图6-2-151）。② 向右转体，右拳经胸前向前翻转撇出，拳心向上，左手落于左胯旁，掌心向下，指尖向前，同时右脚收回后（不要停顿或脚尖点地）即向前迈出，脚尖外撇，眼看右拳（图6-2-152）。③ 身体重心移至

图 6-2-151                                    图 6-2-152

右腿上，左脚向前迈一步；左手上起经左侧向前上划圆弧拦出，掌心向前下方，同时右拳向右划弧收到右腰旁，拳心向上；眼看左手（图 6-2-153、图 6-2-154）。④ 左腿前弓成左弓步，同时右拳向前打出，拳眼向上，高与胸平，左手附于右前臂里侧，眼看右拳（图 6-2-155）。

| 图 6-2-153 | 图 6-2-154 | 图 6-2-155 |

（3）动作要点。右拳不要握得太紧。右拳回收时，前臂要慢慢内旋划弧，然后再外旋停于右腰旁，拳心向上。向前打拳时，右肩随拳略向前引伸，沉肩垂肘，右臂要微屈。弓步时，两脚横向距离同"揽雀尾"式。

（4）功法与健身机理。主要锻炼功法：行功—前进步。此势主练肩、背、腰、胯、臂、腿各部位，有利于锻炼柔韧性和肌肉力量，健肾益胃等功效。

### 22. 如封似闭

（1）动作名称释意。此势动作具有象形之意，两手臂交叉成斜十字，如贴封条状，称为"如封"，继而两掌微微向里引进，然后再向前按出，又好像用手关门一样，称为"似闭"。两掌所运转之动作，在术语上叫作"封格截闭"手法，故取此名。

（2）动作过程。① 左手由右腕下向前伸出，右拳变掌，两手手心逐渐翻转向上并慢慢分开回收；同时身体后坐，左脚尖翘起，身体重心移至右腿，眼看前方（图 6-2-156～图 6-2-158）。② 两手在胸前翻掌，向下经腹前再向上、向前推出，腕部与肩平，手心向前，同时左腿前弓成左弓步；眼看前方（图 6-2-159～图 6-2-161）。

（3）动作要点。身体后坐时，避免后仰，臀部不可凸出。两臂随身体回收时，肩、肘部略向外松开，不要直着抽回。两手推出宽度不要超过两肩。

（4）功法与健身机理。主要锻炼功法：行功—前进步。此势主练胸、肘、腰、腿各部位，有愈肺、健肾、活手足之功效。

### 23. 十字手

（1）动作名称释意。两手腕在胸前交叉，两臂环抱，形状如"十"字而得名。

图 6-2-156　　　　　　　图 6-2-157　　　　　　　图 6-2-158

图 6-2-159　　　　　　　图 6-2-160　　　　　　　图 6-2-161

（2）动作过程。① 屈膝后坐，身体重心移向右腿，左脚尖里扣，向右转体，右手随着转体动作向右平摆划弧，与左手成两臂侧平举，掌心向前，肘部微屈，同时右脚尖随着转体稍向外撇，成右侧弓步；眼看右手（图 6-2-162）。② 身体重心慢慢移至左腿，右脚尖里扣，随即向左收回，两脚距离与肩同宽，两腿逐渐蹬直，成开立步；同时两手向下经腹前向上划弧交叉合抱于胸前，两臂撑圆，腕高与肩平，右手在外，成十字手，手心均向后；眼看前方（图 6-2-163、图 6-2-164）。

（3）动作要点。两手分开和合抱时，上体不要前俯。站起后，身体自然正直，头要微向上顶，下颌稍向后收。两臂环抱时须圆满舒适，沉肩垂肘。

（4）功法与健身机理。主要锻炼功法：开合桩和升降桩。

此动主练两臂及膝腿部，两手相合，重力集中作用于腿部，能坚实腿力。

### 24. 收势

（1）动作名称释意。即套路结束时恢复为起势状态，故取此名。

（2）动作过程。两手向外翻掌，手心向下，两臂慢慢下落，停于身体两侧；眼看前方（图 6-2-165～图 6-2-167）。

图 6-2-162　　　　　　　　图 6-2-163　　　　　　　　图 6-2-164

图 6-2-165　　　　　　　　图 6-2-166　　　　　　　　图 6-2-167

（3）动作要点。两手左右分开下落时，要注意全身放松，同时气也徐徐下沉（呼气略加长）。呼吸平稳后，把左脚收到右脚旁，再走动休息。

（4）功法与健身机理。主要锻炼功法：无极桩。收势不可忽视，含"静"而归一之意，具有平心静气，调整身心作用。

## 第三节　简化太极拳技击原理与用法

### 一、起势

（1）甲手腕被乙攥握时，甲随即将腕部向前贴乙掌心，进而使乙身体重心倾斜后仰跌倒（图 6-3-1、图 6-3-2）；

（2）甲手腕被乙攥握往后拽时，甲双手随即向下向后沉踩，使乙向前扑跌或前栽（图 6-3-3、图 6-3-4）。

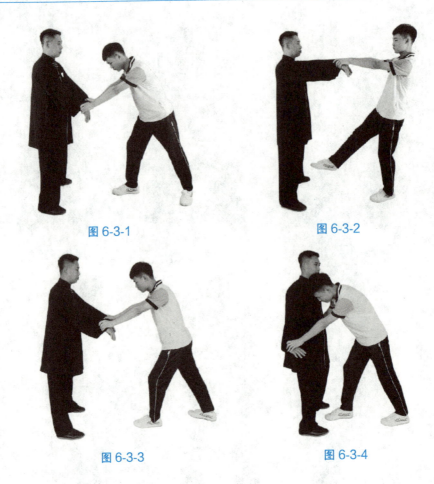

图 6-3-1　　　　　　　　　　　　　图 6-3-2

图 6-3-3　　　　　　　　　　　　　图 6-3-4

## 二、野马分鬃

（1）乙上步用左拳击打甲胸部；甲用左手格抓乙的左腕部（图 6-3-5）。

（2）甲右脚迅速上一步，别住乙方的左腿，同时，左手穿过乙方的左腋下向其颈部穿出，并向右后反别，可使其倒地（图 6-3-6）。

图 6-3-5　　　　　　　　　　　　　图 6-3-6

动作要点：整个动作要求协调一致，充分利用弓腿进身带身靠的力量将乙方跌出。

### 三、白鹤亮翅

（1）乙用左直拳右踢腿同时击打甲方；甲应立即用右手向上、向右挡开乙方的左拳，同时，用左手向下、向左搂其右腿，防开乙方的上下进攻（图6-3-7）。

（2）甲随即用右手向右后方拉乙方的左手，左手搂住其左腿向上、向右弧形上抬，并向右转腰，制乙后倒。

动作要点：防守动作和反攻动作要紧密衔接起来，中间不可有停顿，整个动作要求协调圆活。

图 6-3-7

### 四、搂膝拗步

（1）乙用右拳击打甲方的腹部；甲方迅速用左手向下，向左将其右拳格开（图6-3-8）。

（2）随即甲迅速用右掌向前猛击乙右胸部（图6-3-9）。

图 6-3-8

图 6-3-9

动作要点：防守动作要和进攻动作协调一致。出掌时，要充分发挥蹬右腿和向左转腰的力量，将其击出或击翻倒地。

### 五、手挥琵琶

（1）乙上左步用右直拳击打甲方；甲方身体重心向后坐，右腿屈膝半蹲，左脚尖上勾，避开乙方的冲拳（图6-3-10）。

（2）同时，甲右手向上抓住乙方的右腕并向左用力，左手猛拍其左肘关节，利用双手的合力，使其肘关节受伤（图6-3-11）。

图 6-3-10 图 6-3-11

动作要点：双手用力必须同时进行，发劲要冷弹快猛。

## 六、倒卷肱

（1）乙突然从背后抱住甲；甲方应迅速向下蹲，以防被对方抱起（图 6-3-12）。

（2）随即甲身体重心向后移，左臂向前伸；同时，右臂屈肘，以肘尖向乙方的胸部猛顶，解脱乙方抱腰，击伤对方（图 6-3-13）。

图 6-3-12 图 6-3-13

动作要点：用左肘击乙方的胸部时，头要向右后转，并要猛力向右转腰，以助顶肘之力。

## 七、揽雀尾（掤、捋、挤、按）

### 1. 掤势

（1）乙上步用右拳击打甲；甲立即起左手外格其腕步（图 6-3-14）。

（2）随即甲右脚向前上一步，右腿屈膝半蹲，蹬左腿，成右弓步；同时，左用抓乙右腕向下、向后带拉，右手向乙的右腋下用力掤出，可将乙击出或击倒（图 6-3-15、图 6-3-16）。

图 6-3-14　　　　　　　　　　图 6-3-15　　　　　　　　　　图 6-3-16

动作要点：甲左手向后带拉，使乙有后缩之意，此时，甲应乘乙后缩之势，借其力迅速出右手做"掤"的动作，这样"掤"的效果就好。如不借其力，是无法将对方掤出去的。在掤时，要以腰为主宰，用腰力将乙掤出。

### 2. 捋势

（1）乙上右步用左掌推击甲；甲立即举起左手格其左腕部（图 6-3-17）。

（2）随即甲右脚向前上一步；同时，左手由前向下、向后弧形带拉，右手按住乙的左肩或左肘部由前向下、向后弧形猛捋，可将乙从甲的身体左侧向后捋出或拖倒（图 6-3-18、图 6-3-19）。

图 6-3-17　　　　　　　　　　图 6-3-18　　　　　　　　　　图 6-3-19

动作要点：甲要乘乙向前猛推之势，借其力将乙向后捋出。在捋时，上身要正直，要充分利用上身向左转的力量，使捋的效果更佳。

### 3. 挤势

（1）乙右手抓甲右腕向后引甲；甲顺乙之捋势，右脚向前上一步，同时，左手向自己的右臂方向移动（图 6-3-20、图 6-3-21）。

（2）随即甲身体重心前移，屈右腿，蹬左腿，成右弓步；同时，左手手掌附于右腕内侧，以右小臂平挤乙的胸部，将乙挤出（图 6-3-22）。

动作要点：太极技法，最主要的特点是借力。"挤势"看起来好像是主动进攻之势，其实质却是借对方的捋劲，顺势发力。动作要及时、连贯、协调。

图 6-3-20

图 6-3-21

### 4. 按势

（1）乙用双拳击打甲两太阳穴；甲立即用双手从乙的两臂之间向上架住（图 6-3-23）。

图 6-3-22

图 6-3-23

（2）随即甲身体重心略向后移；同时，用双手由上向下、向后弧形将乙双臂下引，使乙被引进落空（图 6-3-24），而后甲用双手立即向前快速将乙挤出（图 6-3-25）。

图 6-3-24

图 6-3-25

动作要点：甲下引动作必须呈弧形，并要向左转腰，将乙的劲引空后，方可出击，将其按住。

## 八、单鞭

（1）乙上左步用右拳击打甲方；甲立即用右手向上、向后弧形钩其右腕（图 6-3-26）。

（2）随即甲左腿屈膝半蹲，右腿伸直，成左弓步；同时，右手钩住其右腕向后带拉；左手成立掌猛力向其胸击出（图 6-3-27）。

动作要点：击掌时，腰要向右转，利用腰腿之劲发力。整个动作的劲路，应向前、向右弧形发力，方可将对方击出或击翻倒地。

图 6-3-26

图 6-3-27

## 九、云手

（1）乙右脚向前上步，用右拳向甲面部击打，甲用左臂格挡乙右臂（图 6-3-28）。

（2）随即乙迅速出左拳击打甲腹部，甲迅速向左格挡乙左臂，使得其进攻失效（图 6-3-29）。

图 6-3-28

图 6-3-29

动作要点：格挡来拳要迅速干脆。

## 十、高探马

乙用右拳击打甲方；甲身体重心向后坐，右腿屈膝半蹲，左腿微屈膝，并以左脚尖虚点地面，成左高虚步；同时，左掌向下按拍乙方的右拳，右掌向其脸部猛击（图6-3-30、图6-3-31）。

图 6-3-30　　　　　　　　　　　　　图 6-3-31

动作要点：按掌和击掌必须同时进行。发劲时，腰要向左略转，充分发挥"腰为主宰"的作用。

## 十一、右蹬腿

（1）乙用左拳击打甲方；甲方应用双手交叉上架其冲拳（图6-3-32）。

（2）随即甲双手左右分开，化解乙方来拳，并迅速屈膝提起右腿，猛力向乙方的腹部蹬出（图6-3-33、图6-3-34）。

图 6-3-32　　　　　　　　图 6-3-33　　　　　　　　图 6-3-34

动作要点：蹬腿时，脚尖勾起，着力点在脚跟上。腿要先屈后伸，支撑腿要微屈膝站稳，蹬腿要有爆发力。

## 十二、双峰贯耳

（1）乙上左步用双拳击打甲方；甲立即用双手下按（图 6-3-35）。

（2）随即甲右腿屈膝半蹲，左腿伸直，成右弓步；同时，双手握拳由下向外、向上弧形挥臂，并用双拳同时击打乙方的左、右太阳穴，拳眼朝下，拳心朝外（图 6-3-36）。

图 6-3-35　　　　　　　　　　　　　　　　图 6-3-36

动作要点：双拳必须弧形勾击，但弧形不可过大。力要从跟发，发劲要猛，力点要准。

## 十三、左蹬腿

乙上左步用右直拳击打甲方；甲方双手向上左、右分开，并用左手挡格乙方来拳，同时，左腿屈膝上提，并迅速向乙方的腹部蹬击（图 6-3-37、图 6-3-38）。

图 6-3-37　　　　　　　　　　　　　　　　图 6-3-38

动作要点：蹬腿时，脚尖要钩起，着力点要在脚跟上。腿要先屈后伸，支撑腿膝微屈站稳。蹬腿时要有爆发力。

## 十四、下势独立

### （一）仆步下势

（1）乙左脚向前上步，用右拳向甲面部击打；甲迅速下蹲成仆步，躲开乙的进攻（图6-3-39）。

（2）随即甲右腿蹬直成左弓步，左掌向乙方裆部挑击，使其裆部受损或向后倾倒（图6-3-40）。

动作要点：下蹲躲拳要快，变弓步与挑掌要协调一致；挑掌要快速、有力。

图6-3-39　　　　　　　　　　　图6-3-40

### （二）金鸡独立

乙用右拳击打甲方；甲迅速用左手抓住其右腕关节并向后拉，同时右手（屈肘）由其右腋下向上挑起，使其身体前倾，同时，右腿屈膝向上猛提，用右膝猛顶其胸、肋部（图6-3-41）。

动作要点：动作要快速有力，协调一致。顶膝的部位最好是肋骨部位。

## 十五、玉女穿梭

乙上左步用右拳击打甲方；甲立即举起左臂屈肘上架，同时，左腿屈膝半蹲，伸直右腿，成左弓步，用右掌向其胸、腹部猛击（图6-3-42、图6-3-43）。

图6-3-41

图6-3-42　　　　　　　　　　　图6-3-43

动作要点：上架和击掌的劲路不是正前方，而是要求有略微向前、向左的弧形击打。击打时，要充分利用腰腿之劲，其效果更佳。

## 十六、海底针

乙用右脚向甲腹部、裆部蹬踢。甲右脚向右前方上半步躲开来脚，同时迅速用左手向外搂手格挡乙的右腿，接着左脚向前上步，上体前倾，右掌向乙裆部猛插（图6-3-44、图6-3-45）。

图 6-3-44

图 6-3-45

动作要点：闪身、搂挡要快速、灵活；上体前倾与插掌要协调一致，插掌要快速、准确、有力。

## 十七、闪通臂

乙用右手扇甲的右耳；甲立即举起右手向上防开，同时，左腿屈膝半蹲，蹬右腿，成左弓步，用左掌向前击打乙的腰、肋部（图6-3-46）。

动作要点：左掌向前击打要随腰、胯前送和蹬右腿的力量，使击掌更加有力。身体必须中正，收住尾闾，劲由脊背发出。

图 6-3-46

## 十八、搬拦捶

（1）乙上左步用右拳击打甲；甲做"搬"的动作，身体向右转，右脚向前一步，同时，右手握拳肘微屈并向上、向右外拨（图6-3-47、图6-3-48）。

（2）随即甲做"拦"的动作，身体继续向右转，左脚向前上一步，身体重心落在右脚上，成左虚步；同时，右拳变掌将乙的右手向下、向后弧形下压；左手由下向左、向前弧形击乙的右耳（图6-3-49）。

（3）甲做"捶"的动作，左腿屈膝半蹲，蹬右腿，成左弓步；同时，右手握拳向前平伸冲出猛击乙胸部（图6-3-50）。

图 6-3-47          图 6-3-48

图 6-3-49          图 6-3-50

动作要点："搬拦捶"虽有三个动作组成，但要绵绵不断，连贯圆活。"捶"的动作主要是击打乙的胸、腹部，要充分利用蹬腿、转腰的力量。

## 十九、如封似闭

乙上左步用双拳击打甲的双肋部；甲立即用双手向下、向外防开对方来拳，然后，两臂内旋，双手内合，并向前猛力推出，可将乙击翻倒地（图 6-3-51、图 6-3-52）。

图 6-3-51          图 6-3-52

动作要点：整个动作要连贯地进行，中间不可有间断现象，发劲要利用腰、腿之力。由分止合，引劲落空，效果更佳。

# Chapter 6   Simplified Tai-chi Chuan

## Section 1   Brief Introduction to Simplified Tai–chi Chuan

### 1. Brief Introduction to the Creation of Simplified Tai–chi Chuan

"Simplified Tai-chi Chuan" is a boxing method created by adapting and sorting out the old fashion of Tai-chi Chuan, which has been popular among the masses, according to the principle of gradual progress. It changes the old exercise sequence of placing the difficult postures first, removes too many repetitive postures in the original movements, and concentrates the main structure and technical content of the original movements, which is convenient for the masses to master and easy to learn and understand. This set of boxing is divided into eight groups, including twenty-four stances such as "commencement form" and "closing of Tai-chi". Practitioners can practice coherently, or choose to practice in single form or in groups.

### 2. Sequence of Simplified Tai–chi Chuan Movements

Group 1: commencement form of Tai-chi Chuan, partition of wild horse's mane (left style) and (right style), and white crane spreads its wings;

Group 2: brush knee and twist step (left style) and (right style), play the fiddle, step back and whirl arms (left style) and (right style);

Group 3: grasp bird's tail (left style), grasp bird's tail (right style);

Group 4: single whip, wave hands like clouds, single whip;

Group 5: high pat on horse, kick with right heel, stride opponent's ears with both fists, turn and kick with left heel;

Group 6: creep down and stand on one leg (left style), creep down and stand on one leg (right style);

Group 7: fair lady weaves at the shuttle, needle at sea bottom, fan through the back;

Group 8: turn, deflect downward, parry, and punch, apparent close up, cross hands, closing of Tai-chi.

## 3. Explanation on Diagrams

In the text description, where there is the word "meanwhile", no matter whether the movements of a certain part of the body are written first or later, they are required to move together, not in sequence. The direction of movements is based on the front, back, left and right of the human body. No matter how it changes, it always takes the facing direction as the front, the back direction as the back, the left side of the body as the left and the right side of the body as the right. Assuming that the commencement form faces to the south, the direction is specifically explained for some postures with a large inclination in the direction of the closing of Tai-chi.

# Section 2   Diagrams of Simplified Tai-chi Chuan Movements

## 1. Commencement Form

### (1) Movement Description

It means the beginning of the whole set of movements.

### (2) Movement Instruction

Preparation Form: The body is naturally upright and the feet are placed together; The arms droop naturally and the hands are placed on the outside of the thighs; Look forward horizontally (Figure 6-2-1).

Commencement Form: ① The body is naturally upright, the feet are spread to the same width as the shoulders, and the toes are forward; The arms droop naturally and the hands are placed on the outside of the thighs; Look forward horizontally (Figure 6-2-2). ② Lift the arms horizontally forward slowly, with the hands at the same height and width as the shoulders, and put the palms down (Figure 6-2-3). ③ Keep the upper body upright and straight, bend the knees and squat down; Meanwhile, press down the palms gently, and droop the elbows to the position opposite to the knees; Look forward horizontally (Figure 6-2-4).

Figure 6-2-1

### (3) Movement Essentials

① The head and neck are upright, and the chin is slightly retracted. Do not deliberately hold out the chest or tuck in the abdomen. Be concentrated (start with the stand at attention position, then separate the left foot to the left, showing an open step). ② Drop the shoulders, relax the elbows down, and bend the fingers slightly in a natural way. Bend the knees and loosen the waist.The hips should not protrude, and the center of gravity is between the legs. The movements of falling arms and squatting should be coordinated.

### (4) Practicing Method and Fitness Mechanism

The Practicing Method of Yin Yang Movement.

This movement mostly uses two palms to carry out lifting movement, which is beneficial to adjust the breath. Inhale by raising the hands and exhale by lowering the hands. Adjusting breathing in this way can lower one's energy to the navel psychic-center and calm him or her down, thus further preparing for practicing the following movements. In actual practice, the lifting movement is often used to adjust breathing when doing the movements of commencement form and closing of Tai-chi (Figure 6-2-5).

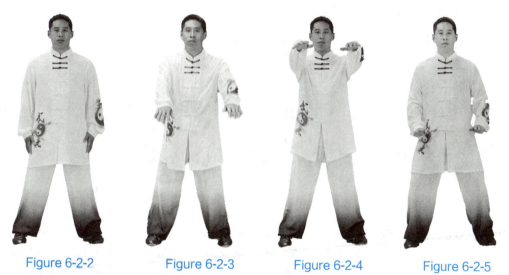

| Figure 6-2-2 | Figure 6-2-3 | Figure 6-2-4 | Figure 6-2-5 |

## 2. Partition of Wild Horse's Mane (Left Style) and (Right Style)

### (1) Movement Description

In this movement, stretch the body, put the hands on both sides, and alternately draw arcs up and down. This movement is like a horse galloping, and the mane on its head is divided into two

bundles, falling on both sides, so it is named partition of wild horse's mane.

### (2) Movement Instruction

① Turn the upper body slightly to the right, and move the center of gravity to the right leg; Meanwhile, fold the right arm in front of the chest, with the palm down, and place the left hand under the right hand through the front of the body, with the palm up. The two palms are relatively ball-shaped, then retract the left foot immediately to the inside of the right foot, with the toes pointing to the ground; Look at the right hand (Figure 6-2-6). ② Turn the upper body slightly to the left, step the left foot forward to the left, push the right heel back, and straighten the right leg naturally, forming a left lunge; Meanwhile, continue rotating the upper body to the left, and the left and right hands are slowly separated from the upper left and lower right with the rotating body. Make the left hand flush with the height of the eyes (the palm is inclined upward), with the elbow slightly bent, and put the right hand beside the right crotch, with the elbow slightly bent as well. The palm is downward, and the fingertips are forward; Look at the left hand (Figures 6-2-7,8).

Figure 6-2-6          Figure 6-2-7          Figure 6-2-8

③ Make the upper body sit back slowly, with the center of gravity moving to the right leg. Raise the tip of the left foot, and it is slightly outward (about 45°). Then, make the sole of the foot step on the ground slowly, and bow the left leg forward slowly. Turn the body to the left, with the center of gravity moving to the left leg; Meanwhile, flip the left hand down, and fold the left arm in front of the chest. Draw an arc to the upper left with the right hand, and then place it under the left hand, with the palms facing each other in a ball shape; Then, retract the right foot to the inside of the left foot, with the toes pointing to the ground, looking at the left hand (Figures 6-2-9, 10, 11). ④ Step right leg forward to the right, and straighten the left leg naturally into a right lunge; Meanwhile, rotate the upper body to the right, and the left and right hands are slowly separated from the lower left and upper right with the rotating body. Make the right hand flush with the height of the eyes (the palm is inclined upward), with the elbow slightly bent; Put the left hand beside the left crotch, with the elbow slightly bent as well. The palm is downward, and the fingertips are forward; Look at the right hand (Figures 6-2-12, 13). ⑤ The same as ③, but in the opposite direction as for left and right (Figures 6-2-14, 15, 16). ⑥ The same as ④, but in the opposite direction as for left and right (Figures 6-2-17, 18).

Figure 6-2-9          Figure 6-2-10          Figure 6-2-11

Figure 6-2-12          Figure 6-2-13

Figure 6-2-14          Figure 6-2-15          Figure 6-2-16

Figure 6-2-17          Figure 6-2-18

### (3) Movement Essentials

The upper body must not lean forward or backward, and the chest must be relaxed and stretched. Keep the arms in an arc when we separate them. When rotating the body, take the waist as the axis. The speed of lunge movement and hand opening should be uniform. When doing lunge movement, as for the stepped foot, we should let the heel hit the ground first, then, make the heel of the foot slowly step on the ground, with the toes forward. Besides, knees should not exceed toes, and hind legs should be straight naturally; The angle between the front and rear feet is about 45°~60° (if necessary, the heel of the rear foot can be pushed back to make corresponding adjustments). As for the lunge of partition of wild horse's mane, the heels of the front and rear feet should be divided on both sides of the central axis, and the transverse distance between them (that is, taking the midline of the movement as the longitudinal axis and the vertical distance on both sides as the transverse) should be kept at about 10-30 cm.

### (4) Practicing Method and Fitness Mechanism

Main practicing method: stepping—forward step.

This movement mainly trains neck, arms, chest, waist, crotch, legs and other parts, and can treat kidney diseases, etc.

## 3. White Crane Spreads Its Wings

### (1) Movement Description

In the course of this movement, the arms spread symmetrically from left to right, up and down, and the middle ridge is straight, which is named after the shape of bird wings and the action of white cranes spreading their wings. It is also said that the movement is named after the posture of lifting and rotating the arms, and there is another saying that it gets its name due to the meaning of double shining with one spreading.

### (2) Movement Instruction

The center of gravity is shifted forward. Take half a step forward with the right foot, and turn the upper body slightly to the left; Turn the palm of the left hand down, bend the left arm flat in front of the chest, make the right hand arc to the upper left, turn the palm up, and hold it in a ball shape relative to the left hand; Look at the left hand (Figure 6-2-19). ② Lean the upper body back, and the center of gravity is shifted to the right leg. Turn the upper body to the right first, face the right front, look at the right hand, then move the left foot slightly forward, with the toes pointing to the ground, forming a left empty step; Meanwhile, turn the upper body slightly to the left again, facing the front, and the two hands are slowly separated from the upper right and lower left with the rotating body. Lift the right hand up and stop it in front of the right forehead, put the palm to the left rear, and put the left hand in front of the left crotch, with the palm down and the fingertips forward; Look forward horizontally (Figure 6-2-20).

Figure 6-2-19                    Figure 6-2-20

### (3) Movement Essentials

When doing the movement of closing of Tai-chi, don't stick the chest out, keep the arms semicircular up and down, and bend the left knee slightly. The rearward shift of the center of gravity should be coordinated with the right hand horizontal lifting and the left hand downward pushing.

### (4) Practicing Method and Fitness Mechanism

The main practicing method is the empty step stance.

This movement exercises chest, back, shoulders, arms, waist and other parts, and can train the longitudinal expansion and contraction of the whole body.

## 4. Brush Knee and Twist Step (Left Style) and (Right Style)

### (1) Movement Description

When doing this movement, brush the knee with one hand, and push forward with another hand (the posture of putting one hand and one foot on different sides in front is a twist step), which is called "brush knee and twist step" according to the meaning of attack and defense. In the course of this movement, the basic skills of martial arts involved are homolateral lunge and heterolateral lunge.

### (2) Movement Instruction

① The right hand falls from the front of the body, and arcs from bottom to back and up to the outside of the right shoulder. Bend the elbow slightly, and place the hand at ear level, with the palm inclined upward; The left hand arcs from lower left to upper and then to lower right, and finally puts it on the right chest with the palm inclined downward; Meanwhile, turn the upper body slightly to the left and then to the right, with the left foot retracted to the inside of the right foot and the toes pointing to the ground; Look at the right hand (Figures 6-2-21, 22, 23). ② Turn the upper body to the left, and step the left foot forward (inclined left) into a left lunge; Meanwhile, push the right hand forward from the ear side, and place it at the same level as the tip of the nose. Put the left hand down over the left knee and fall beside the left crotch, with the fingertips forward; Look at the fingers of the right hand (Figures 6-2-24, 25). ③ Bend the right leg slowly, lean the upper body back, and the center of gravity is shifted to the right leg. Slightly tilt the tip of the left foot outward, then, make the sole of the foot slowly steps on the ground, with the left leg arched forward. Turn the body to the left, and the center of gravity is shifted to the left leg. Put the right foot into the inside of the left foot, with the toes pointing to the ground; Meanwhile, turn the palm of the left hand outward, and use this hand to arc from the left rear to the top, and finally place it on the outside of the left shoulder. Bend the elbow slightly, and place the hand at ear level, with the palm inclined upward; With the rotating body, the right hand first arcs upward, then to the lower left, and finally falls on the left chest, with the palm inclined downward; Look at the left hand (Figure 6-2-26, 27, 28). ④ The same as ②, but in the opposite direction as for left and right (Figures 6-2-29, 30). ⑤ The same as ③, but in the opposite direction as for left and right (Figures 6-2-31, 32, 33). ⑥ The same as ② (Figures 6-2-34, 35).

Figure 6-2-21

Figure 6-2-22

Figure 6-2-23

Figure 6-2-24

Figure 6-2-25

Figure 6-2-26

Figure 6-2-27

Figure 6-2-28

Figure 6-2-29                                   Figure 6-2-30

Figure 6-2-31                Figure 6-2-32                Figure 6-2-33

Figure 6-2-34                          Figure 6-2-35

### (3) Movement Essentials

When the front hand is pushed out, do not tilt the body forward or backward. On the contrary, we should relax the waist and crotch. When pushing the palm, lower the shoulders and elbows, stretch the wrists and palms naturally, and keep in harmony with the movements of relaxing the waist and bowing the legs. When we do the movement of "brush knee and twist step" to form a lunge posture, the transverse distance between the heels should be kept at about 30 cm.

### (4) Practicing Method and Fitness Mechanism

Main practicing method: stepping—forward step.

This movement can exercise waist, ridge, shoulder, arm, knee, leg and other parts, especially beneficial to training waist turning and stepping, and has good effect on kidney and foot health.

## 5. Play the Fiddle

### (1) Movement Description

In the course of this movement, the hands are placed in tandem, swinging and rolling back and forth, which is just like a man holding a pipa. And the movement of the hand at the back (the hand protecting the elbow joint) is like the action of plucking strings, so it is named after this.

### (2) Movement Instruction

Take half a step forward with the right foot, lean the upper body back, and the center of gravity is shifted to the right leg; Turn the upper body slightly to the right, and move the left foot slightly forward to form a left empty step. Make the heel touch the ground, with the toes tilted and the knees bent slightly; Meanwhile, the left hand is lifted from the lower left to the upper, reaching the same level as the tip of the nose, with the palm facing to the right. Bend the arm slightly, retract the right hand and place it on the inner side of the left arm elbow, with the palm facing to the left; Look at the index finger of the left hand (Figures 6-2-36, 37).

Figure 6-2-36                    Figure 6-2-37

### (3) Movement Essentials

Keep the body steady and natural, lower the shoulders and elbows, and relax the chest. When the left hand is lifted up, don't lift it directly, but from left to top and then forward, and the shape needs to be slightly curved. When following with the right foot, make the sole of the foot touch the ground first, and then step on the whole foot. The backward shift of the center of gravity should be coordinated with the upward lifting of the left hand and the retraction of the right hand.

### (4) Practicing Method and Fitness Mechanism

The main practicing method is the empty step stance.
This movement mainly exercises the arms and waist.

## 6. Step Back and Whirl Arms (Left Style) and (Right Style)

### (1) Movement Description

The movement "step back and whirl arms" is named after the retraction and flexion of humerus. It is also known as "step back and repulse monkey": "repulsing" means driving away and expelling. Monkeys are clever and active, and especially like to pounce on people. We can draw the monkey with the hand first, and when the monkey pounces on us, we can take a step back and pull the hand back, while pushing and pressing its head with the other hand. According to this idea, in this movement, the enemy is compared to a monkey, and the action of taking a step back and retracting the hand is like driving away the monkey chasing up, so this movement is also called "step back and repulse monkey".

### (2) Movement Instruction

① Turn the upper body to the right, turn the palm of the right hand (palm up) over the abdomen, and draw an arc from bottom to back and up, lifting it horizontally up. The arm bends slightly, and the left hand turns over immediately, with the palm upward; With the body moving to the right, the eyes look to the right first, and then turn forward to look at the left hand (Figures 6-2-38, 39). ② The right arm bends its elbow and pushes forward, and push the right hand from the ear to the front side, with the palm forward. The left arm bends its elbow with the palm upward, and retreats to the outside of the left rib; Meanwhile, gently lift the left leg and take a step back (inclined left), making the sole of the foot touches the ground first. Then, step on the whole foot slowly, and the center of gravity is shifted to the left leg to form a right empty step. The right foot is straightened with the rotating body with the sole of the foot as the axis; Look at the right hand (Figures 6-2-40, 41). ③ Turn the upper body slightly to the left, meanwhile, the left hand arcs backward and upward with the rotating body, and lifts it horizontally with the palm upward. Then, the right hand immediately turns over the palm, with the palm upward; With the rotating body, the eyes first look to the left, and then turn forward to look at the right hand (Figure 6-2-42). ④ The same as ②, but in the opposite direction as for left and right (Figures 6-2-43, 44). ⑤ The same as ③, but in the opposite direction as for left and right (Figure 6-2-45). ⑥ The same as ② (Figures 6-2-46, 47). ⑦ The same as ③ (Figure 6-2-48). ⑧ The same as ②, but in the opposite direction as for left and right (Figures 6-2-49, 50).

Figure 6-2-38

Figure 6-2-39

Figure 6-2-40

Figure 6-2-41

Figure 6-2-42

Figure 6-2-43

Figure 6-2-44

Figure 6-2-45

Figure 6-2-46

Figure 6-2-47

Figure 6-2-48

Figure 6-2-49

Figure 6-2-50

### (3) Movement Essentials

Don't straighten the hand that pushes forward, and don't draw back the hand directly, but retract it in an arc with the rotating body. When pushing forward, turn the waist and relax the crotch. The speed of both hands should be consistent to avoid stiffness. When we step back, we need to make the sole of the foot touch the ground first, and then step on the whole foot slowly. Meanwhile, the front foot should be straightened with the rotating body with the sole of the foot as the axis. When we retreat the left foot, we should tilt it slightly to the left rear, and when we retreat the right foot, we should tilt it slightly to the right rear, so as to avoid placing the both feet in a straight line. When we step back, look left and right first with the movement of the rotating body, and then turn to look at the front hand. Finally, when we retreat the right foot, the angle of toe outward should be slightly wider, which is beneficial for us to do the following movement of "grasp bird's tail (left style)".

### (4) Practicing Method and Fitness Mechanism

Main practicing method: stepping—backward step.

This movement mainly exercises the waist, ridge, shoulders, back, knees, feet and other parts, which is helpful to the health of kidneys and feet.

## 7. Grasp Bird's Tail (Left Style)

### (1) Movement Description

In Tai-chi Chuan, the opponent's arms are likened to the head and tail of a bird. Holding the head and tail of the bird with both hands and rotating up and down with it is like playing with the bird tail, hence the name. Is it also said that, in the ancient times, before going into a fight, people would tie the hem of the robe into the belt first so as to make moves easily during the fight, so the movement is also named Lazy About Tying Coat.

### (2) Movement Instruction

① The upper torso turns slightly to the right, and along with the turn, the right hand floats up and to the back in a swinging motion until level to the ground with the palm facing up, the left hand is relaxed with the palm facing down, eyes looking at the left hand (Figure 6-2-51). ② The torso continues to turn to the right, the left hand drops naturally, gradually turns over the palm, and swings through the front of the abdomen to the front of the right rib with the palm facing up, and then the right elbow bends, the palm turned down, and pulls to the front of the right chest. The two hands are folded like holding a ball; at the same time, the center of gravity falls on the right leg, the left foot pulls to the inner side of the right foot, the tiptoe taps the ground and the eyes look at the right hand (Figure 6-2-52, 53). ③ The upper torso slightly turns left, the left foot steps forward to the left, the upper body keeps turning to the left, the right leg naturally kicks straight, and the left leg bends its knees to form a bow stance with the left foot forward; at the same time, the left arm wards off to the front left (i.e. the left arm is bent into a bow shape and pushes forward with the outside of the forearm and the back of the hand), at the shoulder level, palm facing inward, the right hand drops to the right side and is placed next to the right hip, palm facing down and fingertip facing forward and eyes looking at the left forearm (Figures 6-2-54, 55).

Figure 6-2-51          Figure 6-2-52          Figure 6-2-53

Figure 6-2-54                    Figure 6-2-55

④ The torso slightly turns to the left, then the left hand goes forward and the palm turns down, the right hand palm turns up and extend forward and up through the abdomen to the lower part of the left forearm; then both hands pull down (Chinese pronunciation is Lv), that is, the upper torso turns to the right, and both hands go right back and up through the front of the abdomen in an arc, until the right hand is at shoulder level with palm facing up, the left arm is bent, level to the ground, in front of the chest with palm facing back, and at the same time the center of gravity is shifted to the right leg; eyes looking at the right hand (Figures 6-2-56, 57).

Figure 6-2-56                    Figure 6-2-57

⑤ The upper torso slightly turns to the left, the right elbow bends inward, the right hand is placed on the inner side of the left wrist (about 5 cm away). The upper torso continues to turn to the left, both hands slowly press forward at the same time, the left-hand palm facing back and the right-hand palm facing forward, and the left forearm is kept in a semicircular shape; at the same time, shift the center of gravity gradually forward to form a bow stance with the left foot at the front, and the eyes look at the left wrist (Figures 6-2-58, 59).

Figure 6-2-58                    Figure 6-2-59

⑥ The left hand palm turns down, the right hand extends forward and to the right through the upper part of the left wrist, at the same height as the left hand, palm facing down, separate two hands to the left and right, with the distance in between the same as the shoulder width, then bend the right knee, the upper torso lowers back slowly to a sitting stance, shifting the weight to the right leg, tilt up the left foot toes, and bend the elbow of both hands back to the front of the abdomen at the same time, both hand palms facing the front down; eyes looking straight ahead (Figures 6-2-60, 61, 62). ⑦ Keep performing the above move, and move the center of gravity forward slowly. At the same time, press both hands forward and up, the palm facing forward, and bend the left leg forward to form a bow stance with the left foot forward, eyes looking straight ahead (Figure 6-2-63).

Figure 6-2-60                    Figure 6-2-61

Figure 6-2-62                    Figure 6-2-63

## (3) Movement Essentials

When warding off, both arms are in an arc shape forward and back. Separating the hands, loosening the waist and bowing the legs must be coordinated. When forming a bow stance, the lateral distance between two heels shall not exceed 10 cm.

When pulling back, do not learn forward the upper torso and do not bulge the hip. Both arms must pull back and turn with the waist at the same time, still in an arc. The whole sole of the left foot touches the ground.

When pressing forward, the upper torso should be upright. The move should be in unity with loosening the waist and bowing the legs.

When pushing, both hands must move in a swinging motion, with the wrist level with the shoulder, and the elbows slightly bent.

## (4) Practicing Method and Fitness Mechanism

Main practicing method: opening and closing stance.

The movement includes the change process of force method of engaging the opponent, warding off, pulling back, pressing forward and pushing. This shows that Tai-chi Chuan emphasizes the four basic strength methods and highlights the importance of basic techniques.

# 8. Grasp Bird's Tail (Right Style)

## (1) Movement Description

Same as "Grasp Bird's Tail (Left Style)".

## (2) Movement Instruction

① The upper torso lowers back to a sitting stance and turns right, shift the center of gravity to the right leg, the toes of the left foot are angled inward, the right hand extends to the right side level to the ground in an arc and then goes from the lower right through the front of the abdomen to the front of the left rib in an arc, the palm facing up, the left arm bends level to the ground in front of the chest, and the left hand palm facing down and the right hand form a shape like holding a ball; at the same time, shift the center of gravity the left leg, the right foot pulls back to the inner side of the left foot, and the tiptoe taps the ground, eyes looking at the left hand (Figure 6-2-64, 65, 66, 67). ② is the same as "Grasp Bird's Tail (Left Style)"③ , but with the opposite side (Figures 6-2-68, 69). ③ is the same as "Grasp Bird's Tail (Left Style)"④ , but with the opposite side (Figures 6-2-70, 71). ④ is the same as "Grasp Bird's Tail (Left Style)"⑤ , but with the opposite side (Figures 6-2-72, 73). ⑤ is the same as "Grasp Bird's Tail (Left Style)"⑥, but with the opposite side (Figures 6-2-74, 75, 76). ⑥ is the same as "Grasp Bird's Tail (Left Style)"⑦, but with the opposite side (Figure 6-2-77).

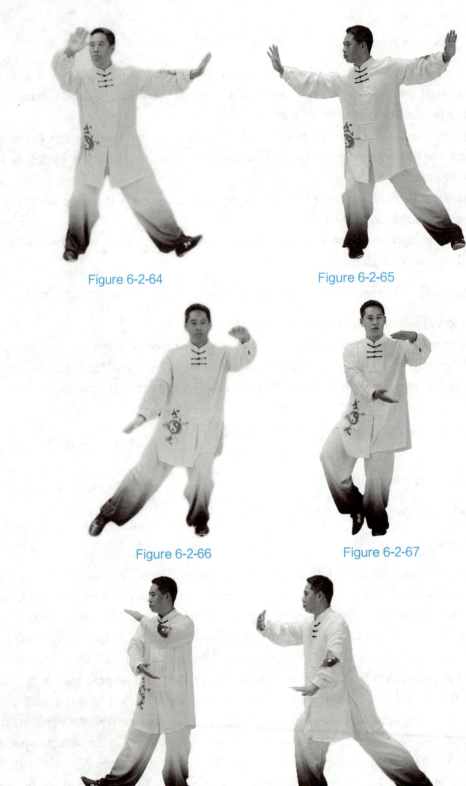

Figure 6-2-64

Figure 6-2-65

Figure 6-2-66

Figure 6-2-67

Figure 6-2-68

Figure 6-2-69

Figure 6-2-70

Figure 6-2-71

Figure 6-2-72

Figure 6-2-73

Figure 6-2-74

Figure 6-2-75

Figure 6-2-76                                    Figure 6-2-77

### (3) Movement Essentials

Same as "Grasp Bird's Tail (Left Style)", but with the opposite side.

### (4) Practicing Method and Fitness Mechanism

Same as "Grasp Bird's Tail (Left Style)".

## 9. Single Whip

### (1) Movement Description

In Tai-chi Chuan, the attacking arm is referred to as a whip. One hand forms a hook shape, and the other brushes against the face or waves out from the chest. It looks like waving a whip while riding a horse, hence the name.

### (2) Movement Instruction

① The upper torso lowers back to a sitting stance, the weight gradually shifts to the left leg and the toes of the right foot are angled inward; at the same time, the upper torso turns left, and the two hands (left hand on top) shift to the left in an arc until the left arm is level to the ground and extended at the left side of the body, palm facing left, the right hand goes through the abdomen to the front of the left side ribs, palm facing inward up, and eyes looking at the left hand (Figure 6-2-78, 79). ② The center of gravity gradually shifts to the right leg, the upper body turns right, the left foot closes up to the right foot, the tiptoe taps the ground. At the same time, raise the right hand in an arc to the upper right (the palm turns from the inward to the outward), and when reaching the right side, form a hook shape. The arm is held at shoulder level, the left hand goes down through the abdomen to the upper right in an arc and stops in front of the right shoulder, palm facing inward; eyes looking at the left hand (Figures 6-2-80, 81). ③ The upper body turns slightly to the left, the left foot steps forward to the left, and the right heels kicks backward to form a bow stance with the left foot forward; while shifting the center of gravity to the left leg, the left-hand palm slowly turns to face the front and pushes forward along with the continued left turn of the upper torso, palm facing forward and fingers at eye level, arms slightly bent; eyes looking at the left hand (Figures 6-2-82, 83).

Figure 6-2-78                Figure 6-2-79                Figure 6-2-80

Figure 6-2-81                Figure 6-2-82                Figure 6-2-83

### (3) Movement Essentials

The upper torso is upright and the waist is relaxed. When completing the movement, the right elbow is lowered slightly, the left elbow faces the left knee vertically, and the two shoulders are sunk. When the left hand turns the palm outward and pushes forward, perform the move along with turning the torso. As we turn the torso, we turn the palm and pushes forward. Don't turn the palm too fast or turn suddenly at the end. All moves shall be performed in a transiting motion, and the upper and lower moves shall be coordinated. If the commencement form faces to the south, the

direction of the single whip (left foot tiptoe) should be east by north (about 15°).

### (4) Practicing Method and Fitness Mechanism

Main practicing method: opening and closing stance.

According to the characteristics of the movement structure, it mainly trains the shoulders and limbs, and has therapeutic effect on shoulder and back pain, hand and foot numbness and other diseases.

## 10. Wave Hands Like Clouds

### (1) Movement Description

Along with the rotation of the waist and spine, the two hands rotate up, down, to the left and to the right respectively, like clouds floating through the sky, hence the name.

### (2) Movement Instruction

① Shift the weight to the right leg, turn the torso gradually to the right, and the toes of the left foot are angled inward; the left hand goes up through the abdomen to the right in an arc to the front of the right shoulder, with the palm tilted backward, and at the same time, the right hand changes to palm facing front right, with eyes looking at the left hand (Figures 6-2-84, 85, 86). ② The upper torso slowly turns left, shifting the center of gravity gradually to the left along; the left hand goes from the front of the face to the left, and the palm gradually turns to the left. The right hand goes from the lower right through the front of the abdomen to front left in an arc to the front of the left shoulder, with the palm tilted inward. At the same time, the right foot closes up to the left foot, forming a small open stance (the distance between the two feet is about 10~20 cm); eyes looking at the right hand (Figures 6-2-87, 88). ③ Turn the upper torso to the right again and at the same time the left hand extends to the right in an arc through the front of the abdomen to the front of the right shoulder, the palm tilted inward, the right hand moves to the right side, the palm turned to the right, and along with it the left leg advances a step to the left; eyes looking at the left hand (Figures 6-2-89, 90, 91). ④ is the same as ② (Figures 6-2-92, 93). ⑤ is the same as ③ (Figures 6-2-94, 95, 96). ⑥ is the same as ② (Figures 6-2-97, 98).

### (3) Movement Essentials

Torso rotation should take the waist and spine as the axis, the waist and hip are loosened, and the body remains at the same level without going up and down. The two arms move along with the rotation of the waist. The moves should be natural, smooth, slow and in unity. When the lower limbs move, the center of gravity shall be stable, the palms of both feet shall touch the ground first and then stand firm, the toes facing forward. The eye follow the left and right hands. In the third move of "Wave Hands Like Clouds", when the right foot follows the last step, the toes are angled slightly inward to facilitate the transition to "Single Whip" movement.

Figure 6-2-84

Figure 6-2-85

Figure 6-2-86

Figure 6-2-87

Figure 6-2-88

Figure 6-2-89

Figure 6-2-90

Figure 6-2-91

Figure 6-2-92

Figure 6-2-93

Figure 6-2-94

Figure 6-2-95

Figure 6-2-96

Figure 6-2-97

Figure 6-2-98

### (4) Practicing Method and Fitness Mechanism

Main practicing method: moving technique—side step.

This movement mainly trains the waist, back, arms and legs, and help prevent and treat hand, foot, waist and back diseases.

# 11. Single Whip

### (1) Movement Description

In Tai-chi Chuan, the attacking arm is referred to as a whip. One hand forms a hook shape, and the other brushes against the face or waves out from the chest. It looks like waving a whip while riding a horse, hence the name.

### (2) Movement Instruction

① Turn the upper torso to the right, and the right hand turns to the right along with it, and forms a hook shape when reaching the right side. The left hand raises to the right and up through the front of the abdomen in an arc to the front of the right shoulder, palm facing inward; the weight falls on the right leg and the tiptoe of the left foot taps the ground, with eyes looking at the left hand (Figures 6-2-99, 100). ② The upper body turns slightly to the left, the left foot steps forward to the left, and the right heel kicks backward to form a bow stance; while the center of gravity moves to the left leg, the upper body continues to turn left, and the left palm slowly turns and pushes forward to perform "Single Whip" movement (Figures 6-2-101, 102).

Figure 6-2-99                    Figure 6-2-100

Figure 6-2-101          Figure 6-2-102

### (3) Movement Essentials

Same as the "Single Whip" above.

### (4) Practicing Method and Fitness Mechanism

Same as the "Single Whip" above.

## 12. High Pat On Horse

### (1) Movement Description

This movement name is pictographic. Its appearance is like standing high on the stirrup to explore the path ahead, or like leaning over the horse.

### (2) Movement Instruction

① The right foot advances a half step, the center of gravity gradually shifts back to the right leg; the right hand in hook shape turns into palm, the palms of both hands turn upward, the elbows bend slightly, and at the same time, the body turns slightly to the right, and the left heel gradually leaves the ground, eyes looking at the front left (Figure 6-2-103). ② The upper torso turns slightly to the left and faces the front, the right hand palm pushes forward by the right ear, the palm facing forward, the fingers at eye level, the left hand pulls back to the front left of the waist, the palm facing upward, the left foot moves slightly forward at the same time, and the tiptoe taps the ground to form a empty step of the left foot, eyes looking at the right hand (Figure 6-2-104).

Figure 6-2-103                    Figure 6-2-104

### (3) Movement Essentials

The upper torso is naturally upright, the shoulders are sunk, and the right elbow are lowered slightly. When shifting the center of gravity with the steps, the torso should not move up and down.

### (4) Practicing Method and Fitness Mechanism

Main practicing methods: empty step stance.
This movement mainly trains the waist, hip, knees and legs, and can treat kidney diseases.

## 13. Kick With Right Heel

### (1) Movement Description

The name of this movement comes from the its characteristics. The performer supports the weight with the left foot and kicks out the right foot, hence the name.

### (2) Movement Instruction

① The palm of the left hand faces upward and extends forward to the back of the right wrist. The two hands cross and then separate to both sides and drop down in an arc, the palms facing down. At the same time, lift the left foot to advance a step to the left front side (toe slightly outward); shift the center of gravity forward and naturally straighten the right leg into a bow stance with the left leg forward, with eyes looking at the front (Figures 6-2-105, 106, 107).
② Both hands draw an arc from the outer circle to the inner circle, both hands crossed in front of the chest, with the right hand outside and both palms facing back, and at the same time the right foot draws close to the left foot, and the tiptoe taps the ground, with eyes looking at the front right

(Figure 6-2-108). ③ Life the two arms in an arc to hold them horizontally on two sides, with elbows slightly bent and both palms facing out, and at the same time bend and lift the right leg, slowly kick the right foot to the right front, with eyes looking at the right hand (Figures 6-2-109, 110).

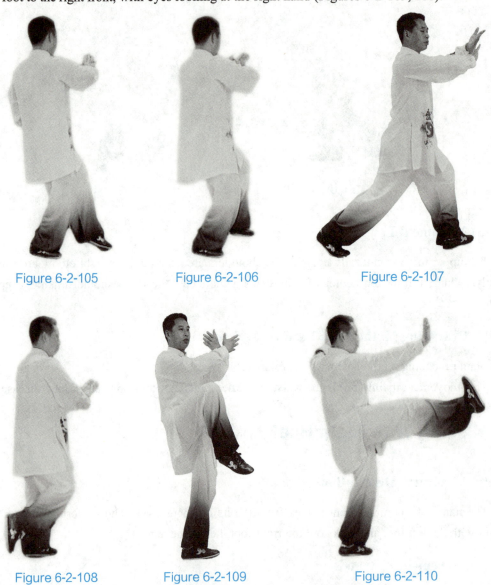

Figure 6-2-105          Figure 6-2-106          Figure 6-2-107

Figure 6-2-108          Figure 6-2-109          Figure 6-2-110

### (3) Movement Essentials

Keep the body stable and don't lean forward or backward. When separating the hands, keep the wrist and the shoulders level. When kicking, slightly bend the left leg, the right foot tip angled inward, and issue force on the heel. Separating hands and kicking must be coordinated. The right arm and right leg face each other vertically. If the commencement form is to the south, the direction of the kick should be due east by south (about 30°).

### (4) Practicing Method and Fitness Mechanism

Main practicing methods: Yin Yang stance and opening and closing stance.

This movement mainly trains the legs and exercises the flexibility and muscle strength of the legs.

# 14. Stride Opponent's Ears With Both Fists

### (1) Movement Description

This movement name is pictographic. Both hands go from back to front to strike the opponent's both ears, which is like two mountains falling down and is extremely powerful, hence the name.

### (2) Movement Instruction

① The right leg pulls back, the knee bends and holds level to the ground, the left hand goes from back up and to the front of the body, both hands turn the palms up, and both hands lower in an arc at the same time, falling on both sides of the right knee, eyes looking forward (Figures 6-2-111, 112). ② The right foot falls to the front right, and the center of gravity gradually moves forward, forming a bow stance with the right foot forward, facing the front right; at the same time, both hands drop and slowly form fists, and go up and to the front in an arc from both sides to the front of the face to form a clamp shape, the two fists facing each other at ear level, thumbs tilted down and inward. (The distance between the two fists is about 10~20 cm), and eyes looking at the right fist (Figures 6-2-113, 114).

Figure 6-2-111                    Figure 6-2-112

Figure 6-2-113          Figure 6-2-114

### (3) Movement Essentials

When completing the movement, the head and neck are upright, the waist and hit are relaxed, the two fists are loosened, the shoulders are sunk and the elbows are lowered, and both arms are kept in an arc. The bow stance and body direction of "Stride Opponent's Ears With Both Fists" are the same as that of "Kick With Right Heel". The horizontal distance between the heels of the bow stance is the same as that of the "Grasp Bird's Tail".

### (4) Practicing Method and Fitness Mechanism

Main practicing method: opening and closing stance.
This movement mainly trains the shoulders, arms, elbows and wrist.

## 15. Turn and Kick With Left Heel

### (1) Movement Description

The name of this movement comes from the its characteristics. The performer turns 90° from the front to the left, and then kicks the left heel, hence the name.

### (2) Movement Instruction

① The knee of the left leg bends and the torso lowers back to a sitting stance, shifting the weight to the left leg, the upper torso turns to the left, the right foot toes are angled inward, and the fists change to palms and go from top to the two sides in an arc to be level to the ground, the palms facing forward; eyes looking at the left hand (Figures 6-2-115, 116). ② Shift the center of gravity of to the right leg, pull the left leg to the inner side of the right foot, and the tiptoe taps the ground. At the same time, both hands swing from the outer circle to the inner circle and fold the arms in front of the chest, with the left hand on the outside and both palms facing the inward; eyes looking straight to the left (Figures 6-2-117, 118). ③ Separate the two arms to left and right in an arc left to be level to the ground, the elbows slightly bent and both palms facing out. At the same time, bend and lift the left leg, kick the left foot slowly to the front left; eyes looking at the left hand (Figures 6-2-119, 120).

Figure 6-2-115                                      Figure 6-2-116

Figure 6-2-117                                      Figure 6-2-118

Figure 6-2-119

Figure 6-2-120

### (3) Movement Essentials

Same as "Kick With Right Heel", but with the opposite side. Kicking with the left foot and angled 180° to kicking with the right food (i.e. due west by north, about 30°).

### (4) Practicing Method and Fitness Mechanism

Main practicing methods: Yin Yang stance and opening and closing stance

This movement mainly trains the legs and exercises the flexibility and muscle strength of the legs.

# 16. Creep Down and Stand On Left Leg (Left Style)

## (1) Movement Description

Creeping down: bending the legs to squat in the movement to lower the torso is called creeping down or pushing down.

Golden Pheasant Stands on One Leg: the appearance of this movement is "one foot is lifted and one foot supports alone" with one hand up and one hand down like a rooster standing on one leg, hence the name.

## (2) Movement Instruction

① The left leg pulls and bends level to the ground, the upper torso turns right, the right palm forms a hook shape, the left hand palm floats up and to the right and down in an arc, stands in front of the right shoulder, with the palm tilted inward, and the eyes look at the right hand (Figures 6-2-121, 122). ② The right leg slowly bends and squats, and the left leg extends from the inner side out (relatively backward) to form a crouch stance with the left foot forward; the left hand drops (palm facing out) down and to the left, and goes along the inner side of the left leg forward, eyes looking at the left hand (Figures 6-2-123, 124).

Figure 6-2-121                    Figure 6-2-122

Figure 6-2-123

Figure 6-2-124

③ Shifts the center of gravity forward with the left heel as the axis, the toe is turned outward as far as possible, the left leg form a bow stance forward, the right leg kicks back, the tiptoe of the right foot is angled inward, the upper torso turns slightly to the left and lifts up forward. At the

same time, the left arm continues to extend forward (palm is vertical) with the palm facing right, the right hand forms a hook shape and drops with the hook tip facing backward, eyes looking at the left hand (Figure 6-2-125). ④ The right leg slowly lifts and bends to form the posture of "standing on the left leg". At the same time, the right hand changes from hook shape to palm, and swing forward in an arc from the lower back along the outer side of the right leg. Bend the arm above the right leg to have the elbow face the knee, palm facing left. The left hand drops next to the left side of the hip, palm facing down and fingertip facing forward, eyes looking at the right hand (Figures 6-2-126, 127).

Figure 6-2-125

Figure 6-2-126                                    Figure 6-2-127

### (3) Movement Essentials

When squatting on the right leg, the upper torso should not lean forward too much. The left leg is straight, the toe of the left foot angled inward, and the soles of both feet touch the ground. The tiptoe of the left foot and the heel of the right foot step on the central axis.

The upper torso should be upright, the leg we stand on should bend slightly, and the toes naturally point down when the right leg is lifted.

### (4) Practicing Method and Fitness Mechanism

Main practicing method: Yin Yang stance.

Creeping down: this movement mainly trains the back, knees, legs and ankles, and exercises spine and leg strength.

Golden Pheasant Stands on One Leg: this movement mainly trains the lumbar spine and both legs and improve balance.

## 17. Creep Down and Stand on One Leg (Right Style)

### (1) Movement Description

The same as Creep Down and Stand on One Leg (Left Style).

### (2) Movement Instruction

① Drop the right foot in front of the left foot, with the foot on the ground; Then turn the heel around the front of the left foot and turn the body to the left; At the same time, raise the left hand flat to the back into a hook; Circle the right hand while turning and put it in front of the left arm, with the palm obliquely backward; Look at the left hand (Figures 6-2-128, 129). ② The same as the ② of the Creep Down and Stand on One Leg (Left Style), only with opposite directions (Figures 6-2-130, 131). ③ The same as the ③ of the Creep Down and Stand on One Leg (Left Style), only with opposite directions (Figure 6-2-132). ④ The same as the ④ of the Creep Down and Stand on One Leg (Left Style), only with opposite directions (Figures 6-2-133, 134).

Figure 6-2-128

Figure 6-2-129

Figure 6-2-130

Figure 6-2-131

Figure 6-2-132          Figure 6-2-133          Figure 6-2-134

### (3) Movement Essentials

After the tip of right foot touches the ground, it must be lifted a little, then crouch the left foot. Other essentials of this movement are the same as the Creep Down and Stand on One Leg (Left Style), only with opposite directions.

### (4) Practicing Method and Fitness Mechanism

The same as Creep Down and Stand on One Leg (Left Style).

## 18. Fair Lady Weaves at the Shuttle

### (1) Movement Description

This movement is meant to mimic the movement of shuttles. It's called Fair Lady Weaves at the Shuttle because this movement is slow and soft, just like a fair lady flexibly and delicately weaves at the shuttle from side to side.

### (2) Movement Instruction

① Turn the body slightly to the left and land the left foot forward, with the toe out and right heel off the floor; Bend the knees into a half-sitting posture, and hold the hands like we're holding a ball on the left chest (left upper and right lower); Then bring the right foot to the inside of the left foot, point the toe to the ground, and look at the left forearm (Figures 6-2-135, 136, 137). ② Turn the body to the right, step forward with the right foot and bend the knees to form a right lunge; At the same time, raise the right hand in front of the face and rest it on the right forehead, with the palm obliquely upward; Move the left hand to the lower left first and then forward (the height of the tip of nose), and move the palm forward; Look at the left hand (Figures

6-2-138, 139, 140). ③ Shift the weight slightly back and tip the right foot slightly out; Then shift the weight to the right leg, with the left foot following, step the left leg on the inside of the right foot, and point the toe to the ground; At the same time, put both hands like we're holding a ball on the right chest (right upper and left lower) and look at the right forearm (Figures 6-2-141, 142). ④ The same as ②, only with opposite directions (Figure 6-2-143, 144, 145).

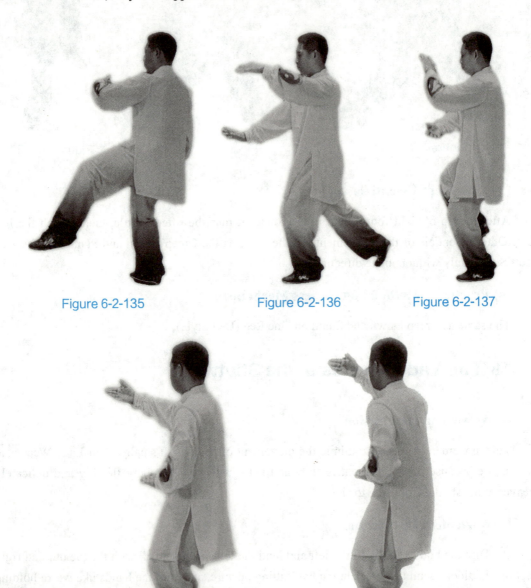

Figure 6-2-135          Figure 6-2-136          Figure 6-2-137

Figure 6-2-138                    Figure 6-2-139

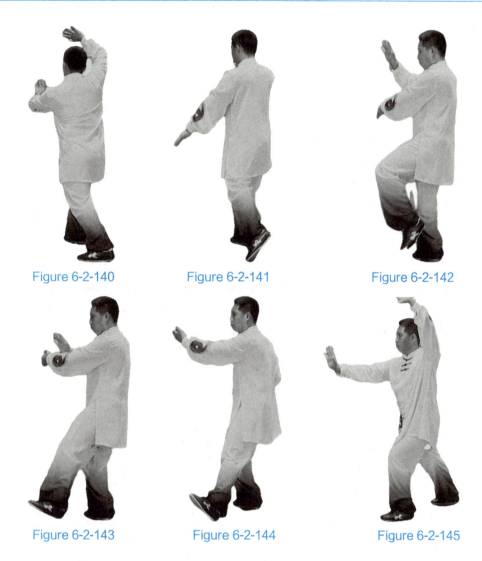

Figure 6-2-140          Figure 6-2-141          Figure 6-2-142

Figure 6-2-143          Figure 6-2-144          Figure 6-2-145

## (3) Movement Essentials

After the movement, face diagonally forward (If we start the movement facing the south, the directions of "working at shuttles" are due west by north and due west by south with a angle of 30°). After we push the hand forward, do not bend the upper body forward. Avoid lifting shoulders when hands are up. When we raise one hand and push the other forward, coordinate the bent leg with the waist. When we're making a bow stance, the lateral distance between the heels shall be the same as the movement of Brush Knee and Twist Step (about 30 cm).

## (4) Practicing Method and Fitness Mechanism

Main practicing method: Opening and closing stance.

This movement mainly exercises the shoulder, elbows, wrist, waist, legs, to build the dexterous stretching strength of these parts.

## 19. Needle At Sea Bottom

### (1) Movement Description

Sea bottom means the *Huiyin Point(perineum)*, four figures are the "needles", and this movement is meant to attack (that is why it's called Needle At Sea Bottom). Some people believe that it's called Needle At Sea Bottom because we can use the figure to poke or stab the nerves of the crotch (the *Huiyin Point*, or Sea Bottom) of the enemy.

### (2) Movement Instruction

Step the right foot forward for half a step, shift the weight to the right leg, move the left foot forward slightly, point the toe on the ground and make an empty stance; Turn the body slightly to the right, put the right hand down (from the forward to the back of the body), and lift it up to the ear; Then make it follow the turn of the body to the left, and insert it to the lower front by the side of the right ear, with the palm facing the left and fingertips obliquely downward; At the same time, circle the left hand to the lower front to the left hip, with the palm down and fingertips forward; Look at the lower front (Figures 6-2-146, 147).

Figure 6-2-146          Figure 6-2-147

### (3) Movement Essentials

Turn the body first to the right, then to the left. After the movement, face the due west. Do not lean the upper body too far forward. Avoid bow and hip protruding. Bend the left leg slightly.

### (4) Practicing Method and Fitness Mechanism

Main practicing method: Yin Yang stance.

This movement is mainly to practice the strength of the waist.

## 20. Fan Through The Back

### (1) Movement Description

This movement is meant to mimic the sudden unfolding of a folding fan, with the spine like the shaft of the fan, and the arms like the framework of the fan. The arms spread laterally as the waist rotates and the strength comes from the back. That's why it's called Fan Through The Back.

### (2) Movement Instruction

Turn the upper body slightly to the right, step the left foot forward, and bend the knees into a left lunge. At the same time, lift the right hand from the front of the body, lift the bent arm, and stop it above the front of the upper right. Turn the palm obliquely upward, with the thumb downward. Raise the left hand and push forward by the chest(the height of the tip of nose), with the palm forward. Look at the left hand (Figures 6-2-148, 149, 150).

Figure 6-2-148          Figure 6-2-149

Figure 6-2-150

### (3) Movement Essentials

After the movement, the upper body shall be naturally straight and upright, and we shall relax the waist and crotch; Do not fully extend the left arm, but extend the back muscles. While pushing and raising the palms, the hand and bow stance should be coordinated. When we're making a bow stance, the lateral distance between the heels shall be the same as the movement of Grasp Bird's Tail (no more than 10 cm).

### (4) Practicing Method and Fitness Mechanism

Main practicing method: Opening and closing stance.

This movement mainly exercises the back. The strength comes from the back and acts on the arms and legs.

## 21. Turn, Deflect Downward, Parry, And Punch

### (1) Movement Description

This movement is meant to attack. While turning, move the force of the enemy to the left or right with both hands, and block the opposing hand with the upright left palm. Then hit the costal part or the chest of the enemy with the right fist. That's why it's named Turn, Deflect Downward, Parry, And Punch.

### (2) Movement Instruction

① Make a sitting stance and shift the weight to the right leg, with the left toe inward and the body turning to the right rear; Then shift the weight to the left leg; At the same time, move the right hand to the right rear (fisted), circle it to the left side by the abdomen, with the heart of the fist upward. Place the left palm in front of the head, with the palm obliquely downward, and look ahead (Figure 6-2-151).② Turn the body to the right, and move the right fist forward by the chest(turning the fist while moving it), with the heart of the fist upward. Move the left hand to the left of the crotch, with the palm downward and figures forward; At the same time, after the right foot is withdrawn (do not pause or point the toe), step forward and turn the toe outward, and look at the right fist (Figure 6-2-152). ③ Shift the weight to the right leg and take a step forward with the left foot; Circle the left hand forward from the left, with the palm facing the lower front; Then circle the right fist in the right to the right of the right waist, with the heart of the fist upward; Look at the left hand (Figures 6-2-153, 154).④ Make a left lunge while punching the right fist forward (the height of the chest), with the eye of the fist upward; put the left hand in the inside of the right forearm and look at the right fist (Figure 6-2-155).

Figure 6-2-151                                    Figure 6-2-152

Figure 6-2-153              Figure 6-2-154              Figure 6-2-155

### (3) Movement Essentials

Don't hold the right fist too tight. When the right fist is recovered, slowly turn the forearm inward and circle it, then turn it outward and stop at the right waist, with the heart of the fist upward. When punching forward, extend the right shoulder slightly forward with the fist, sink the shoulder to the elbow, and bend the right arm slightly.

### (4) Practicing Method and Fitness Mechanism

Main practicing method: Walking method—forward steps.

This movement mainly exercises the shoulders, back, waist, crotch, arms and legs. It aims to build flexibility and muscle strength and it's good for kidney and stomach.

## 22. Apparent Close Up

### (1) Movement Description

The name of the movement is pictographic. Two arms are crossed to form a tilted cross like sealing up, called "ru feng". Both palms come together, draw both arms backward towards the body and then push forward, as if closing the door with hands, called "si bi". The circling actions of both palms are called "sealing and closing", which the movement is hence named after.

### (2) Movement Instruction

① The left palm moves forward beneath the right wrist; the right fist becomes a palm; both palms open gradually, turning upward simultaneously; both palms are gradually apart and drawing back towards the body slowly. Roll back into a sitting stance, with the left toes up and the body weight shifted to the right leg; gaze forward (Figures 6-2-156, 157, 158).

Figure 6-2-156          Figure 6-2-157          Figure 6-2-158

② Turn the palms facing outward in front of the chest; push the palms down in front of the abdomen, then push both palms upward and forward; both wrists are at the shoulder height, with palms facing forward; the left leg steps forward to form a bow stance; gaze forward (Figures 6-2-159 160, 161).

Figure 6-2-159          Figure 6-2-160          Figure 6-2-161

### (3) Movement Essentials

The upper body shall not lean backward when in a sitting stance; do not stick the butt out; when drawing back both arms towards the body, keep both shoulders and elbows slightly loose and facing outward; do not retract both arms in a straight line. When both hands are pushing forward, the distance between should not be wider than the shoulders.

### (4) Practicing Method and Fitness Mechanism

Main practicing methods: forward steps in Tai-chi walking method.

The movement is mainly practiced on the chest, elbows, the waist and legs. It stimulates and strengthens lungs, kidneys, limbs and flexibility.

## 23. Cross Hands

### (1) Movement Description

Cross wrists in front of the chest, with both arms wrapped around, looking like a cross.

### (2) Movement Instruction

① Bend knees in a sitting stance. Shift the wight to the right leg. The left toes are buckled. While turning the body to the right, draw the right hand in an arc out and across to the left hand. Both hands are raised horizontally with palms up and slightly bent elbows. Meanwhile, the right toes are turning outward along with the body rotation, taking a right bow stance; gaze at the right hand (Figure 6-2-162).

② Slowly shift the body weight to the left leg, buckle the right toes and then immediately retract them towards the left . Both feet are shoulder-width apart. Gradually straighten both legs and take an open stance; meanwhile draw both hands downward in front of the abdomen and then draw them upward in an arc and cross them in front of the chest. Both arms are fully rounded with wrists at the shoulder level. The right hand is crossed outside with both palms backward; gaze forward ( Figures 6-2-163, 164).

### (3) Movement Essentials

When both hands are apart and wrapped around, the upper body shall not lean forward. After standing up, the body should be held upright naturally, slightly extending the crown of the head towards the sky and tucking the chin in . When both arms are wrapped around, they should be round and comfortable, with the shoulders and elbows sinking down.

### (4) Practicing Method and Fitness Mechanism

Main practicing methods: opening and closing stance, Yin Yang stance.

| Figure 6-2-162 | Figure 6-2-163 | Figure 6-2-164 |

The movement is mainly practiced on both arms, knees and legs. With both hands holding, the weight is focused on both legs and hence legs would be strengthened.

## 24. Closing of Tai–chi

### (1) Movement Description

The movement is taken when the whole routine is completed and restored to the commencement state.

### (2) Movement Instruction

Turn both hands outward with palms down; gradually move both arms downward until they're fully extended downward; hands rest against both sides of the thighs; gaze forward (Figures 6-2-165, 166, 167).

| Figure 6-2-165 | Figure 6-2-166 | Figure 6-2-167 |

### (3) Movement Essentials

Relax the whole body when both hands apart are dropping; meanwhile slowly sink the breath to the lower belly (the exhalation is slightly longer then the inhalation). When the breathing is steady, step to the right with the left leg until the left foot is immediately beside the right foot. Rest and walk.

### (4) Practicing Method and Fitness Mechanism

Main practicing method: infinite stance.

The closing movement should not be neglected. It helps the practitioner achieve togetherness through tranquility, cultivating calmness and nurturing body and mind.

## Section 3   Simplified Tai-chi Chuan Attacking Principles and Application

## I. Commencement Form

(1) As the wrists of A are grasped by B, A soon puts the wrists forward against the palms of B, so that B leans back and falls over (Figures 6-3-1, 2);

Figure 6-3-1                                    Figure 6-3-2

(2) As the wrists of A are grasped and dragged backward by B, A moves both hands downward and pull, causing B to fall forward (Figures 6-3-3, 4).

Figure 6-3-3                                    Figure 6-3-4

## II. Partition of Wild Horse's Mane

1. B steps forward and punches A at the chest with the left fist; A grabs B's left wrist with the left hand. (Figure 6-3-5)

2. A's right foot promptly steps forward to block B's left leg. At the same time, the left hand passes through B's left armpit to reach his neck, and press to the right and back to make B fall to the ground. (Figure 6-3-6)

Figure 6-3-5                          Figure 6-3-6

Movement Essentials:

The whole movement shall be coordinated and smooth. Fully use the bow and arrow step to bring the force out to cause B to fall out.

## III. White Crane Spreads Its Wings

1. B extends the left fist straight forward and kick with the right foot at the same time to hit A; A shall immediately raise the right hand up and to the right to block B's left fist, and at the same time lower the left hand down and to the left to hold B's right leg to prevent attacks from B's upper and lower torso. (Figure 6-3-7)

2. Then use the right hand to grab and pull B's left hand, and the left hand holds B's left leg up and to the right in an arc, turn the waist to the right, and cause B to fall back.

Movement Essentials:

The defense move should be closely followed by the return and attack move with no pause in between. It is required that the entire movement is coordinated and smooth.

图 6-3-7

## IV. Brush Knee and Twist Step

1. B hits A's abdomen with the right fist; A shall quickly lower the left hand down and to the left to block B's right fist. (Figure 6-3-8)

2. Then A quickly hits the right side of B's chest with the right palm. (Figure 6-3-9)

Figure 6-3-8　　　　　　　　　　　Figure 6-3-9

Movement Essentials:

The defense move and the attack move should be coordinated. When striking with the palm, give full play to the power of kicking with the right leg and twisting the waist to the left, and knock B out or down.

## V. Play the Fiddle

1. B advances the left step and hits A with the right fist straight forward; A shifts the center of gravity to the back, bend the knee of the right leg in a half stance, and the tiptoe of the left foot angled upward to evade the B' punch. (Figure 6-3-10)

2. At the same time, A lifts the right hand to grasp B's right wrist and exert force to the left, and the left hand beat B's left elbow fiercely, so as to use the joint force of both hands to hurt B's elbow. (Figure 6-3-11)

Figure 6-3-10　　　　　　　　　　　Figure 6-3-11

Movement Essentials:

Both hands must exert force simultaneously, and the force should be sudden, explosive, fast and fierce.

## VI. Step Back and Repulse Monkey

1. B suddenly wraps his arms around A from behind; A shall quickly squat down to avoid being lifted up by the opponent. (Figure 6-3-12)

2. Presently, A shifts the center of gravity to the back, and extends the left arm forward. At the same time bends the right arm at the elbow and hits B's chest with the elbow tip to break loose from and hurt B. (Figure 6-3-13)

Figure 6-3-12　　　　　　　　　　Figure 6-3-13

Movement Essentials:

When hitting B's chest with the left elbow, turn head back to the right and turn waist to the right with great force to help the elbow hit harder.

## VII. Grasp Bird's Tail (Ward Off Slantingly Upward, Pull Back, Press Forward, Push)

### 1. Ward Off Slantingly Upward

(1) B steps forward and hit A with the right fist; A immediately raises the left hand to fend off B's wrist. (Figure 6-3-14)

(2) Presently A steps forward with the right foot, bends the right leg and squats, kicks the left leg and forms a bow stance with the right leg forward; at the same time, uses the left hand to grab B's right hand at the wrist and pulls B to the back and down, and then uses the right hand to push B at the right armpit forcefully to knock B out or down. (Figures 6-3-15, 16)

Movement Essentials:

A pulls B to the back with the left hand to make B want to retract. At this moment, A should take advantage of B's retraction and rapidly use the right hand to make the "ward off" move. In this way, the "ward off" would be highly effective. Without leveraging, we'd be unable to ward off the opponent. When making the move, we should use the waist as the core to issue force, using the waist force to ward B off.

| Figure 6-3-14 | Figure 6-3-15 | Figure 6-3-16 |

### 2. Pull Back

(1) B advances a step with the right foot and pushes and hits A with the left palm; A immediately raises the left hand to block B's left wrist. (Figure 6-3-17)

(2) Then A advances a step with the right foot; at the same time, the left hand pulls B from the front down and to the back in an arc, and the right hand presses and holds B's left shoulder or left elbow and pulls it from the front down and to the back in an arc, which can pull B out or down from A's left side to the back. (Figures 6-3-18, 19)

| Figure 6-3-17 | Figure 6-3-18 | Figure 6-3-19 |

Movement Essentials:

A should take advantage of B's strong push forward and use B's force to pull B back. When pulling back, keep the upper torso upright and make full use of the force issued by turning the upper torso to the left, to make the pull back more effective.

### 3. Press Forward

(1) B extends the right hand to grasp A's right wrist and pulls A backward; A advances a step with the right foot along B's pull, while the left hand moves towards the right arm. (Figures 6-3-20, 21)

Figure 6-3-20               Figure 6-3-21

(2) Then A shifts the center of gravity to the front, bends the right leg and kicks the left leg to form a bow stance; at the same time, place the left palm at the inner side of the right wrist, press B's chest with the right forearm to press B forward. (Figure 6-3-22)

Movement Essentials:

The most important feature of Tai-chi technique is to leverage force. "Press forward" form seems to be an active attack, but it actually uses the "pull back" force of the opponent to issue force along. Moves should be timely, smooth and coordinated.

### 4. Push

(1) B hits A's both temples with both fists; A immediately put his hands up between B's arms. (Figure 6-3-23)

Figure 6-3-22               Figure 6-3-23

(2) Then A shifts the center of gravity slightly to the back; at the same time, uses both hands

to push B's arms down and to the back in a swinging motion, to lead B into empty space (Figure 6-3-24), and then A immediately pushes B forward with both hands. (Figure 6-3-25)

Movement Essentials:

A must push B's arms down in a swinging motion, and turn the waist to the left. After emptying B's force, A can attack and push B.

Figure 6-3-24                    Figure 6-3-25

## VIII. Single Whip

1. B steps forward with the left foot and hits A with the right fist; A immediately swing his right hand up and back in to grab B's right wrist. (Figure 6-3-26)

2. Then A bends the left leg and half squats, straightens the right leg to form a bow stance; at the same time, the right hand grasps B's right wrist and pulls back; turn the left palm outward and push out towards B's chest. (Figure 6-3-27)

Figure 6-3-26                    Figure 6-3-27

Movement Essentials:

When attack with the palm, turn the waist to the right and leverage the strength of the waist and legs. The whole movement should issue force forward and to the right in a curve.

## IX. Wave Hands Like Clouds

1. B steps forward with his right foot and hits A with his right fist; A then sticks out his left arm to block B's right arm. (Figure 6-3-28)

2. B immediately punches A's abdomen with his left fist; A quickly turns left to block B's left arm to fail A's attack. (Figure 6-3-29)

Figure 6-3-28                    Figure 6-3-29

Movement Essentials:

Punch blocking should be swift and decisive.

## X. High Pat On Horse

B punches A with the right fist; A shifts the center of gravity to the back, bend the right knee in a half squat posture, slightly bends the left knee, and touches the ground with the left foot on the toe to form a high empty stance; at the same time, presses the left palm down and beat B's right fist, and the right palm hits B on the face. (Figures 6-3-30, 31)

Figure 6-3-30                    Figure 6-3-31

Movement Essentials:

Pressing and hitting with the palm must be performed simultaneously. When issuing force, the waist should turn slightly to the left fully leverage the waist as "the core to issue force".

## XI. Kick With Right Leg

1. B hits A with the left fist; A shall cross the hands and lift them up to fend off B's fist. (Figure 6-3-32)

2. Then, A shall separate the hands to the left and right to weaken B's attack, and rapidly bend the knees, lift the right leg, and kick B's abdomen. (Figures 6-3-33, 34)

Figure 6-3-32                    Figure 6-3-33                    Figure 6-3-34

Movement Essentials:

When kicking, the toes are angled inwards, and the force centers on the heels. The legs should be bent first and then extended, the supporting leg should be slightly bent to stand firm, and the kick should issue explosive force.

## XII. Stride Opponent's Ears with Both Fists

1. B takes a step forward with the left foot and hits A with both fists; A immediately presses them down with both hands. (Figure 6-3-35)

2. Then A bends the right leg and squats, straightens the left leg to form a bow stance; at the same time, both hands make fists, swing the arms in an arc from bottom out and up, and both fists hit B's left and right temples at the same time, with the thumb facing down and the palm side facing out. (Figure 6-3-36)

Movement Essentials:

Both fists must attack in a swinging motion, but the swing angle shall not be too large. Issue force from the core of the body, the force should be heavy, and the force point should be accurate.

Figure 6-3-35                    Figure 6-3-36

## XIII. Kick with Left Leg

B steps forward with the left foot and hits A with the right fist straight forward; A separates both hands upward and to the left and right, and block B's fist with the left hand. At the same time, A bends the left leg and lift it up, and quickly kicks B's abdomen. (Figures 6-3-37, 38)

Figure 6-3-37                    Figure 6-3-38

Movement Essentials:

When kicking, toes should be angled inward and the focus should be on the heels. Legs should be bent first and then extended. Slight bends the knee of the supporting leg and stands firm. Be explosive when kicking.

## XIV. Creep Down and Stand On One Leg

1. Do a drop stance and creep down

(1) B steps forward with his left foot and hits A's face with his right fist; A quickly squats to

form a drop stance to dodge B's attack. (Figure 6-3-39)

(2) Then A kicks straight with his right foot to form a bow stance with his left foot forward; A sends his left uplifting palm to attack B's crotch, so that B's crotch will be hit or B will fall back. (Figure 6-3-40)

Figure 6-3-39                    Figure 6-3-40

Movement Essentials:

Be swift to squat to dodge fists; be coordinated to form a bow stance along with an uplifting palm; be swift and forceful to perform an uplifting palm.

2. Golden Pheasant Stands on One Leg

B hits A with the right fist; A quickly grabbed B's right wrist joint with the left hand and pulled it back. At the same time, the right hand (bending elbow) goes through B's right armpit and lifts B up to tilt B's body forward. At the same time, the right leg bends the knee and lift up forcefully, and use the right knee to hit B's chest and ribs. (Figure 6-3-41)

Movement Essentials:

The movement should be fast, forceful and coordinated. The best place to hit with the knee is the rib part.

Figure 6-3-41

# XV. Fair Lady Weaves at the Shuttle

B steps forward with the left foot and hits A with the right fist; A immediately raises the left arm, bends the elbow and block B on the top. At the same time, the left leg bends and half squats, straightens the right leg to form a bow stance with the left foot forward, and hit B's chest and abdomen with the right palm. (Figures 6-3-42, 43)

Movement Essentials:

The moves of raising arm to block and hitting with the palm is not performed straight forward, but in a slightly swinging motion forward and to the left. When attacking, fully use the strength of the waist and leg to achieve better effect.

Figure 6-3-42          Figure 6-3-43

## XVI. Needle At Sea Bottom

B does a push kick towards A's abdomen and crotch. A takes a half step to the right front with his right foot to dodge B's kick foot, and at the same time A immediately does a left elbow butt to block B's right leg; then A takes a step forward with his left foot, leans forward, and gives a thrust palm fiercely towards B's crotch. (Figures 6-3-44,45)

Movement Essentials:

Be swift and agile to do dodging and elbow butts; the upper body should lean forward to be coordinated when one does a thrust palm; be swift, precise and forceful to perform a thrust palm.

Figure 6-3-44          Figure 6-3-45

## XVII. Fan Through The Back

B uses the right hand to slap A at right ear; A immediately raises the right hand up to block the attack. At the same time, A bends the left leg and half squats, kick the right leg and form a bow stance with the left leg forward, and hit B at waist and ribs with the left palm. (Figure 6-3-46)

Movement Essentials:

When attacking with the left palm forward, use the force of the waist, turning the hit forward and kicking the right leg to make the palm attack more powerful. The torso must be upright, contract the coccyx part, and force from the back.

图 6-3-46

## XVIII. Deflect Downward, Parry, And Punch

1. B steps forward with the left foot and hits A with the right fist; A performs the "deflect downward" move, turning the body to the right, advancing a step with the right foot, and at the same time clenching the right fist and bending the elbow slightly up and to the right. (Figures 6-3-47, 48)

Figure 6-3-47

Figure 6-3-48

2. Then A performs the "parry" move, continuing to turn the torso to the right, advancing a step with the left foot, and place the center of gravity on the right foot to form an empty step with the left foot; at the same time, changing the right fist to palm to press B's right hand down and back in an arc; the left hand strikes B at the right ear from bottom to the left and forward in an arc. (Figure 6-3-49)

3. A performs the "punch" move, bending his left leg to half squat, kicking the right leg and form a bow stance with the left foot forward; at the same time, clenching the right fist and stretching it straight forward to hit B hard at the chest. (Figure 6-3-50)

Figure 6-3-49          Figure 6-3-50

Movement Essentials:

Although the movements consist of three moves, they shall be performed continuously and smoothly. The "punch" move is mainly to hit B at the chest and abdomen. When performing this move, make full use of the strength of kicking legs and turning waist.

## XIX. Apparent Close Up

B steps forward with the left foot and hit A's both ribs with both fists; A immediately lower both hands down and outward to fend off the opponent's fists. Then, A rotates both arms inward, brings both hands together inward, and push forward with a strong force, which can knock B to the ground. (Figures 6-3-51, 52)

Figure 6-3-51          Figure 6-3-52

Movement Essentials:

The whole movement should be performed smoothly without interruption. Leverage the strength of waist and legs to issue force. Separate the hands first and then bring them together can fail the opponent's attack and make the move more effective.

# 附录 简化太极拳路线图

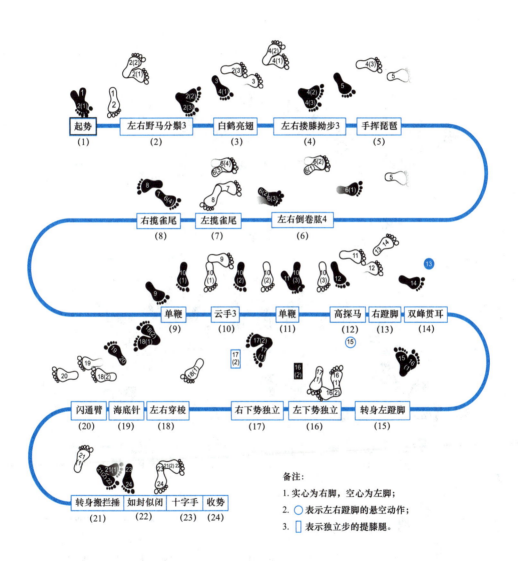

备注：
1. 实心为右脚，空心为左脚；
2. ○ 表示左右蹬脚的悬空动作；
3. ▯ 表示独立步的提膝腿。

255

# Appendix Road Map of Simplified Tai-chi Chuan

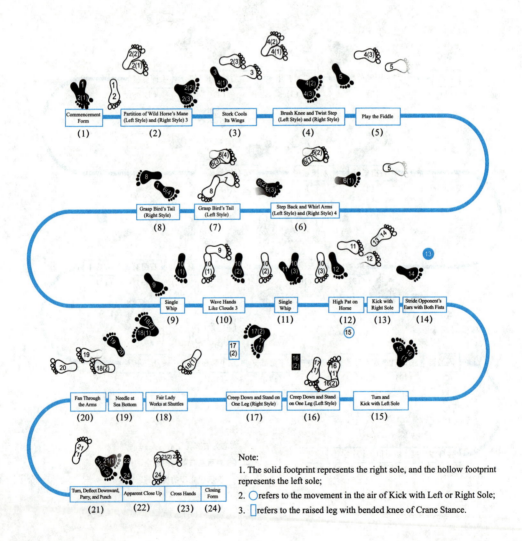

| | | | | |
|---|---|---|---|---|
| Commencement Form | Partition of Wild Horse's Mane (Left Style) and (Right Style) 3 | Stork Cools Its Wings | Brush Knee and Twist Step (Left Style) and (Right Style) | Play the Fiddle |
| (1) | (2) | (3) | (4) | (5) |

| | | |
|---|---|---|
| Grasp Bird's Tail (Right Style) | Grasp Bird's Tail (Left Style) | Step Back and Whirl Arms (Left Style) and (Right Style) 4 |
| (8) | (7) | (6) |

| | | | | | |
|---|---|---|---|---|---|
| Single Whip | Wave Hands Like Clouds 3 | Single Whip | High Pat on Horse | Kick with Right Sole | Stride Opponent's Ears with Both Fists |
| (9) | (10) | (11) | (12) | (13) | (14) |

| | | | | | |
|---|---|---|---|---|---|
| Fan Through the Arms | Needle at Sea Bottom | Fair Lady Works at Shuttles | Creep Down and Stand on One Leg (Right Style) | Creep Down and Stand on One Leg (Left Style) | Turn and Kick with Left Sole |
| (20) | (19) | (18) | (17) | (16) | (15) |

| | | | |
|---|---|---|---|
| Turn, Deflect Downward, Parry, and Punch | Apparent Close Up | Cross Hands | Closing Form |
| (21) | (22) | (23) | (24) |

Note:

1. The solid footprint represents the right sole, and the hollow footprint represents the left sole;

2. ◯ refers to the movement in the air of Kick with Left or Right Sole;

3. ▯ refers to the raised leg with bended knee of Crane Stance.

256

# 致 谢

　　本教材由广州铁路职业技术学院张竹筠教授（武术六段）和陆军特种作战学院范伟教授牵头策划，由广州铁路职业技术学院基础课部和国际合作学院共同完成，是一部武学和传统体育文化内容综合呈现的立体化双语教材。本教材的出版得到业界同仁热心支持和鼎力帮助，全体编者表示衷心的感谢！

　　首先感谢北京航空航天大学飞行器设计与力学系王幼复教授（武术七段）为本教材题写书名！感谢国内外著名电影电视及舞台剧制作人、编剧及导演，中国功夫及武术演艺国际推手傅华阳先生以及美国佛罗里达州肿瘤和血液病临床研究所张文卿医学博士分别作序。

　　为高定位高质量完成教材的目标，主编主创人员先后三次组织专家论证会，在此感谢李朝旭（广州体育学院武术学院三级教授）、陈娟（陈氏太极拳第十二代嫡宗传人）、任荣伟（中山大学管理学院工商管理系教授）、韩彬（广东广播电视台主持人）、徐春龙（清华大学广东校友会秘书长）、康涛博士、李兆飞（番禺区政协委员，戴家形意拳、武派太极拳第七代传人）、冯建福（图书资料研究馆员）等专家的指导和建议！

　　感谢向成军副教授、张倩菡女士为教材所进行的大量英文翻译工作！

　　感谢代流通老师为教材编写推进做了大量的组织和联络工作！

　　众人拾柴火焰高，本教材是集体智慧的结晶，再次致谢所有参与者及其家人的付出和支持！

全体编者

2021 年 11 月 16 日

# Acknowledgements

This text book is led by Professor ZHANG Zhujun (ranking level 6 in National Martial Arts) of Guangzhou Railway Polytechnic and Professor FAN Wei of Special Operation College of PLA, and is completed by Department of Basic Courses and International Cooperation School of Guangzhou Railway Polytechnic. It is a multi-dimensional bilingual Chinese and English text book that presents Chinese martial art and traditional sports culture in depth. The text book is published with the support received from various parties, for which we, the authoring team, are deeply indebted.

First of all, we would like to thank Professor WANG Youfu (ranking level 7 in National Martial Arts), Department of Aircraft Design and Mechanics, Beihang University , for inscribing the book's title! We would also like to thank Mr. FU Huayang, a world famous producer, scriptwriter and director for movies, TV and theatres as well as an international promoter of Chinese kung fu and martial arts, and ZHANG Wenqing, MD, Oncologist and Hematologist of Florida Cancer Specialists and Research Institute, for writing the prologue.

To ensure achieving the writing objectives of this text book with high standard and quality, the main authors and editors have organized three expert panel discussions. And we would like to thank the participating experts as follows. LI Chaoxu, Level-3 professor, School of Martial Arts, Guangzhou Sport University; CHEN Juan, direct descendant of the 12th generation of Chen-style Tai-chi Chuan; REN Rongwei, professor of Department of Business Administration, School of Management, Sun Yat-sen University; HAN Bin, TV host of Guangdong Radio and Television Station; XU Chunlong, Secretary General of  Guangdong Alumni Association, Tsinghua University; Dr. KANG Tao; LI Zhaofci, CPPCC member of Panyu District, and descendant of the 7th generation of Dai-style Xing Yi Chuan (Form-and-will Boxing) and Wu-style Tai-chi Chuan; FENG Jianfu, literature research librarian.

We would like to thank Associate Professor XIANG Chengjun and Ms. ZHANG Qianhan, for their incalculable help with the translation work!

258

We also extend our thanks to DAI Liutong for his great help with organizing and liaison to make the writing project progress smoothly!

This text book would not have been possible without the corporation and devotion of all partners. Their wisdom is well encapsulated in this book. And again, we would like to thank them all as well as their family members for their devotion and support!

Sincerely,

The authoring team

November 16th, 2021